C24.

D0876135

WITHDRAWN

Robert John Walker: A Politician
from Jackson to Lincoln

923
WI53s

ROBERT JOHN WALKER

A Politician from Jackson to Lincoln

BY JAMES P. SHENTON

1961

New York and London

Columbia University Press

Library of Congress Catalog Card Number: 61-11283
Manufactured in the United States of America

To the memory of

E M I L E . H U R J A ,

a gentle man

who had a dream

cATJan16'62

135670

Acknowledgment

MANY PEOPLE HAVE MADE this book possible; a full listing would be impossible. The few mentioned are a symbolic tribute to the many assistants. The sentiments expressed are inadequate re-compensation of their efforts. All failings are my own.

The Social Science Research Council of Columbia University generously provided a grant to meet clerical expenses. Henry Tobin also generously aided me at a critical moment of research.

Richard Hofstadter and Dwight Miner urged a much needed cutting of the original manuscript. Henry Graff never stinted in his help. Thomas C. McClintock, David Rothman, and Robert E. Zegger located sources and generously transcribed notes. John E. L. Clubbe read it with care, used ruthlessly a blue pencil, and defended the result with unfailing good humor. David Sloan, Richard Abrams, Bernard Wishy, and Edward McLeroy have carefully read manuscript and proof. Robert J. Walker, III, a generous grandson, allowed me long and free access to his grandfather's papers. The Staffs of the Library of Congress, the National Archives, the Columbia University Library, and the Pennsylvania Historical Society—to name but a few—have given me ample proof of the heavy debt all researchers owe them. Edwin A. Miles and Holman Hamilton answered some urgent queries. Eileen Menegus and Ann Laverty not only typed it but said they enjoyed reading it.

Mrs. Gudrun Hurja Hunt permitted me full use of her late husband's papers and has my pledge to complete a larger work on the era in which Mr. Walker flourished. Her late husband, when seriously ill, gave me a morning in which he shared his thoughts on the career of Robert J. Walker. And to two men I humbly extend my gratitude: Harry J. Carman and Allan Nevins who instilled in me a love for history and an awareness of a humanity that makes their mentorship a goal to achieve.

JAMES P. SHENTON

Foreword

THE IDEOLOGY which the United States champions dates back to the Declaration of Independence and to the Constitution's Bill of Rights. Throughout the history of the Republic this ideology with its emphasis on freedom of the individual—not absolute freedom, but freedom to think, to believe, to disbelieve, to will, to choose, to inquire, to criticise, and to differ—has prevailed.

In the long and embittered struggle between the North and the South which eventuated in the Civil War or the War Between the States, as it is sometimes called, our ideological pattern was both challenged and defended. With passing years this struggle between the planting South and the industrial North, with its legacy of blighted hopes, ruined lives, and bitter memories, has been an enormously rich area for historical research. Literally hundreds of books, diaries, and articles have appeared and the end is not yet, as the outpouring of manuscripts occasioned by the first centennial anniversary of the conflict has indicated.

In a very real sense Professor Shenton's admirable volume on Robert John Walker adds to this growing literature.

Though his approach is biographical, the author does not belong to the Carlylian school. His task, he fully realizes, is not to make the subject of this portraiture a hero, but to marshall all of the relevant material which will enable the reader to comprehend for himself the kind of person Walker was and his impact upon the ideas, men, and events of his time. As seen in the pages of this volume, Walker, being human, had both strengths and weaknesses and was the product of his social-cultural background.

Born of Scots-English ancestry in the hamlet of Northumberland, sixty miles north of Harrisburg, Pennsylvania, on July 19, 1801, Walker's life spanned the first two thirds of the nineteenth century. He died in Washington, D.C. on November 11, 1869. Barely five feet two inches tall and weighing scarcely one hundred pounds he had a massive head which tended to accentuate his diminutive physique. Though small of stature he had a first-rate mind, enormous physical and mental energy, and a driving quest for the acquisition of material wealth. His desire to be in the limelight politically was insatiable.

Joining the Democratic party, young Walker campaigned for Andrew Jackson. Following his father's death in 1824, Walker moved to Natchez. The story of Walker's activities both in and out of politics not only in Mississippi but elsewhere is intriguing; a story which includes every major problem on the political horizon from the middle 1820's to the eve of the Civil War: Texas, land speculation, the disposal of public lands and the Pre-Emption Act, the struggle over the national bank, the establishment of the independent treasury, Indian affairs, boundary disputes, tariffs, railroad transportation, the slavery issue, Kansas governorship, presidential campaigns, and Cabinet appointments.

The role of Walker in connection with each of these issues and problems is superbly handled by Professor Shenton. Not only does he portray the real Walker but helps the reader to understand the character and psychology of the people of the United States in the first sixty years of the nineteenth century. Unquestionably, this volume sheds considerable new light upon the events and movements which helped to shape Walker's career and to which he, in turn, gave direction.

The author's concluding chapters entitled "A Sixty-Year-Old Public Man" and "The Search" are especially illuminating in view of some of the vexing problems confronting the United States today. Now even more than in Walker's time the ideological foundation so basic to the nation's pattern of life is being challenged as never before. It is imperative that we review our historical past to the end so that we may the better understand the origin of our ideology and its philosophical import.

When it is remembered that for many years those interested in biographical study, and especially in Walker and his influence on the American scene, hesitated to embark on a study of Walker because of the persistent belief that the necessary source material for a biography was not available, our indebtedness to Professor Shenton is the greater.

HARRY J. CARMAN

Contents

Introduction

"A MERE WHIFFET OF A MAN" was the description of one contemporary. Others characterized him as "land-mad," besmirched with "corruption," preoccupied with "self-seeking advantage"; some, however, thought it appropriate to designate him as "one of the truly great statesmen of the Republic."

For "a mere whiffet of a man," Walker provoked a surprising amount of exaggerated characterization. Much of it was deserved, for in his tempestuous political career, extending from Jackson to Lincoln, he made decisions which profoundly shaped the direction of American politics, and he conceived visions of American economic growth which, though premature, proved prophetic. In his young America, his penchant for the grandiose scheme proved congenial.

Yet, despite the prominence of his role, he has remained an elusive subject for the biographer. Ever since William Dodd in 1914 reminded the world of his existence and suggested the need for a biography, occasional essays have scrutinized moments in his career or reiterated Dodd's conclusion that he was an imperialist of gargantuan appetite. As recently as 1953, *Pravda* revived words of his to prove the antiquity of America's aggressive aims in the Pacific. No political history of the 1840's and the 1850's fails to mention him, but only in a subordinate way. Nearly a century after his death, he seems destined to remain a footnote to history.

Time and again, other biographers have started to do research on his life, only to despair of finding the evidence with which to complete the task. In the eleven years that I have searched for

the "man," I, too, have come to wonder whether the complete
story will ever be told. But, as the evidence has slowly accumulated, I have concluded that the available evidence comes reason-
ably close to capturing the essence of the man.

There are, however, certain defects in the evidence that must
be mentioned. Only four hundred letters written by Walker have
survived; many of these are mutilated fragments or brief notes
written in his curious shorthand: the sole survivors of Walker's
habit of stuffing his pockets with numerous notes to remind him
of his myriad activities. But they are a scattering of material in
a career that extended over almost five decades. There are years
for which no original evidence exists to prove that Walker lived.
Fortunately, a goodly body of correspondence *to* him has survived the vicissitudes of time.

The largest single collection of Walker letters (now on loan
deposit from his grandson, Robert John Walker III, at the Library of Congress) consists of three volumes of correspondence,
newspaper clippings, several of his public papers, and a eulogis-
tic memoir written by his eccentric sister, Martha Walker Cooke.
These volumes were preserved by his spinster daughter, Sophia,
but they are limited primarily to the period from 1840 to 1858.

A second collection which came also from Sophia exists at
the New York Historical Society. It is a miscellaneous collection
of letters from eminent Americans and a scattering of equally
eminent Britishers of the middle nineteenth century. As in the
Library of Congress deposit, the letters cover the period 1840–
1858. An unusual trove of letters both to and from Walker exists
in the Salmon P. Chase letters at the Pennsylvania Historical
Society. These have the merit of being the only surviving, and
nearly complete, correspondence between Walker and another
man. Oddly, one of these letters found its way into the Autograph
Collection of the University of Indiana.

There exists two important collections of Walker materials in
private hands. One is a Walker Letterbook, the possession of the
late Professor Ralph Ferguson of the University of Pittsburgh,

which survived the destruction of the Civil War. It had come
to Professor Ferguson by way of a woman who had received it
as a gift from a veteran of the Grand Army of the Republic. He
had looted it from a great mansion house, probably that of John
Tyler, in Virginia before it had been put to the torch. The letters
cover the period from 1844 to 1849. The other collection belongs to the widow of Emil Hurja. She has permitted me full use
of original letters and research notes that her husband accumulated over the years.

When I met Mr. Hurja in 1952, he generously permitted me
to use the Walker Papers at the Library of Congress, and he
shared with me his dream of writing a biography of Walker.
He offered to permit me to examine his collection of Walker
letters at a subsequent date, but before I had a chance to reclaim
his offer, he died. Six years later, Mrs. Gudrun Hurja Hunt gave
me access to the materials. Unlike other Walker Collections, this
one contained letters from almost every period of his life.
Though there are less than two hundred, they often proved to
be the missing links to evidence found elsewhere. There also
existed fifteen notebooks that contained notes which most often
paralleled my own research. These proved an excellent check
for my own notes.

Much of the remaining material exists scattered in numerous
collections of contemporary manuscripts. Of particular use were
the W. W. Corcoran Collections at the Library of Congress. In
the letterbooks of this shrewd banker one can trace some of the
financial vicissitudes of Walker. Of equal value are the papers
of James K. Polk, George Mifflin Dallas, and James Buchanan.
I discovered, however, that in almost all collections of the period
there are numerous references to Walker. From the tone of these
references and from the ample references to him in newspapers
of the day, I feel that I have gained a sense of the man. Lively,
controversial, and contentious, Walker, no matter how elusive,
proved a quarry worth pursuing. I have enjoyed the chase.

One final word of warning is necessary. Where the evidence

has been slight, I have had to make only a minimal presentation. For months during 1858, 1859, and 1860, I found no evidence. During his complex business dealings of the 1850's, dealings which persuaded an earlier searcher that Walker had the makings of a "robber baron," he kept only the barest of records. Many of his business correspondents complained at the infrequency of his communications. Perhaps his reluctance to commit these dealings to paper is a tacit admission of their dubious nature. And finally, the absence of materials for his youth may be explained by the maxim: the young live, rather than write. What evidence remains reveals a man of stupefying energy, driven by the demon success. Though he puzzled many of his own generation, none denied his verve for life. And it was only when he had died that anyone thought of assigning a final description. Then, and only then, he was called "a gentleman of the old school of politics." The description would have made Mr. Walker unhappy; he disliked being dated.

1. The Young American

IN EARLY JULY of 1835 hundreds of planters and farmers gathered throughout the state of Mississippi to form vigilante committees to meet a feared slave insurrection. Additional hundreds gathered at Livingston to witness the hanging of two white men who had confessed agitating the slaves to rebellion. Before July ended, six white men and fifteen slaves would go to the gallows for suspected subversion. In Madisonville, north of Jackson, a diminutive man launched his campaign for the Democratic nomination to the Senate. Before the crowd standing patiently under the merciless rays of the sun, his harsh, grating voice delivered an unnerving message. The Whigs under Henry Clay, he charged, deliberately fostered insurrection by denouncing slavery as morally degrading to both owner and slave. Despite the protests of his advisors, he continued his attack, and, as one recorded, "used it effectively, to alarm his hearers, a large majority of whom were planters and slave-holders." Robert John Walker had found the issue with which to launch his political career.[1]

Since the slavery issue had never before been raised in Mississippi, one might have anticipated that Walker felt genuine fear. The reverse was true. Even as he campaigned, he privately intervened with Mississippi's Governor Runnel for the commutation of a young white man's death sentence for "Negro stealing." Not only was the sentence too severe but the stolen slave was "a *handsome* young mullato girl for whom the unfortunate convict had conceived a strong attachment." The sins of the flesh, Walker understood, and rightly so, for he possessed them in abundance.[2]

Yet, the opinions Walker expressed about slavery were compounded of political necessity and a genuine conviction that slavery must one day end. But he predicated such termination on the slave being removed from the white community. When pressing in 1844 for the annexation of Texas, he defended Texas as supplying a funnel through which the slave population could move into Mexico where their absorption into the Mexican population would be assured. Though only a remote possibility, this proposal ceased to make sense when he subsequently demanded the total annexation of Mexico. Though he insisted upon humane treatment for his own slaves, he did so believing the Negro innately inferior to the white man. When arguing in court against the right of a master to emancipate his slaves at will, he raised the possibility that Mississippi might be confronted as a result with the choice of "a government of intelligent white freemen, or of ignorant negro slaves." Many years later, during the Civil War, he claimed, much to the astonishment of his listeners, to have freed his slaves in 1838. Unfortunately, evidence contradicts him, for in 1841 Walker refused to negotiate with a creditor who offered to liquidate his $30,000 debt in return for 2,300 acres of land and 17 slaves.[3]

The man who pursued this ambiguous course could hardly be described as physically prepossessing. Anyone viewing him from a distance might well have concluded that he was a boy rather than a man. Five feet two inches in height, he weighed scarcely one hundred pounds. His massive head accentuated his diminutive physique. As he aged his skin withered, giving him an appearance that one uncomplimentary host compared to that of a pigmy. Of the masses of brunette curls that crowned his head he had an inordinate pride, and when they began to grey, he did not hesitate to dye them black. He possessed a great pride and a trigger-like temper. He issued without hesitation challenges to duels with no less personages than Henry Clay, Thomas Hart Benton, and Jeremiah Black. All declined, probably assuming that if they accepted, Walker would be honor bound to seek to kill. It was agreed that Walker possessed turbulent energy which he devoted to a restless struggle to achieve honor and wealth, a combination which often proved contradictory. Everything he did was done with "fierce indignation." [4]

The unquiet journey of Robert John Walker began in the hamlet of Northumberland, some sixty miles north of Harrisburg, Pennsylvania. Only fragments of evidence substantiate that his birth occurred on July 19, 1801, to Jonathan and Lucretia Walker. He joined a brother, Duncan Stephen, and two sisters, Marianne and Charlotte Corday. In 1807, his youngest sister Martha was born. Two brothers and a sister had died in infancy. The family drew its origins from English and Scottish stock—an ancestry of which Walker always felt inordinately proud. Time and again he felt obliged to remind his listeners that a great-grandfather had served at Blenheim and later had been killed by Indians early in the French and Indian War. His paternal grandfather had seen action in the ensuing Indian Wars. But details of Walker's ancestry are few; even the date of his father's birth is uncertain. All that is known is that it occurred sometime in 1756, and that Jonathan Hoge Walker was either the third or fourth of four sons. The Walkers apparently prospered as farmers, lawyers, and land speculators. According to family tradition, Jonathan Walker joined the Revolutionary Army in 1776 to serve under Colonel St. Clair in the ill-fated Canadian expedition, and subsequently took part in militia action against "the Indians and Tories." The official records only indicate that he served as a "private . . . of the 3rd class of Cumberland county militia." Even this limited service would have involved him in the bloody Seneca Wars. His son never forgot that his father in his youth had revealed a sturdy courage. It goaded him to emulation, at least verbally. [5]

The range of Jonathan's influence upon his son is at best conjectural. Robert John remained remarkably reticent about his parents (and he made only the barest references to his wife and children). Perhaps the son harbored resentment against a father who ruled his children with an iron hand and who insisted upon steady compliance with his will. Nor could the son ever quite forget that his father towered well over six feet, and that he apparently viewed his son's diminutive stature with tolerance. Throughout his adult life, Walker struggled to attain that which had always eluded his father—wealth.[6]

The father intensely believed in the importance of education, completing his own at the age of thirty at Dickinson College in Pennsylvania. He read law with Stephen Duncan whose son-in-law he became in 1790, when he married Lucretia Duncan. His marriage provided him with extensive connections in the Pennsylvania legal community. Jonathan promptly identified himself with the Masonry of Mifflin County after being admitted to practice the law there. In 1791, he settled at Northumberland, where within two years he was performing the duties of deputy attorney general for Northumberland County. He also speculated extensively in land, apparently a family weakness. Before his youngest son's birth, he had gained considerable stature as a lawyer in the upper Susquehanna Valley.[7]

Jonathan revealed a radical inclination when he savagely castigated capital punishment in a series of legal articles published at his own expense during the 1790's. Capital punishment, he contended, penalized the criminal for a failure in his education. He believed crime resulted from a social rather than an individual fault. He admitted that the great Italian penologist, Caesare Bonesama Beccaria, had influenced his thought. So much so that he named his third son, who died before Robert's birth, Beccaria. When subsequently serving as president judge of the Fourth Pennsylvania Judicial District and as presiding judge of the Pennsylvania High Court of Errors and Appeals, he invariably viewed his judicial task as one which should deter rather than punish crime.[8]

Throughout his life, Jonathan took a staunchly liberal view of women's rights. He believed women should play an active role in politics. A strong admirer of the *Girondists* in the French

Revolution, he rejected the excesses perpetrated in the name of revolution. When Charlotte Corday assassinated Marat, one of the radical leaders in the French Assembly, he pronounced the deed as one of exquisite heroism. The subsequent execution of his heroine so moved him that he named his second daughter Charlotte Corday, hoping that she would not hesitate to emulate her namesake if the safety of her country so required. When discussing education, he described it as best when it worked to instill in the student, both male and female, the will to achieve the "greatest happiness for the greatest number." In his household, his daughters "were instructed by him in Latin and Greek," and were subjected along with the sons to a regimen based upon "principles of rectitude, habits of mental industry and self-control." He instilled in his children a propensity for liberal thinking. His youngest son, though never acknowledging this debt to his father, would be irresistibly drawn to the novel idea, and would dream of a world governed by an immutable law of progress.[9]

The judge placed his youngest son under the guidance of a Cameronian divine. The harsh discipline of this Calvinist teacher left its mark. It created in Robert John Walker a marked antipathy for sectarian belief, but it also left him with a strong preference for the "more awakening appeal of ardent and eloquent extempore prayer and preaching." Though he never entered an evangelical sect, he shared the Fundamentalist's sharp distaste for "Papal mummeries." When, many years later, his sister-in-law, Constantia Bache, flirted with "Puseyism," and its insistence upon the Church of England as "the only *true* church," Walker exploded, denouncing it as an effort "to expunge the Reformation, to extinguish the lights of the last three centuries, and replunge the human soul into the dark cell from which it began to emerge in the days of Luther." A commitment to the "apostolic succession," he protested, "rests wholly . . . on Catholic tradition," and leads inevitably to Papal allegiance with a consequent subservience to men "who were transcendent in villainy." When pressed, he dismissed the Bible as a "book that abounds . . . in . . . metaphysical expressions," a reflection of its *oriental* origin. Stubbornly, he argued, "the Church of Christ is a spiritual existence, . . . the temple of which is the converted soul." [10]

But his Cameronian training also instilled in him a compulsion to constant industry, a need which would wreak havoc on the grown man's frail body. His intense energy, driving ambition, and stubbornly inquiring intelligence found expression in his wide search for knowledge.

Jonathan Walker was determined that his youngest son should have the benefits of the best education. Early in the autumn of 1817, Robert registered at the University of Pennsylvania. Family connections assured him of ready access to the best social circles in the Quaker City. But there existed an uncomfortable fact: he had status without substance. His presence at the University had been made possible because of a generous extension of credit by the Reverend Dr. Samuel Wylie, an old family friend. This gentleman's charities had provoked the description "proverbial . . . if . . . not always discriminating" from a friend; less restrained souls settled for describing them as "grotesque." The minister's impulsive generosity caused Judge Walker to protest when contracting for credit: "The terms which you state are too low; you will sink money by it, which I cannot . . . permit." [11]

Though distant from parental authority, Robert found his life in Philadelphia thoroughly supervised. Jonathan determined his curriculum, assigning his son, "general literature, Hebrew, and the Romance languages." In pursuit of the latter, the judge pressed his son to room with a French friend of "pure morals," who would enable the youth to converse in French. In addition, he enjoined him to observe "the Lord's day," with the flat warning that failure to do so would result in swift termination of his college studies.

Time and again, Jonathan warned his son to prepare for

migration to Natchez, Mississippi, where his wife's brother had already settled. As his rheumatism made circuit riding in the bleak Pennsylvania winter uninviting, the sub-tropical warmth of the Mississippi riverport became ever more alluring. All thought of changing residence ended, however, when James Monroe was elected to the Presidency. The creation by Act of Congress April 20, 1818, of the United States Court for the Western District of Pennsylvania, resulted in Monroe appointing Jonathan Walker its judge. Walker accepted the post with alacrity, admitting that "the irresistible advance of age" made further circuit riding impossible. And there existed his gnawing fear that if he were to die, his family would be left destitute. For the time, no further discussion of southward migration occurred.[12]

The parental injunctions had their effect, for Walker's behavior proved a model of rectitude. Constant application to study enabled him to complete *magna cum laude* the two year sequence at the University in early August, 1819. At eighteen he returned to Pittsburgh to read the law with his father. In the summer of 1820, his father appointed him court clerk, a post which paid a thousand dollars a year and for which a substitute clerk could be hired to do the necessary work, for two hundred dollars a year. After his admission to the bar, the young man, with a secure income, returned in 1821 to the University of Pennsylvania to study for his Master's degree, receiving it in 1822.[13]

Again he returned to Pittsburgh which he envisioned "must be the Emporium of the western country, the depot of its commerce and ultimately to become its supplier." To an uneasy Dr. Wylie, who pressed for a repayment of the more than one thousand dollars he had advanced to educate Walker, went the bland assurance that he had "determined not to be a *loco* motive animal but to settle myself permanently in this place." The man, who would achieve world-wide fame as a vigorous proponent of free trade, reflected the sentiments of Pittsburgh when he sweepingly denounced congressional opponents of a protective tariff.

He pronounced his heartfelt advocacy for a strong national government committed to a vigorous program of internal improvements. One hears the voice of John Quincy Adams in these sentiments, but Adams represented a fading past, and the young lawyer, amenable to the main chance, flirted with a bold departure.[14]

To the surprise of his Whiggish father and his Federalist brother, Walker joined the newly organized Democratic party which in return elected him a member of the Pittsburgh Democratic Committee. The judge, who had hitherto refused to indulge in partisan politics, wavered before finally agreeing to support the congressional candidacy of William H. Wilkins and permit his youngest son to use the family's prestige to advance the new party. Wilkins, already President of the Bank of Pittsburgh, chafed at the restrictions placed on state banks by the Second Bank of the United States. Before long, he would be rapidly advancing through Democratic ranks in a political career that culminated in his appointment as Secretary of War by John Tyler. The bubbling energy of Walker intrigued him, and the two men soon became inseparable. At the Wilkins home, the young man met Mary B. Bache, the niece of Mrs. Wilkins. Within a brief time Walker conducted a tender courtship with the girl; one that ended in marriage.[15]

Assured of his father's patronage, increasingly active in both law and politics, Walker now campaigned publicly for the presidential candidacy of Andrew Jackson. His early espousal of Old Hickory's political aspirations gave him a prominence that belied his youth. The Allegheny County Democracy chose him with three other delegates to represent it at the Democratic state convention held at Harrisburg in early March, 1824. Along with William Wilkins and two other delegates he supported the candidacies of Jackson and Calhoun, although he had originally expressed a preference for Albert Gallatin in the second place. In the same year his own political aspirations received a jolt when he ran fifth among seven candidates for the four state assembly seats assigned to Allegheny County.[16]

In the midst of success, however, several bleak facts stood out.

His political setback had only temporary consequences; however the security of his court clerkship depended upon his father. A rapid decline in the old man's health made it imperative that he migrate to a warmer climate. The Wylie debt remained unpaid and pressing. Jonathan's assets consisted largely of farmlands that could be sold only at considerable loss. Late in 1823, Robert Walker set out to establish a legal practice in New Orleans with his father; their journey ended at Natchez where Jonathan died on March 24, 1824. Obliged now to administer the estate of his father, Walker abandoned thoughts of setting up a practice in New Orleans and returned to Pittsburgh. The illness of his father also ended his clerkship, leaving him without a fixed income.[17]

What would have happened to him had he decided to remain in Pennsylvania is conjectural. He had already many influential relatives and friends, and he added to his abundance of distinguished connections when he married Mary Bache at Christ Church, Philadelphia on April 4, 1825. Mary remains an elusive figure; she seems to have been as overshadowed by her husband as Lucretia Walker had been by Jonathan. Both women were apparently content to be wives of active, prominent men. Home and children seemed their sole concern. The only noticeable permanent influence that Lucy had had upon her children was to instill in them a fondness for composing poetry—often maudlin in tone and message. Mary would occasionally betray a certain puzzlement at her husband's restless energy, and, as Presidents Pierce and Buchanan were to learn, she occasionally exerted a negative influence on his political activities.[18]

Marriage also secured him membership into one of the most tightly knit family groups in America. Mary's father, Richard, was postmaster of Philadelphia, a post which had been a family sinecure since its creation by his grandfather, Benjamin Franklin. Her uncle, Benjamin Franklin Bache, had been the vociferously antifederalist editor of the *Aurora*. Her maternal grandfather, Alexander J. Dallas, had been James Madison's Secretary of the Treasury. Uncle George Mifflin Dallas had already served his diplomatic apprenticeship with Albert Gallatin at Ghent and would rise to the Vice Presidency in Polk's administration. Brother Alexander Dallas Bache had begun to display the scientific interests that would lead to his appointment as Superintendent of the United States Coast Survey. The Dallas mansion on Philadelphia's Fourth Street and their great country house, Devon, were symbolic of the family's condition: they were rich, conservative, and ambitious. Robert John shared their ambitions.[19]

The undeviating steadfastness with which the Bache-Dallas clan pursued its interests within the Pennsylvania democracy, would have provided ample opportunity for advancement within Pennsylvania politics had Walker chosen to remain in Pittsburgh. However, migration to Natchez was settled upon in the winter of 1826, after Duncan Walker had sent his brother an urgent plea to join him in his law practice. Walker believed the quickest path to power, prestige, and possession lay in the direction of the booming Southwest. With his wife and his vivacious sister Charlotte he went south, leaving behind the promise of Pittsburgh. But his Pennsylvania connections remained to aid and buttress his hopes. They also served to give lie to the belief that the Jacksonian democracy thwarted privilege. As a skeptical John Quincy Adams subsequently observed, success in the New America depended on how loud you "bawled Democracy." [20]

And a new spirit was abroad in the land, one which chaffed at the inhibitions of the past and, rejecting the notion of limits, insisted upon the emancipation of individual enterprise. Captivated by a vision of a society regulated by human decency, young Americans preached experiment and equalitarianism, and demanded the chance to conquer the future. Robert John Walker shared that vision. A free man in a free society, he dreamed the passionate dream that America's present was the world's future. He could hardly contain his eagerness; he revealed in his youth the constant of his character—the future was progress.

2. The Confidence Man

NATCHEZ, 1826, was a peculiar blending of gentility and aggressive expansion. It knew flush times as thousands of settlers and gangs of slaves poured into the Mississippi valley. But its sophistication had also made it increasingly suspect in the eyes of its rough-hewn neighbors. In the town had settled a small clique of Pennsylvanians, well-connected in the North, pushing in their ambitions and versed in the ways of democratic politics, and who quickly recognized what might be made of a rift between the "Natchez aristocrats" and the "pine woods" settlers. They resolved to court the backwoods settlers whose votes spelt political dominance.[1]

No single Pennsylvanian proved more successful in this courtship than Robert John Walker who remained only nine years but left Mississippi with one of its Senate seats. There is no record when he arrived in Natchez, only the certainty that he joined his brother Duncan's law practice. In this, he proved unusually adept, using his keen mind, already well versed in legal nuances, to corrupt the law without breaking it. Such legal activity put him in heavy demand. Joseph Baldwin recalled:

What country could boast more largely of its crime? What more splendid role of felonies! What more terrific murders! What gorgeous bank robberies! What more magnificent operations in the land offices! Such . . . levies of black mail, individual and corporate! Such flourishes of rhetoric on ledgers suspicious of gold which had departed forever from the vault! And in INDIAN affairs!—the very mention is suggestive of the poetry of theft—the romance of a wild and weird larceny! Swindling Indians by the nation! Stealing their land by the township!

Everywhere there abounded evidence "of the second great experiment of independence: the experiment, namely, of credit without capital, and enterprise without honesty." [2]

Walker swiftly adjusted to these circumstances. When offered an appointment in 1828 to the highest Mississippi court, he rejected it. Unlike Edward Turner who had been Duncan's first law partner, he turned his back upon the judiciary, preferring to explore the Sherwood Forest of Mississippi high finance. He remembered too vividly that his father's long years of judicial service had left him poor. The son was determined to escape that fate. [3]

The absence of hard currency had led to the construction of an elastic credit system based on land. As the need for new credit increased, the value ascribed to land expanded. There resulted a spiralling inflation of land value which allowed landowners to believe they were becoming rich. To this opportunity Walker responded without inhibitions, and soon created an empire of plantations and slaves founded on credit. He assumed monetary obligations in the expectation that if he were pressed, the law provided a loophole through which to escape the consequences. Once, without a moment's hesitation, he endorsed a friend's note for $150,000. The Young American revelled in his newly found wealth. [4]

By 1830 both Walkers had become major figures in the Mississippi bar. Their practice extended into Louisiana and the demand for their services exceeded their ability to comply. Complicating matters, Duncan's health, never robust, suffered from the humid climate of the lower Mississippi. Furthermore, his imagination had been stirred by tales of the wealth that existed in Texas. The father and uncle of Mary Walker had already investigated the fertile promise of the new territory, and, in their frequent returns to Natchez, gave stimulating accounts of the sudden wealth awaiting the early comer. In 1834, after a quick visit to Texas, Duncan, convinced of Lone Star prospects, relinquished his practice to Robert and migrated. There he purchased large tracts of land near San Antonio, land which subsequently provided his brother with a material interest in the future of Texas.[5]

Though unwilling to hold appointive office, Walker plunged into partisan politics. Having earlier identified himself with Jackson's campaign for the Presidency, it was logical that in 1828 he should draw up the Mississippi democracy's manifesto supporting the old general. When the incumbent Senator Thomas B. Reed unexpectedly died, creating a vacancy for the unexpired five years of his term, Walker, despite his protestations, obtained two votes in a legislature which finally chose Robert H. Adams, a close friend of Duncan Walker. Everyone noted that it had been as a "Jackson man" that Adams had won. Despite his overwhelming support from the Natchez commercial and banking community, the pine woods delegates had cared only that Adams supported Old Hickory. The lesson had not been lost to Walker. He would never permit anyone to forget his youthful espousal of Jackson's cause. It would always supply him with one of his major arguments for votes.[6]

In 1832, when the young lawyer bid for a House seat, he campaigned on the importance of re-electing Jackson. Although the electorate gave the incumbent president a thumping margin of victory, Walker lost his bid. Some thought because in the vehemence of his support of Jackson, he had forgotten to remind his listeners of his own aspirations. After the campaign he joined J. F. H. Claiborne, the historian of Mississippi, in editing the local Jacksonian journal. His restless energy also propelled him further into politics and into an ever expanding speculation in land. This latter enterprise ultimately provided both the opportunity and the necessity to gain political office.[7]

Walker had not been alone in his speculations. Skyrocketing prices had convinced other young men that fortunes existed in land sales. William M. Gwin, whose evangelical intensity for self-promotion deeply impressed the ambitious Pennsylvanian, joined Walker in exploiting Indian lands. Some 1,000,000 acres of Cocchuma land, ceded under the Treaty of Dancing Rabbit

Creek, occupied the attention of a syndicate organized by the two men and joined by Henry S. Foote, John A. Quitman, and Joseph Davis. Each member of the syndicate was permitted to buy $1,000 worth of shares. Eventually, about 150 speculators from Mississippi, Tennessee, and Alabama participated in the enterprise. The syndicate allowed squatters to purchase their own improved land at cost, provided it did not exceed a quarter section. If the squatter insisted upon bidding against them, he was threatened with loss of all his land through syndicate bidding. As a result, about seventy percent of the Cocchuma land opened for sale passed into the syndicate's hands, enabling each shareholder to realize an average profit of $301 on his shares.[8]

The organizers of the syndicate, moreover, had supplemented their profits by retaining substantial amounts of land. Walker, in partnership with a Thomas Barnard, purchased 1,774 acres for about $1.25 an acre; subsequently, Barnard sold Walker his interest in 1,600 of these acres for $4,300. Simultaneously, Walker and Quitman jointly purchased a considerable tract of land in Coahoma County. In 1846, Quitman offered to accept a clear title to these lands and a $5,000 cash payment as full settlement of two judgments totalling $20,500 that he held against Walker. Rather than relinquish his share, Walker paid $2,500 on the judgments and agreed to make further payments at convenient intervals. He had also endeared himself during the syndicate purchases to numerous squatters by defending their disputed claims. On paper, at least, the syndicate made a handsome profit, but much of it had been in the form of promissory notes rather than hard cash. And it had had to borrow heavily to finance its purchases.[9]

As a member of the "Mississippi Regency," the state's Democratic leadership, Walker had been able to use political influence to get credit. At Natchez, he borrowed at least $10,000 from the sinking fund of the Planters' Bank—a fund expressly set aside to pay for state bonds, then held in London.[10] Since Governor Hiram Runnels had also joined the syndicate, the Bank proved unusually generous in its loans, though some of the less fortunate charged that it behaved like a legislative harlot. As the demand for credit facilities grew, a compliant legislature issued new bank charters increasing bank capitalization from $6,000,000 in 1833 to $52,500,000 in 1838. Legislative banking reached a climax in 1837 with the incorporation of the Union Bank whose $15,500,000 capitalization was backed by the physical property and slaves of the state. The whole rickety structure collapsed in 1838 when, after the Union Bank had advanced planters a credit of sixty dollars on each bale of their cotton, a decline of the price to thirty-eight dollars per bale left the Bank with enormous losses. In 1840, its liquid assets consisted of $4,349 in specie to redeem immediate liabilities of $3,-034,154.[11]

A desperate legislature finally followed the suggestion made by the new governor, Alexander McNutt, that the state repudiate $5,000,000 in Union Bank bonds held largely in Great Britain. The Planters' Bank bonds, though not repudiated, were left unpaid until 1852, when the Mississippi voters elected a legislature pledged not to redeem the Planters' Bank obligations. Within this fiscal wilderness Walker had at first flourished, only to be almost crushed by an irredeemable burden of debt.[12]

Walker first realized his hazardous condition when he felt the pinch of the sharp contraction resulting from Jackson's decision to remove public deposits from the Second Bank of the United States. His own extensive land and slave holdings had residual value, but his numerous note endorsements made him liable for rapidly mounting debts as borrowers failed during the Panic of 1837 to meet their obligations. Except for one near disastrous occasion, however, the young speculator kept his nerve. But that indiscretion had involved a denunciation in the spring of 1834 of Old Hickory to John Black, the incumbent Whig Senator from Mississippi. Delightedly, Black had read: "the public voice demands restoration of the deposits, and the creating of a bank to supply the general currency." He heartily endorsed Walker's conclusion that, "A state bank can no more supply and govern the general currency, than a state government can direct and control the affairs of the nation." Throughout his apostasy there ran the lament: "the country must be relieved from the frightful scenes of distress which have ruined us!!!" Gwin remembered gleefully how Walker "wept like a child" when he subsequently recalled his momentary desertion of Jackson.[13]

Whether he would have departed further from the Jacksonian camp is a moot point, for George Poindexter, the senior Senator from Mississippi, launched an investigation of the Cocchuma land sales. This brilliant eccentric had replaced John C. Calhoun as the President's *bête noir* after he had invoked senatorial courtesy to block the appointment of Samuel Gwin, an impetuous young friend of Jackson, to serve as land office register at Mount Salus, Mississippi. Old Hickory, never complacent in defeat, took the reverse as a personal rebuff. Twice again he submitted the appointment only to have the Senate reject it. A thoroughly irate President then refused to nominate anyone to the office until the Senate repealed the resolution upon which the Mississippi Senator had based his opposition: the one of February 3, 1831 disapproving the appointment of residents of one state to posts in another state. Jackson was completely victorious when the Senate dutifully repealed the resolution, and, to complete Poindexter's humiliation, he finally forced the appointment of Gwin to the Cocchuma land office.[14]

Poindexter launched his investigation to repay his earlier treatment by Jackson. Whatever the intention, Walker realized he could not escape involvement. His purchases at Cocchuma on his own account and in partnership had totalled 76,597 acres. Of this total 25,776 acres had been purchased on assignment for squatters, an action which proved most rewarding when the legislators of the counties, which were erected out of the Cocchuma purchases, voted almost solidly for Walker in 1836 in his successful bid to replace Poindexter in the Senate.[15]

When confronted with investigation, Walker rose to defend his gains. His excursion into heresy ceased as he contritely rejoined the Jackson camp. The Jacksonians determined to punish Poindexter for his affront by removing him from the Senate. The vivid stump personality, however, of "Old Poins," as the Whigs affectionately called Jackson's enemy, made it imperative that his opponent possess equivalent forensic power. With some unease the Mississippi democracy examined the credentials of the displaced Pennsylvanian; many of the delegates looked askance at his wavering over the removal of the deposits. A "terrible agony" gripped Walker as he considered how his indiscretion might deny him the nomination. But all was not black, for only once had he faltered. He could point out that he had staunchly supported the President in his dispute with Calhoun over nullification; a doctrine which he contended, would grant, if accepted, "that the American Congress shall possess such powers only, as South Carolina believes they may possess." Furthermore, the staunch protectionist of Pittsburgh championed a revenue tariff in Natchez. Nor did his wide popularity in the new Cocchuma counties fail to impress itself upon the Democracy. A candidate who had the support of a bloc of sixteen counties in the state legislature would be the candidate to defeat, rather than elect.[16]

The advantages outweighed the disadvantages; none more so than the belief that Jackson fondly recalled the young man's energetic efforts on his behalf when he first tried for the Presidency. Whether a shadow of suspicion over Walker's orthodoxy ever darkened the presidential mind at this time is doubtful. It is likely that given the primitive loyalties of Jackson, the old General needed to know little other than the young man had challenged the foul Poindexter. Most Democrats soon agreed that "the fierce invectives" with which Walker defended Jacksonian measures made him a near match for the sarcastic and often ironic "Poins." In November, 1834, the Democratic convention meeting at Jackson confirmed, although with some vigorous dissent, Walker's nomination. Ahead lay a year long struggle to get the election won.[17]

The Democrats now pressured Governor Runnels, a fellow Jacksonian, to convene a special session of the legislature for early 1835 to elect a senator. To secure Democratic control of the legislature, Runnels also issued writs of election to the sixteen counties erected out of the Choctaw cession permitting them to elect representatives to the lower house. The Democrats expected these new legislators to secure for them a heavy majority in the lower house with which to counterbalance Whig control of the state senate.[18]

The Whigs promptly charged that the election of the new delegates would violate the constitutional provision that the Senate should have at least one-fourth the lower house's membership. They also challenged the eligibility of the new members to serve until the next regular legislative session. The Whig senators refused to share in an election which they argued would be based on a fraudulent Democratic majority. The House Democrats countered with the charge that the Senate unconstitutionally interfered with the qualifications of its membership. The Senate then adjourned *sine die,* leaving the House no alternative but to follow its lead. As a result Poindexter's seat in the Senate remained vacant. The Jacksonians cried fraud, confident that the election of Walker was now "ensured." The *Globe* crowed that Poindexter would "not get ten votes . . . if his name were proposed." The checkered marital adventures of "Old Poins," and his extensive borrowings from the Bank of the United States were exploited to prove his private and public immorality. The struggling Senator reeled under the attack.[19]

Rarely had the Whiggery proved more inept. Thoroughly distraught, they were persuaded by Duff Green, nursing bitter grievances at Jackson's repudiation of Calhoun, to reopen the Cocchuma fraud charges. The Democrats pointed out that the

Whig Senator John Black had pronounced the Cocchuma syndicate both legal and proper. Moreover, whatever chance existed that Walker might be denied the seat depended on the Whigs breaking his control of the new counties. Every Mississippian knew that the settlers in these counties "were . . . either members of the [syndicate], or were in favor of it." They could hardly be expected to admit indulging in fraudulent behavior. The Whig attack only solidified the region's determination to support Walker.[20]

A genuine danger threatened Walker when his fellow Democrat, the "piney-woods" orator, Franklin E. Plummer, disgruntled at his failure to obtain the Democratic nomination, decided to run as an independent candidate while supporting the Whig ticket. The care with which Plummer cultivated his backwoods constituents had already earned him two terms as congressman. A thoroughgoing democrat, he regularly announced his opposition "to the aristocracy, whether composed of birth, of wealth, of learning, or of talents." Having deserted the Democrats, he accused them of being "aristocrats in principle and feeling, and democrats only in name." He caustically asked, "Where was Walker when I was defending the Hero of New Orleans from the attacks of his enemies in his struggle with the Bank?" Plummer soon found himself charged with a sellout to the enemy Whigs, who supposedly financed his campaign for their own nefarious purposes.[21]

The Democrats, however, doggedly identified their candidate as the personal choice of Jackson. William Gwin persuaded Andrew Jackson Donelson, the President's secretary, to send a presidential statement describing Walker as "amongst the first in point of talents, attainments and political integrity." Not willing to risk losing a single "pine-woods" vote, Walker changed his address from Natchez to Madisonville, a little hamlet in the heart of the state. His plantation there, which reverted back to its original owner after the election, enabled Walker's partisans to declare: "Citizens of Mississippi, Walker's interests are yours; he is a cotton planter; it is his only vocation." [22] In the foreseeable future, the pineys would be his constituency.

Massive treatises poured forth from his pen, demonstrating, in gorgeously embellished phrases, the evident superiority of the Jacksonians. The impressionable yeomen stood in awe as the little politician orated for hours without a note. He denounced Poindexter for traitorously allying himself "with the great monied power of the North, which had already ruined the South financially and would next turn its batteries against our domestic institutions." To allay doubts about his own reliability on the bank question, Walker revealed he had written a second letter to Black arguing that removal "was certainly unnecessary for the Bank was dying under the veto, and why convulse the country by kicking the bank into its grave before the expiration of its charter in 1836." He suggested cautiously that Jackson outline the replacement bank he had mentioned in his veto address. [23]

Though Walker knew he trod on dangerous ground, he also knew that many conscientious Jacksonians harbored doubts about the wisdom of a program that eliminated the Bank without a suitable replacement. His cautious criticism also enabled him to suggest to Natchez that, after all, he remained reliable. But, above all, it initiated a conservative stance on fiscal questions that would be his for life.

As the time for election drew near, the Whigs threw caution to the winds in their effort to defeat Walker. Senator John Black proposed that he resign his seat to provide room for both Plummer and Poindexter—a plan that was dropped when it became apparent that Plummer delegates preferred Walker as their second choice. Bitter desperation drove Poindexter to fight harder. Samuel Gwin, smarting from the Cocchuma investigation, chose to bait the Senator with hisses during an angry speech. Isaac Caldwell, the former law partner of "Old Poins," challenged Gwin to a duel. Within a few days Caldwell was dead and Gwin condemned to a lingering death from his wounds.[24]

Surrounded by large crowds from the near countryside, the state legislature voted on January 9, 1836. The first ballot gave Walker thirty-six votes only seven votes short of a majority. A steady desertion of votes from Plummer finally gave Walker the victory on the fifth ballot. The Whigs gloomily accepted the Jacksonian triumph. John A. Quitman, the Whig president *pro tempore* of the state senate, soon to be reconciled with the new Senator, regretfully informed his wife, "We are . . . chained to the car of Van Buren for six years." Poindexter faded into retirement. Walker, betraying "an eagerness altogether unbecoming" a fledgling Senator, hastened to Washington to take his seat.[25]

3. Texas

ON FEBRUARY 22, 1836, Senator Thomas Hart Benton of Missouri presented the credentials of the new Senator from Mississippi to Vice President Van Buren who administered the oath of office. Walker, exhausted from a laborious journey by river boat and stage coach in the dead of winter, was distracted by the illness of his wife who had been forced to remain behind with their daughter Mary in Maysville, Kentucky. A few days later he endured a "severe domestic bereavement" when his brother Duncan succumbed to tuberculosis while in Cuba.

It was Duncan who had laid the basis for his brother's interest in Texas.[1] In 1834, Duncan had purchased a considerable amount of land in the territory, and the following year transferred these lands to his brother.[2] Shortly afterward, he was imprisoned by the Mexicans who accused him of agitating for Texan independence. When he was released in 1836 his health had been irretrievably wrecked. He died in Cuba. The anguish of a grief stricken Walker burnished the steely hatred he subsequently felt for Mexico. This personal tragedy helped to shape the course of history.[3]

When Texas declared itself independent of Mexico, the Mississippian made himself its unofficial representative on the floor of Congress. On April 26, 1836, though supporting American neutrality in the dispute between Mexico and Texas, he called for public support of "a people who are imitating . . . our own Revolution." Despite the Senate's hesitancy to recognize Texan independence, the little Senator persisted in pressing the case for Texas. On May 9, 1836 he read before a startled Senate a

letter from Mexico reporting that Santa Anna had assured the
French and British ministers "that he would drive the Texans
across the Red River, and into the territories of the United
States; and that, if the Texans were protected there, he would
drive them to Washington, and burn it too, as the British had
done." The triumph of the Texans at San Jacinto on April 21,
1836, moved Walker to press once again for recognition.[4]

Shortly afterward, Senator William C. Preston of South Carolina announced he had decided to relinquish direction of the
pro-Texas senators to "second the views of the gentleman from
Mississippi, and follow in his wake." Privately it was assumed
that the views of Walker on Texas now accorded with those of
President Jackson. Although Walker claimed his information
on Santa Anna's threat to invade the United States had been received in a letter of March 26, 1836, an identical letter from
Anthony Butler, the American Minister to Mexico, had been in
the President's possession since December, 1835. Efforts to
persuade the Senate to recognize Texan independence proved
fruitless during the first session of the 24th Congress, but Walker
immediately took up the fight in the second session. Four days
before the Old General left the Presidency, the Senate approved
a resolution submitted by Walker recognizing Texas independence.[5]

The Texan envoys to Washington, Memucan Hunt and William
H. Wharton, treated the Mississippian as their unofficial representative in Congress. Both described his efforts as "high minded
and disinterested." They were frequently reminded "that it was
a Representative of the state of Mississippi" who aided them.
Since the cause of Texas happened to be particularly attractive
to his constituents, Walker saw no reason why he should not
exploit his role. During his first campaign for the Senate he had
urged annexation; now he began a nine year campaign for the
union of the two republics. In response to clamorous requests
from Texans he visited the San Jacinto battle field in the spring
of 1837. Before the assembled dignitaries of the new republic

he heard himself described as "our champion in our direst conflict with the enemy, our savior in the thrilling hour of dismay." Walker replied "with the thunders of . . . eloquence." It was evident that his support of the annexation of Texas had pushed him, despite his junior standing, into the forefront of the Senate's leadership.[6]

Unfortunately for the hopes of Texas, Van Buren, now President, remained notoriously cool to the prospect of expansion. The administration's indifference to annexation of any land angered Walker. In 1839 his anger almost led to open bitterness when Van Buren tried to peacefully settle the dispute over the Maine–New Brunswick border. Never restrained when faced with the prospect of territorial expansion, Walker declared in the Senate that forcible seizure, even if it meant war with Great Britain, was justified.[7] His relations with the administration had been already strained in the early months of 1837 when Van Buren proposed a hard currency system. The Senator promptly threatened a "war to the knife" unless it was modified. During a particularly heated debate over the issue, Walker offered to duel Thomas Hart Benton, a leading proponent of an "exclusive gold and silver currency." [8] The collapse of the banks that followed the Panic of 1837, however, persuaded Walker to abandon pet banks and paper currency which he now denounced as the main supports of the "whole wretched banking system." His swift shift to a hard currency and the Independent Treasury soon made him a major prop for administration policy in the Senate.

Walker's constant concern for territorial expansion led him to take an interest in public land policy. The efforts of Henry Clay to distribute the proceeds of public land sales among the states brought a sharp response from the frontier states. At stake in their estimation was the establishment of a pre-emption and graduation program which would permit settlers to buy land at prices commensurate to the value of the land and which would eliminate the fiscal disabilities of the underdeveloped states. They assumed that any contraction of Treasury income would

be made up by higher tariff charges and they also foresaw that
the older, more populous states would receive most of the public
land funds. Walker, who had inaugurated his congressional
career with a "lecture" to Clay on the errors of Whiggery,
offered a series of amendments to the Clay proposal. Though
Walker failed in his efforts to attach the principle of graduation
or to limit public land sales to actual settlers, the Clay bill was
subsequently rejected by a presidential veto. Walker had now
become the chief proponent of pre-emption with the graduation
and reduction of public land prices.[9]

The impending termination of the Pre-emption Act of 1834
moved the spokesman for the Mississippi frontier to propose a
permanent pre-emption act which would provide "for the sale
and entry of all the public lands in forty acre lots, and . . .
equalized the grants of public lands among the new States, in
which the public lands are situated." He also pressed for the
right of every "actual settler on the public lands at any time
before the 1st of January, 1836 to pre-empt a quarter section." [10]
Over the stubborn opposition of Henry Clay, Walker succeeded
in having his measures switched from the hostile Committee on
Public Lands to a special committee of which he was chairman.
Its favorable report of June 15, 1836, came to naught since the
Whig majority in the Senate declined to act.[11]

The displacement of the Whigs from control of the Senate in
December, 1836, ensured for Walker the chairmanship of the
Committee on Public Lands. Ironically he gained control of the
very committee that hardly two years before had investigated
his land speculations. The committee promptly repudiated Clay's
proposals on land sales and returned its own bill early in
January, 1837. Uneasily aware of his own reputation as a speculator, Walker urged that public lands be sold only to actual
settlers. Unless this provision were made, "vast quantities of
these lands would pass into the hands of a few capitalists."
Memories of his own actions stirred as he argued "it was the
system that was wrong; and so long as it was continued, any

denunciation of those who purchased large bodies of the un-occupied lands was worse than ridiculous." [12]

A system that invited the ambitious to "come and get it" could only terminate by impoverishing "the many, and enriching the few." In urgent words he evoked a coming class struggle as he warned: "It will create a war of capital against labor, of the producer against the non-producer; of the cultivator against the speculator; a war in which this Government will be arrayed on the side of the speculator." The agrarian dream came alive again as the Senator assured his listeners that the proposed legislation would encourage "agriculture, that mother of freemen, that nurse of virtue, liberty and independence." [13] Senator Thomas Ewing of Ohio could hardly be blamed for afterward finding it "a little remarkable, that those who denounce these 'speculators' the most loudly and most frequently . . . are those who under-stand them best, and who are themselves the most deeply en-gaged in the vocation which they thus condemn." [14]

The eloquence of the Mississippian and the presence of a Democratic senatorial majority determined the event; Walker's land bills were approved by the Senate on February 9, 1837, but the House adjourned without considering the measure. Early in December of 1837, Walker resumed his efforts to obtain pre-emption rights for settlers who were not covered by earlier pre-emption laws. This time the House confirmed the measure and Van Buren signed it into law in June, 1838.[15]

But a rapidly developing economic crisis diverted his atten-tion from public to private affairs. The Planters' Bank that he had solemnly assured the Senate was "perfectly solvent" and for which "he would himself handle the insurance coverage—if his resources permitted—for less than one 20th of one per cent" neared collapse. His intimate friend William Gwin, fully in-formed of the Planters' circumstances by Walker, warned Clai-borne that Secretary of the Treasury Woodbury was preparing to compel certain of the state's "pet banks" to return "for near a million" in federal funds.[16] No longer able to conceal the rickety credit system upon which his own investments were based, Walker lashed out at "new loans, increased tariff, and the issuance of more paper money." The hard money wing of the party now had a firm ally. Thomas Hart Benton, only recently at odds with Walker, listened approvingly as the Mississippian denounced interest bearing Treasury notes which would "find their way to England and . . . would . . . result in debt to a foreign power." When it was suggested that his constituents were in favor of restoring the Bank of the United States, he announced he would resign his seat to allow the people of Mississippi to vote for someone who supported the Bank. He considered the Sub-Treasury system the "best calculated to relieve the present distressed state of the country." Pet banks he renounced in favor of a firm separation of government and banking. His conversion to *Loco Foco* doctrines was so complete that he announced his intention to make the divorce of government and banking his re-election issue in 1840.[17]

A personal difficulty now threatened Walker's continued membership in the Senate. His precarious health broke, and he feared a lung affliction similar to that which had taken the life of his brother. The severity of his illness forced him to absent himself from the Senate for long periods.[18] Prodded by his doctors he agreed to go south in search of a more favorable climate. It was not until May, 1839, that he was pronounced cured. The havoc which disease had wrought upon his physique had so weakened him that Walker announced from Natchez on May 1, 1839, that he would not try for re-election. The announcement brought a flood of Democratic pleas that he reconsider his withdrawal. The Mississippi democracy had already sustained severe political reverses in 1838 when the state's two House seats were filled by Seargeant S. Prentiss and Thomas J. Word, both Whigs. An even greater blow was the election of John Henderson, a Whig, to replace Democrat Thomas Williams in the Senate in January, 1839. The party could hardly be expected to view with detachment the loss of its strongest candidate, especially when it was assumed the Whigs would nominate for the Senate the spellbinding orator, S. S. Prentiss.[19]

Public pleas registered by Governor McNutt, Gwin, and Federal Judge Samuel J. Gholson against his withdrawal, forced a reluctant Walker to reconsider and announce to the Mississippi democracy that his obligations to it were "beyond the power of language to express. For such a party," he continued, "there is no honorable sacrifice which I am unwilling to make." His campaign issues were to be the Independent Treasury and "whether this shall be a government of the banks or the people." Since Prentiss favored a restoration of the Bank, the resulting campaign raged as a straight-out fight between the pro- and anti-bank supporters. The increasing numbers of Mississippians who moved toward support of Governor McNutt's repudiation stand gave Walker a decided advantage. The Whig cause suffered from the indifference to victory of their candidate, who confessed privately to his mother, "If not elected, I shall feel no disappointment, for I have seen as much of public life as I wish." [20]

Unable to campaign because his recent illness had adversely affected his throat, making public speaking impossible, Walker commenced writing letters which his opponent accurately complained were "as long as the Mediterranean." J. F. H. Claiborne who reluctantly played host to the invalid Senator agreed to write in support of Walker's campaign. It was he who reiterated that his candidate had received the hearty endorsement of Calhoun, which moved one opposition journal to describe it as "a certificate . . . to recommend Mr. Walker to the Nullifiers." [21] Actually this open courting of southern sentiment directed most of the campaign attack not against Prentiss but against his close friend, Henry Clay. Walker accused Prentiss of intending to make Mississippians "the slaves and vassals of the northern manufacturers." He further indicted his opponent for supporting land legislation intended to complete the degradation of Mississippi. The campaign served to accentuate Prentiss's disgust "with politics, and . . . the notoriety" which it attached to his name. Perhaps, too, the eloquent Whig felt a pang of conscience in opposing the man who had allowed him, a schoolmaster from Maine, to study law in his office.[22]

The Mississippi Whiggery suffered an overwhelming defeat in 1839. The returns from the November election ensured the re-election of Governor McNutt; they sent Albert G. Brown and Jacob Thompson into the House and they gave the Democracy a top-heavy legislative majority. The legislature met on January 9, 1840 to elect Walker with seventy votes on the first ballot. Re-elected, but still weak from his illness, he returned to Washington to resume his seat for the first session of the 26th Congress. It was an aggressive and ambitious senior Senator who returned to demand fuller recognition from the party leadership.[23]

Since he had based his election campaign upon the Independent Treasury, Walker aggressively defended it in the Senate. The recurring feud with Clay broke out again when that gentleman savagely castigated Van Buren for surveying "unconcerned the widespread ruin and wretchedness before him, without emotion and without sympathy." [24] Walker hurried to defend his chief's laissez faire attitude in the midst of economic crisis. Denouncing Clay for a "total absence of all decorum," the debate rapidly deteriorated until Clay offered to accept Walker's challenge to duel. The none-too-objective observer Philip Hone concluded that Walker had abused Clay "grossly." Although the duello was not invoked, the relations between the two men had become so strained that neither could speak of the other without bitterness.[25]

In the presidential campaign of 1840, Walker, still recuperating from his illness, gave reserved support to Van Buren. Along with Buchanan he expected the re-election of the shrewd New Yorker unless "the elements of opposition be combined in favor of Harrison." Though firmly attached to the hard money policies of Van Buren, the Mississippian skeptically viewed the President's opposition to territorial expansion. The 1840 defeat of the

Little Magician provoked in Walker little more than an amused indifference. Increasingly he became preoccupied with the future of Texas. Once again he explored its chances of statehood. Success hinged on northern willingness to admit Texas in order to maintain the sectional equilibrium in the Senate. Time and again he reminded the South that Texas could be divided into four or more states. Not content with Texan expansion, he pressed for division of Florida into two territories that could later be made into two more southern states. Walker had converted expansion into a struggle to overcome the limitations imposed on the peculiar institution by the Missouri Compromise.[26]

The election of Harrison did not promise fulfillment for the Texas advocates. But a malicious fate assigned the ancient Whig thirty days as President. His death brought him freedom from the hoards of office-seekers; it also gave the Presidency to the states' rights Democrat, John Tyler, who had defected to the Whiggery. It was not long before the Whig leadership and the President were at odds over their national and states' rights principles. One Walker correspondent described the Whigs as a "mongrel party" and chortled as its President and party leadership feuded. Unknown as yet to the Mississippian, the death of Harrison had placed an annexationist in the Presidency. Within a short time their mutually shared interest in Texas enabled Walker to ". . . whisper . . . Democracy and the Presidency into the ear of Mr. Tyler." [27]

At first, Walker had grave suspicions of Tyler. He warned his wife Mary that Tyler's appointments were forcing him to accept a position from which he would have to denounce Tyler "in a decided & emphatic manner." On the floor of the Senate Walker actually demanded a clarification of the Presidential powers that had devolved upon Tyler.[28] But any prospective hostilities between the two men ended when they united in opposition to the establishment of the Fiscal Bank of the United States. The Democrats fought a delaying action against renewal, offering endless amendments designed ostensibly to secure the new bank against the abuses perpetrated by the Second Bank of the United States. The Whigs accused them of deliberately seeking to consume "time and making the final bill odious." Time and again the Senate voted down proposals preventing the new bank from conducting discount business, to place the appointment of the government directors in the hands of Congress, and denying it the right to grant loans to corporations.[29] When it became apparent that the Whigs would pass the bill into law, Walker confidently predicted that Tyler would veto the congressional decision. A stunned Whiggery heard that prediction confirmed on August 16, 1841, when the clerk read Tyler's veto message. A hissing gallery spectator escaped punishment only after the "happy" Mississippian interceded. He understood Whig outrage and pitied them for being cheated of the fruits of their 1840 triumph.[30]

Soon after, Buchanan eager for the 1844 Democratic presidential nomination, angrily charged that "Tyler is endeavoring to throw himself into the arms of the Democratic party." Clay Whigs were being turned out of office as rapidly as Democrats were found who could "humbug" Tyler "by reassuring him of his growing popularity." [31]

As the ties between Tyler and the Whigs dissolved, Walker assumed the role of unofficial spokesman for the administration in Congress. A mutual antagonism to the bank found a complement in Tyler's enthusiasm for the annexation of Texas. The presence of Walker on the Committee on Public Lands permitted him ample opportunity to press the presidential views on Texas. Long afterward, Claiborne, living in a defeated South, ungenerously recalled that his erstwhile friend had been the "Delilah" of the Tyler administration. It was an exaggerated description as Walker himself made clear when Gwin proposed to exploit his friend's supposed influence upon Tyler. The President, Walker confessed, was receptive to his suggestions, but he was no captive.[32]

The political advantages of Texas complemented his growing interest in Texas lands. Walker shrewdly advised Gwin and Claiborne on their purchase of "near 600,000 acres of land at & around the three forks of Trinity in Texas." From Richard Bache, his father-in-law who was now settled near Dallas, Walker received reliable information about the prospects of Texas land speculations. But his heavy obligations prevented him from exploiting his own holdings. Hard-pressed, he disposed of his inherited holdings in Texas, but even this money barely scratched the surface of his indebtedness. As security for an outstanding debt of $42,500, contracted during flush times, the Senator in 1841 put up several notes he held against Gwin, which in turn were secured by two plantations of nearly 2,800 acres and 108 slaves. Though Walker subsequently declared that even at this early date he held the "peculiar institution" in abhorrence, he had not forgotten the security value of slaves.[33] In 1843, he informed his cousin Stephen Duncan, who was pressing for repayment of a note, that he had managed to reduce his total liabilities since 1837 from $200,000 to about $30,000. He had sold his lands and slaves only when no other alternative existed. His senatorial salary had been attached and he managed the support of his family only with income earned from arguing cases before the Supreme Court.[34] Whenever possible he retired his outstanding obligations with paper—depreciated currency and notes he held against others were preferred. The only means he did not employ, hard currency, he evidently did not possess.[35]

His friend Gwin had noted that creditors were somewhat deferential to his senatorial friend. They did not choose to provoke an official reprisal. Gwin chose, therefore, when similarly harassed, to make a "successful bid" for a congressional seat in 1841. As he remembered it, the House seat gave him a refuge from dunning creditors.[36] It also launched him upon an effort to raid the Treasury. Prior to his departure from Mississippi he had agreed to serve as agent for the Chicksaw Indians in the administration of investments made by the government for the

Indians. Under the agreement made between the federal government and the Chicsaw tribe covering the cession of their tribal lands, the government had agreed to administer funds received to compensate the Chicsaw as their lands were sold. Annual interest payments had been promised to the dispossessed tribesmen. Gwin discovered that payments of $112,042.99 had been inadvertently charged against the Chicsaw capital account rather than against the Treasury. Furthermore, although the Chicsaw funds were supposed to be invested only in "safe and valuable" stocks, a considerable amount had been invested in stocks of dubious value which returned no interest. The chiefs and commissioners of the Chicsaw nation delegated to their agent full authority for negotiating a settlement, and as a dutiful agent Gwin presented the matter to the Treasury Department. Secretary of the Treasury, G. M. Bibb, adjusted the matter by transferring the full sum to the Chicsaw account.

A perfectly legitimate transaction soon passed into the category of dubious, if not fraudulent financing. Gwin promptly presented the Treasury Department an assignment from the Chicsaw chiefs which transferred $56,021.49 to his personal account. The transfer was confirmed by the second auditor of the Treasury but instead of being paid was passed by the Comptroller to the Indian Office for administrative examination. Members of the Chicsaw nation immediately protested the payment as excessive. The account remained in the Indian Office until 1850 when Secretary of the Interior Ewing, upon the advice of Attorney-General Reverdy Johnson, finally released the payment to Gwin.[37]

Throughout the early stages of this drawnout dispute, Walker aided his friend indirectly. On several occasions he attempted to obtain congressional authorization for the Chicsaw nation to try the validity of its conflicting arguments in court. Gwin lobbied energetically in behalf of the proposed bills on the assumption that his chances for a final settlement would brighten considerably if he could put his claim to a legal test.[38]

However, once Walker had been appointed Secretary of the Treasury, he confirmed Gwin's suspicion that although he "professes great friendship" he always took care that friendship would not endanger his own career.[39] There is no evidence that Walker ever indulged in illegal acts, but his identification with known speculators cast suspicion upon his honesty. It also led to the accusation that he supported the annexation of Texas because he expected monetary reward.

A public accusation appeared, charging that the Senator from Mississippi supported annexation because he owned land in the territory and held Texas script. The charge received a prompt denial by an announcement that both forms of property had been relinquished. The public was invited to remember that similar stands on Texas had already been taken by John Quincy Adams in 1825 and Henry Clay in 1827 and also by Andrew Jackson and Martin Van Buren in 1829.[40] No evidence has been discovered showing that Walker held any bonds or script either in the 1840's or 1850's. His assertion in 1850 to the government banker, W. W. Corcoran, a gentleman who would have readily known if it were otherwise, "that I have not now, never have had & never expect to have any interest . . . direct or indirect in Texas Stock, bonds, script or debt of any kind," suggests that in this instance the Mississippian told the truth.[41]

An explanation other than material reward lay at the base of Walker's preoccupation with Texas. Annexation was an issue that had on various occasions gripped Mississippians. In 1843, the state legislature declared the annexation of Texas an issue of "an import infinitely grave and interesting to the people of the lower South." [42] Since his political future depended upon the continuing support of Mississippi, and it was suspected—mistakenly—by some that he aspired to the 1844 Democratic Vice Presidential nomination, his actions were a response to popular pressure.[43] He also shared the sentiments of his constituents. Throughout his life he dedicated his energy to the fulfillment of continental expansion. His support for Texas annexation accentuated an already intense personal vision of the American manifest destiny.

The single-minded devotion that Walker gave to the cause of Texas determined his stand at the 1844 Democratic convention. Although he publicly affirmed an undying friendship for Van Buren, he privately made it known that he was "decidedly against Mr. Van Buren." [44] Charles Jared Ingersoll, the aristocratic Philadelphian, a vigorous proponent of annexation, heard Walker read approvingly the conclusions of a fellow Mississippian who had declared "that either Van Buren or Clay will get votes for president of several States, as the one or other declares for Texas." [45] In the eyes of Richard M. Johnson, the quixotic former Vice President, Walker and Senator A. H. Sevier of Arkansas were his "right and left bower in the present canvass." This gentleman, acutely embarrassed by pecuniary difficulties, assured his fellow debtor that he would look to his guidance on Texas "in the event of ever having power again to serve my country." But as both men realized, it would be Van Buren against the field.[46] Transcending the Texas issue was a gnawing fear that even an espousal of annexation by Van Buren would not be enough to prevent a second defeat. The mutual distaste between Tyler and Van Buren precluded a reunification of the Democracy if either man were the nominee.[47]

While Walker pursued his devious course toward Van Buren, he knew that Jackson wholeheartedly supported his campaign for annexation. Old Hickory insisted that *"the present golden moment* to obtain Texas must not be lost, or Texas must from necessity be thrown into the *arms of England,* & be *forever* lost to the United States." [48] The old man's immense prestige made it unlikely that anyone who publicly rejected annexation would receive the nomination. In addition, Jackson kept Sam Houston from openly opposing annexation. This raucous Texan vacillated on the advantage of annexation. As one Walker correspondent apologized, when attempting to explain Houston's indecision, "I am sorry to say that he was on several frolics previous to leaving. When *sober*, he was for annexation: but when *drunk*, or in liquor, he would express himself strongly against the measure!" [49] Wearily the old general, racked with illness, pleaded with Houston to do nothing to forestall annexation. Anxiously, he read Walker's plea that the Texas President take advantage of the Tyler administration's sympathy toward annexation lest a delay of "the measure one or two years" lose Texas forever.[50]

Matters worsened when Anson Jones succeeded Houston to the Presidency of Texas. Jones, a former New Yorker, was known to be "without feeling for annexation." [51] His emphatic statement "That annexation was a good question for the Candidates of the Presidency; but a large portion of the Democracy were opposed to it in the U.S. and that it would be lost sight of by the Tariff" made the prospects for future negotiations look bleak.[52] Texans expressed themselves with increasing frequency in favor of a British alliance. When General Duff Green, the American consul-general to Texas, threatened President Jones with a revolution if he were to reject annexation, the enraged President shouted: "No damn demagogue should dictate to him or rule his course of action. That if a Revolution did occur, he would find him prepared for it." [53] Furthermore, Jones gave every indication that he would expel the aggressive Green from Texas. Even if Texas were to seek annexation Walker realized that Democratic dissension precluded the necessary two-thirds majority needed in the Senate to ratify the annexation treaty.

An uncomfortable impasse had been reached. As the Democratic party prepared to designate its 1844 candidate, no choice seemed possible but Van Buren. Such a decision would have made annexation an unlikely prospect. The immediate problem facing the annexationist camp was to obtain time to prevent the Little Magician's nomination. It was with this purpose that Walker visited the office of Silas Wright on February 26, 1843. The New York Senator had long been recognized as the spokesman for the former president in Washington. The Mississippian asked Wright to delay the Democratic convention. Traditionally, candidates were chosen a full year before the elections. In a long conversation, the two men agreed that although the nomination of Van Buren was certain, a delay would help mollify the various dissidents within the party. Grudgingly, Wright agreed to have the convention convene in May of 1844. He asked Walker and Ohio's Senator Benjamin Tappan, whose commitment to Van Buren would one day lead him into the Free Soil ranks, to canvass Democratic congressmen on the acceptability of a May convention.[54]

As the leader of the annexationists, Walker realized he must remain aloof from any effort to obtain a nomination for himself at the Baltimore convention lest it force a tightening of the opposition to Texas. When the Democratic convention at Jackson, Mississippi evinced a desire to support his candidacy for the Vice Presidency, the Senator unconditionally withdrew his name. A supporter of Polk at the convention noted with relief that "Mr. Walker had more prudence and foresight than his friends and he withdrew." [55] When Secretary of State Abel Upshur was killed in the U.S.S. *Princeton* explosion during the Washington Day celebration of 1844, rumors circulated that Walker had been designated his successor. Jackson assured Houston that the talents of the little Mississippian would remain in the Senate where they were most needed. It was one thing to be an unofficial spokesman for Tyler, as the Senator himself realized: it was quite another to become a member of the official family. Furthermore, "Little Bob" had no intention of undermining the hopes of Van Buren and at the same time embracing the hopeless political future of Tyler.[56]

Amidst the tumult over Texas there came unsettling information that Old Hickory was almost bankrupt. Immediately, the Democratic faithful sought ways to relieve the General's dilemma. None proved more active than Walker who delegated for himself the task of obtaining for the retired President a refund with interest of the $1,000 fine levied against him for refusing to comply with a writ of habeas corpus after the Battle of New Orleans. On Saint Valentine's Day, 1844, the Senator wrote the Hermitage that "The bill passed without any proviso by the triumphant vote of 30 to 16." A Treasury draft for $2,732.90 reached the penniless old man shortly afterward.[57]

Humanitarian preoccupations did not divert Walker from the question of Texas. Nursing a wrenched back and a sprained ankle, caused when a hack in which he had been riding broke an axle, he eagerly responded to the plea from the Carroll County, Kentucky democracy that he assist them in their campaign for the annexation of Texas. Former Congressman William O. Butler, a long-time friend of Walker, who regaled listeners with tales of the days when he had been Jackson's aide-de-camp, and George Sanders, a "poor" and unscrupulous office seeker, had composed the request, well-aware it would give the Mississippian his chance to make Texas the dominant issue at the Baltimore convention. They also maliciously anticipated that it would force Clay to state his stand. Both men served their cause well.[58]

On February 5, 1844, Walker responded by issuing his *Letter on the Annexation of Texas*, a long, devious essay, which argued for immediate annexation. The *Letter* created an immediate sensation. Every section of the nation was given a logical reason for advocating annexation: the New Englanders were promised new markets; the Southerners new land into which to expand; the abolitionists would have a funnel with which to siphon the slave out of the South into Mexico and freedom; and the British-baiters would have a chance to twist the lion's tail. Since the *Letter* could never hope to obtain an attentive hearing in either Whig or antiannexationist Democratic journals, it was printed in pamphlet form. By the tens of thousands the *Texas Letter* was distributed across the nation.[59]

From all sides readers lauded the essay. Richard Rush, a Philadelphia patrician and a friend of the Walker family, assured Walker that: "Could your letter be *read* throughout the middle and northern states by large classes now strongly prejudiced against Annexation, . . . it would sow the seeds of conviction." From Richard M. Johnson, eager to obtain patronage for his Indian school from the War Department now headed by Walker's uncle, William Wilkins, came the pronouncement that the letter was a "120 pounder." The abolitionist, Lewis Tappan, who informed the Mississippian that he intended "to touch the subject of slavery with the torch—of truth and moral suasion," responded to the funnel theory as one of "sound philosophy." George Bancroft, Boston Brahmin and historian of a divinely inspired America, saw the letter as another reason for his "most decided support of Texas." The evidence proved to Walker that he now had an issue with which to reshape the course of the Democracy.[60]

Upon a hapless Van Buren descended numerous letters insisting he make known his stand on Texas. The wily politician was finally cornered. Reluctantly he declared against annexation. Van Buren's long political career entered into the shadows; that of the nearly bankrupt Senator from Mississippi was reaching its zenith.[61]

Early in June, 1844, the Senate unexpectedly rejected annexation. Andrew Jackson, depressed at the result, demanded "why friend Walker did not press a treaty for . . . annexation through the House of Representatives when he saw the Senate would not approve?" Answering his own question, he sardonically wrote, "it appears to me that this great and important national question was lost sight of for President making." Privately Walker admitted as much, but he knew that once the election result was in, Congress would agree to a joint resolution annexing Texas, thereby putting the question beyond need of a two-thirds Senate vote. For the moment, he meant to exploit Texas as an issue to defeat Van Buren at Baltimore and then to elect a Democratic candidate who favored annexation. A few months delay in annexing Texas seemed to Walker a cheap enough price for such a result. Jackson would therefore have to wait.[62] And at Baltimore the ruthless game would be played out.

4. The Substance of Power

DURING THE YEARS from 1844 to 1849 Walker achieved his greatest power. He became first "president-maker" and then Secretary of the Treasury. His decisions substantially affected the future of the Republic. But whatever his original expectations and his final achievements, he left the Treasury Department in 1849 a politician without a future.

No one who came to Baltimore to nominate a Democratic presidential candidate in 1844 had any idea of the portentous decisions of the near future—decisions which would almost double the nation in size and establish the conditions within which the conflict between nationalism and sectionalism would ultimately be fought. If any common purpose united the delegates, it was their determination to nominate a winner.

Baltimore impressed the political visitors with its dynamic vigor for life. The western wealth that poured into the city by the Baltimore and Ohio Railroad created a bustle which hardly disguised the severe dislocations that afflicted the city. But the delegates, preoccupied with politics, accepted the endless activity of Baltimore as a natural aspect of the urban life which was slowly beginning to characterize the nation.[1]

The city appeared properly impressed when three trains each of thirty-eight railway cars arrived from Washington loaded with Democratic politicos and hostile Whig observers.[2] It was fascinated with Samuel F. B. Morse's new telegraph which enabled Washington to be kept fully informed of the convention's proceedings. It expected, as did many Democrats, the renomination of Martin Van Buren, who had a certain majority of the convention's votes on the first ballot.[3] What it did not know was that there existed determined and conniving opposition to Van Buren.

The Old Magician's delegates looked to New York for their guidance. That state's delegation under the leadership of Benjamin Franklin Butler and John Van Buren was confident of ultimate success. It knew that "Old Martin's" letter opposing the annexation of Texas had lost him support among the party's expansionists, but the Whigs could not derive any benefits from his stand since their candidate, Henry Clay, had been equally emphatic in his opposition to annexation. Assuming that Clay would not attempt to shift his position, they ignored the caginess of the gaunt Kentuckian. Nor had the Van Buren leaders fully considered the possibility that to gain the advantage of the Texas issue, the convention might reject Van Buren and nominate an expansionist candidate. Equally threatening was the opposition of conservative Democrats to Van Buren's radical financial and tariff policies.[4] Ample evidence existed to show that discontent ran rampant even among the Van Buren delegations.

Early in May, 1844, a seven man Mississippi delegation, pledged to Van Buren, announced that it felt the pledge no longer binding as both the convention that had instructed it to vote for Van Buren and the Mississippi state legislature had declared for the annexation of Texas. Obviously, they could not fulfill both expectations. Walker, a member of the delegation, seized upon this development to ensure support of a pro-annexation candidate. Shortly afterward the delegation issued a manifesto arguing that Texas was not a sectional but a national question. "To the South," it asserted, "it gives peace and security, to the North & West, new & ever augmenting home markets." Determined to remove any doubt on its stand, the delegation concluded with the flat declaration that "only those who sustain this great and truly American measure shall receive our cordial & undivided support." [5] Anyone who had read *The Texas Letter* knew who had sparked this development.

Control of the Mississippi delegation gave Walker the instrument he needed to manipulate the decisions of the Baltimore convention. He pledged the delegation to support efforts to reestablish the 1832 and 1833 Democratic National Convention rules "which required a majority of two-thirds to make a nomination." Careful to avoid the accusation that they supported a sectional candidate, the delegation agreed to oppose not only Van Buren but also Calhoun. Then, with prodding from Walker, it agreed to back a resolution calling for the 1832 rules with Walker designated to cast the delegation's vote.[6] Adoption of the two-thirds rule would neatly solve the ethical problem of casting pledged votes. Van Buren could obtain his majority which hardly approached two-thirds and not seriously endanger the well-laid plans of the pro-Texas managers. Unless the Van Buren leaders were able to start an unexpected stampede toward their candidate, they were beaten. Walker's activities within his own delegation were but a prelude to his even more subtle maneuverings within the convention itself, where his behavior led one delegate to describe him as "a man of the mole policy—who works underground and in the dark." [7]

At no time did Walker indicate a strong preference for a candidate; his sole aim appears to have been to thwart Van Buren's hopes. Actually Texas provided a pretext to eliminate the former president, for as early as 1842 Walker had considered checking Van Buren by organizing the friends of "all the other candidates . . . against him." [8] He did so because he believed that even if Van Buren were nominated, he would not win. At the same time he flirted with the idea of supporting Calhoun whose opinion on Texas was correct and who commanded the support of Tyler. Even this commitment had been predicated on the assumption that the states' rights Democrat Tyler would be unable to get the Democratic nomination. But neither Calhoun nor Tyler would receive his support if either candidacy threatened to split the Democratic party, for Walker had asserted, "There must be no disunion in the Democratic

ranks in the next great contest, and those who attempt to produce
it will fall never to rise again." [9] In the faction-ridden Democracy, his insistence upon a winner guaranteed his role as the
guiding spirit of the anti-Van Buren party. Since he belonged to
no faction, he could be trusted by all.

Indifference to the final candidate, provided he supported
Texas annexation, was an important but not the strongest in-
gredient in Walker's campaign. Improvising as circumstances
dictated, he left the Van Burenites perpetually bewildered, unable to forestall the attrition of their support. A Calhoun delegate, Francis Pickens, who constantly attended Walker, concluded that "though Walker fights nobly, he does not see the end
of his moves." [10] The opposition to Van Buren first threatened
not to support the Democratic slate should he triumph. When
Butler and John Van Buren refused to panic, Walker and his
fellow intriguers next turned to the imposition of the two-thirds
rule. To achieve success in this effort the conspirators had to
capture the post of presiding officer. This could not be accomplished once the convention had been seated, for, since all or-
ganizational decisions would be majority decisions, the Van
Buren majority possessed the strength to organize the convention. Walker did not propose to wait until the seating of the
convention.

Twenty minutes before the convention was scheduled to open
on May 27, Romulus Saunders, a brash, uncouth North Carolinian, strode to the platform and addressed a startled, partially
seated convention. He nominated to preside over the convention
a close friend of Buchanan, Hendrick Wright, who was prepared
to put his "private political capital in the Balance of the big
scales at Baltimore" to frustrate Van Buren. The Van Buren
management caught off guard and unwilling to lose any support
within the powerful Pennsylvania delegation allowed Wright
to take up the gavel. Flushed with victory, Saunders pressed for
a vote on the two-thirds rule. Pandemonium threatened until
someone reminded the delegates that God had not yet been

invoked to give them wisdom. An interlude of prayer may not
have stilled anger, but it did permit a semblance of order to
return, quelling the furious threats of some delegates to quit the
"fraudulent convention." [11]

Saunders roared again to the attack. His crude English re-
sounded across the stifling convention hall as he demanded the
immediate institution of a two-thirds rule. When he had finished
speaking, the tattered Democracy seemed rent beyond repair.
Throughout the day the debate raged. Walker, abandoning all
caution, defied the Van Buren managers to prove that their candidate was still the party's choice. Now irrevocably committed to
the defeat of Van Buren, he threatened a party split unless a
Texas candidate received the nomination. New York's Senator
Daniel Dickinson complained of the Mississippian's harsh, grating voice which ached in his ears as he sought to make sense out
of the snarling accusations.[12] When Benjamin Franklin Butler
finally gained the floor, he worked himself into a passion. Shak-
ing with emotion, he screeched his denunciation of the two-
thirds fraud. For two hours his anger found expression in violent
denunciations of the men who sought to deprive his candidate of
his just due. When he ceased speaking, the Van Burenites roared
their approval. For a flickering moment, it appeared Butler had
turned the tide. As the Van Buren demonstration grew in intensity, Walker, swiftly and calmly, moved the chair to adjourn
the convention. Wright, committed to Buchanan's candidacy,
immediately complied. Van Buren's last chance had been successfully parried.[13]

During the night of May 27th and the morning of the 28th,
Hendrick Wright worked to split the powerful Pennsylvania
delegation. The Van Buren supporters led by Henry Simpson
fought hard to prevent a split. Their efforts ran afoul of the
ambitions of "a certain Pennsylvania Senator." [14] Buchanan
might not obtain the presidential nomination but he intended if
possible to establish his claim upon a cabinet post. When the
convention reconvened on the 28th, the fight over the two-thirds

rule resumed. The tedious round of speeches suddenly soared with Walker's passionate rebuttal of Butler's denunciation. Amidst guffaws, as Walker mimicked Butler's indignation, the preliminary skirmishes ended. Walker concluded his speech with a motion that the two-thirds rule be adopted. As the votes were slowly tabulated, the Van Burenites knew they had been defeated. A few votes defected from Massachusetts, half the pledged delegation from Pennsylvania bolted, and finally Virginia voted as a unit for the two-thirds rule. The façade of Democratic unity seemed shattered. But even as Walker found himself engulfed by enthusiastic admirers, his mind concerned itself with the reestablishment of a united Democratic front as the party turned to nominating its candidates.[15]

The first roll call of the states gave Van Buren 146 votes. Although a majority, it was obvious he would never receive the necessary two-thirds. During the subsequent seven ballots, Van Buren steadily lost votes to the vigorous expansionist Senator Cass of Michigan. Walker, himself, cast his first ballot for Buchanan. On the second, he switched his support to Cass whose strength in the western delegations made him Van Buren's strongest opponent. While the struggle for the nomination raged between Van Buren and Cass, Andrew Jackson Donelson, Old Hickory's nephew, occupied his time with "a good deal of private management for the nomination of James K. Polk as vice-Presidential candidate." [16] George Bancroft, the historian-politician who led the Massachusetts delegation supporting Van Buren, realized when Virginia cast its seventeen votes for Cass on the seventh ballot followed by defections elsewhere, that Cass's nomination could not long be delayed. Adjournment after the seventh ballot was followed by the news that Kentucky's eccentric Richard M. Johnson had withdrawn and had instructed his delegates to support Cass. Bancroft now realized that only the swiftest action would prevent a Cass nomination and a refusal by Van Buren to support the Democratic slate.

Not only did Van Buren harbor a deep distaste for Cass, but

numerous Van Buren delegates protested efforts "to make Mr. Cass," the party candidate "in whose favor not a delegate was chosen by the people, notwithstanding the exertions of his friends and the length of time they had been canvassing in his favor." [17] An obstreperous New York was hardly the most promising omen for election. Hastily, Bancroft pressed for the compromise nomination of Polk. The Tennessee delegation, led by Andrew Jackson Donelson, Gideon Pillow, and Polk's intimate friend, Cave Johnson, snapped up Bancroft's proposal. Immediately, the Tennesseans went to work pressing Polk's nomination upon other southern delegations. The magic word spread that Old Hickory had groomed "Young Hickory" for precisely this contingency. Bancroft argued with the weary New York leaders that Polk was their logical alternative since he had been their vice presidential choice. Butler, who possessed a letter from Van Buren authorizing him to withdraw his name "if in his deliberate judgment he should find it necessary" remained noncommittal, but suggested to Bancroft that he would be willing to support Polk if he obtained substantial support on the eighth ballot outside the Van Buren camp.[18]

On the eighth ballot, Polk received forty-four votes. Bancroft had swung thirteen votes to him from Massachusetts and New Hampshire, while the Tennesseans had secured the twenty-eight votes of Alabama, Louisiana, and Tennessee. Three votes came from Pennsylvania and Maryland. Butler had his evidence. He withdrew the name of Van Buren and "declared his intention to vote for James K. Polk, who fully came up to the Jeffersonian standard of qualification, being both capable, honest, and faithful to all his trusts." Later he explained to Van Buren:

the name of Governor Polk was spoken of as a better one than any person before the convention. His state [Tennessee] deserved nothing from New York; but he had not been a party to the conspiracies and plots by which we had been destroyed, and his nomination, it was most obvious would not only give us a sound Democrat . . . but flounders with a single blow . . . the plots . . . set afoot by Tyler, Calhoun,

Woodbury, Buchanan, Johnson, Stewart, and above all, as most likely to get the benefit of them, Lewis Cass.[19]

Walker had kept his delegation tied to Cass for seven ballots partly to indicate that he would accept nothing less than a candidate pledged to annex Texas. But his behavior also supplemented his clever campaign to convince the Van Burenites that in accepting Polk they were frustrating the designs of the more conspicuous opponents of their leader. Obviously, the author of the two-thirds rule was hardly the man to obtain surrender from Butler. The strength of the Polk nomination rested upon the belief that it was made and supported by men who were not active in defeating Van Buren. Yet, Walker subsequently claimed that the nomination of Polk had been his doing, it having been achieved "with the aid of General Jackson." The old general's conviction that Van Buren had destroyed his chances in opposing Texas had led to his discussing with Polk in early May the possibility that he might get the presidential nomination. Polk had prepared his manager Cave Johnson for this contingency. Furthermore, Walker had been pledged to Polk's candidacy for Vice President from the outset of the convention. When he shifted his support on the ninth ballot to Polk, seemingly following the lead of the Van Buren managers, he had good reason to be jubilant: he had defeated Van Buren; he had a pro-Texas nominee; and the party had united behind the seemingly unforeseen candidate.[20]

Once Polk had been securely nominated, Walker worked to mollify the disgruntled supporters of Van Buren. "New York," he declared, "had made a noble sacrifice"; it was therefore only just that the convention nominate New York's Senator Silas Wright for the vice presidency. His motive was evident, for Wright, although doubting Van Buren's nomination, as early as May 7, still was loyal to his old chief. With Wright on the ticket, New York's democracy would give its wholehearted support to the campaign; otherwise there was the chance that New York might remain passive.[21] Wright's nomination received near unanimous convention support, with only eight Georgians dissenting. The latter received unexpected support from Wright, who did not choose to accept a nomination after the rejection of Van Buren. A weary convention returned to the task of finding a suitable vice presidential candidate.[22]

The refusal of any New York supporter of Van Buren to accept the nomination, and the equal certainty that no New Yorker hostile to Van Buren would be nominated by a convention intent upon soothing "Old Martin," considerably narrowed the region from which a candidate could come. A balanced ticket called for an easterner to offset the southwesterner Polk. New England or Pennsylvania seemed most logical. Walker promptly nominated Pennsylvania's former Senator George Mifflin Dallas, or more exactly, Uncle George. The nomination made political sense as Pennsylvania had a notorious propensity for intra-party feuding. Dallas, who was closely identified with Philadelphia and the eastern Pennsylvania commercial classes, would secure the support of a substantial proportion of Pennsylvania's democracy. His presence on the ticket also reassured those Pennsylvanians who looked askance at southern demands for a revenue tariff. Once the nomination had been confirmed, an elated Walker left Baltimore for Philadelphia to inform Uncle George of his good fortune. Senator Dallas received the news at five-thirty in the morning of May 31, as a jubilant Walker and his tipsy friends whooped through a war dance in the Dallas parlor. Uncle George privately viewed the honor as both empty and superfluous, but undemanding. And so he accepted it as any indifferent gentleman would.[23]

Once the convention had adjourned, the exhausted delegates fled the stifling heat of Baltimore. Walker, whom the convention had designated to manage the presidential campaign, returned to Washington to plot grand strategy. His efforts soon obtained "the zealous cooperation of Silas Wright and Daniel S. Dickinson in New York, upon whose vote the contest turned." Although Van Buren received bitter denunciations of Buchanan by Simpson and of Tyler by Butler, Walker's name did not appear among the perfidious in the many letters "Old Martin" received to console him in the hour of defeat. In fact, the former President understood the actions of Walker; he had fought for Texas but had not sought the presidential nomination. Van Buren and his managers could not help but respect the brilliant lesson in politics Walker had given them.[24]

Nomination is not election, but in Polk's case this truism had been complicated by his lack of a national reputation. As it turned out, this proved a political advantage for it permitted the presentation of Polk as everyone's candidate. News of his nomination took Polk unaware at his Columbia, Tennessee home. He quickly adjusted to the idea and promptly subscribed to Walker's description of himself as no longer "a Representative of a single State—but of the Democracy of the whole Union." He expressed his desire to hear from Walker "frequently pending the contest, and will thank you for any suggestions which you may think useful." [25]

Walker, worried over the unhealed split between Tyler and the Democratic party, took quick advantage of Polk's invitation and presented the problem to the President. After several hours of conversation with Tyler, Walker knew that the incumbent President had no thought of running on an independent ticket, though he believed his public withdrawal would have little effect upon his supporters who were "exasperated by the assaults of the *Globe* and other [Democratic] presses." Although he desired a Polk-Dallas victory, Tyler morosely concluded, that his friends "would either remain neutral, or many of them join Mr. Clay" since "they considered themselves proscribed and invited not to join [the Democratic] party." The number of votes involved was estimated at "about 150,000, . . . chiefly republicans who voted for the Whigs in 1840." [26]

The intentions of the Tyler faction appeared particularly urgent when his Philadelphia supporters "resolved to run separate Tyler electoral tickets for Congress and state and county offices." Should these plans mature the movement might be "adopted throughout the Nation." [27] Walker urged Polk to do everything he could to encourage "union and cooperation" for "it would be *decisive* in our favor." To accomplish this purpose, he advised Polk to write a private letter to a judicious friend, "which could be shown in confidence to Mr. Tyler, expressing such views as you entertain of his services to the democratic party, and welcoming his friends as brethren, and equals back into our ranks." A similar letter from Jackson promising that, after Tyler's withdrawal, his friends would be admitted to the party ranks and be fully entitled to "equal rights and consideration with any other portion of the democracy." Walker believed this would eliminate the threat of Tyler tickets.[28] Upon receipt of Walker's letter, Polk sent it to Jackson at the Hermitage, but the cagey old politician warned that any such move by Polk would "damn you and destroy your election." [29] As Jackson had himself written a letter "most kind and respectful to Mr. Tyler, . . . expressing . . . a deep anxiety for his withdrawal . . ." the need for Polk to do likewise had diminished.[30]

From the Hermitage flowed letters supporting Walker's efforts to soothe the ruffled feelings of Tyler's supporters. Francis Preston Blair received instructions "to support Polk and Dallas, let Tyler alone, and leave Calhoun to himself." [31] In a letter to Major Lewis, a long time friend, Jackson proposed that the "great popularity" a prompt withdrawal by Tyler would bring should be for the incumbent a sufficient incentive.[32] As Old Hickory had requested, this letter was shown by Walker to Tyler who then decided to "withdraw from the canvass." [33] Walker's purpose had been achieved but mainly through the efforts of the shrewd old general who feared that any letters passing between Polk and Tyler might be used at a future date to prove the existence of "another Adams-Clay bargain." [34]

The elimination of the threatened Tyler schism permitted Walker to formulate the political program upon which Polk would campaign. The outline of this program had been set forth by the Mississippian in 1842 when he specified that the next contest must be fought "under the banner of free trade and hard money." [35] No sooner had Polk been nominated than Walker wrote him that he could be defeated only by the tariff question. Pennsylvania's pro-tariff sentiments made it unlikely that an "out and out free trade candidate" would receive its votes. Despite his proclivities for free trade, Walker realized that "the tariff was stronger now throughout the Union, than it ever was before, and in Pennsylvania, New York, Connecticut, and New Jersey, it was irresistable." The Pennsylvania legislature, though controlled by Democrats, had passed unanimous resolutions in support of the tariff, and with many new factories and prospering older establishments dotting the state, its sentiment was unlikely to change. Obviously Polk "could not remain silent" on the tariff "without defeating the ticket"; but it was equally certain that he would have to come forth with a tariff plank acceptable to both the free trade extremists in the South and the protectionists of Pennsylvania. [36]

Walker, after consultation with fellow Democrats, both pro- and anti-tariff, suggested that Polk's views on the tariff "be expressed in the shape of a 'desire for a result.' " To his earlier plea that the candidate support "incidental protection," Walker now proposed a two point program that allowed for:

A revenue tariff, not to exceed the wants of the government, administered in a spirit of republican simplicity . . . and that within the range indicated . . . all should delight to see every branch of domestic industry deriving such incidental aid, as would enable it to realize fair and reasonable profit, and maintaining such wholesome competition, as would prevent the monopoly of our markets by foreign products and manufactures. [37]

The day after Walker forwarded these tariff views to Polk, the nominee expressed substantially the same views in a letter to John K. Kane, a former Federalist who had ardently embraced the Jacksonian doctrine and whose support of Jackson in the bank war had led to "temporary social ostracism" in his home

city of Philadelphia. Polk felt that Kane, an intimate friend
of Dallas, should consult with the vice presidential candidate
and also with Henry Horn, a former Jacksonian congressman, to
determine whether his letter should be published. It was decided
to allow a reading by judicious people who would be favorably
influenced by what Polk had asserted:

I am in favor of a tariff for revenue, such an one as will yield a sufficient amount to the Treasury to defray the expenses of the Government economically administered. In adjusting the details of a revenue
tariff, I have heretofore sanctioned such moderate discrimination, as
would produce the amount of revenue needed, and at the same time
afford reasonable incidental protection to our home industry. I am opposed to a tariff for protection merely and not for revenue.[38]

The similarity of views on the tariff expressed by Walker
and Polk gave rise to the charge that Walker had composed the
Kane letter. When the charge was brought to Polk's attention in
September, 1845, by his nephew J. Knox Walker, then serving
as the presidential private secretary, the President immediately
pronounced it false. Polk, always chary of anything suggesting
he play the puppet, summoned Walker who agreed the charge
had no validity and helped prepare a denial for publication
by Ritchie in the party organ, The Union.[39] Nevertheless, Polk
had written his letter partially in response to Walker's urging
that he clarify his views. Nor did their parallel views work to
Walker's disadvantage, for it predisposed Polk to view with
favor his claim to the Treasury Department where a workable
tariff policy would ultimately have to be formulated.

During the summer of 1844, Walker remained in Washington.
By late August, he had franked almost 170,000 campaign leaflets
and pamphlets. A flood of Walker's speeches in abridged form
covered the country. In Richmond alone some 80,000 were distributed. Hundreds of thousands of copies of his Texas Letter
poured forth into the nation, though whether its plea for annexation swayed many votes is questionable. Estimates of the
Letter's influence ranged from the editorial comment of a North

Carolinian newspaper describing it as "the Archimedean lever of the election" to that of a Van Burenite who having returned from "the South and the confines of Texas" was confident "that the excitement we have witnessed originated with a few interested managers, and is quite limited in extent and degree to the Calhoun and Tyler factions, and I have not met with more than one Democrat in that region, who has said that he would regulate his vote by any question connected with Texas." [40] Supreme Court Justice Catron concluded otherwise, informing Walker that, "From Tennessee south you are the leader." [41] In addition, there came innumerable invitations from southern barbecue committees, all wishing "to see our noble Senator, and take him by the hand, and thank him for his efforts to restore Texas to the Union." All were declined by the busy little Senator, now preoccupied with the task of electing "a Chief Magistrate who would restore to us Texas and Oregon, and replant the banner of the Republic upon the banks of the Del Norte and the shores of the Western Ocean." [42] Texas had considerably less appeal in New England, compelling George Bancroft to threaten the New England manufacturer with a British "monopoly of the Texas market under a virtually exclusive treaty," [43] unless they supported its annexation hopes.

Surprisingly, Van Buren, who had every reason to view the Texas issue with distaste, did not protest its use for getting votes. Most contemporaries accepted his silence as an effort to keep the party intact, but two years later Stephen Douglas, then an Illinois congressman, "let the cat out of the bag." In a speech delivered from the House floor, Douglas noted "that the Baltimore resolutions were offered by Mr. B. F. Butler, the friend of Van Buren, and that the Oregon and Texas resolutions were drawn up by Mr. Walker." This revelation led the *Journal of Commerce* to wonder:

These resolutions pledged the Democratic Party for the re-annexation of Texas and the reoccupation of Oregon. Mr. Van Buren and many of his prominent partisans had committed themselves against the annexation of Texas . . . Mr. Butler was his friend, acting for him in convention: why did he move the Texas resolution? What were the arguments urged by Walker to induce Mr. Butler to move a resolution creating a party test, requiring Mr. Van Buren to take back what he said, and to stultify himself? [44]

The answer, as the *Journal* probably knew, was patronage pledges. Although Butler eventually received appointment as a district attorney from Polk, Silas Wright believed that Polk had pledged himself to "the appointment of Butler to the State Department." [45] That Van Buren's supporters believed such an understanding existed was evident in their effort to elect Polk. The willingness of Wright to surrender his senatorial security for the hazards of the New York governorship in order to strengthen the party ticket within the state was but the most generous effort. "Old Martin" helped the ticket substantially when he reassured the "New York Committee Protesting the Baltimore Convention" that "I have known Messrs. Polk and Dallas long and intimately—I have had frequent opportunities for personal observations of their conduct in the discharge of high and responsible public duties. . . . They are both gentlemen possessed of high character . . . and able to discharge the duties of the station for which they have been nominated." [46] The discords that had threatened at Baltimore faded as a united Democracy worked to elect its ticket. Lurking in the minds of many were the expectations of patronage; for the Van Burenites there existed the security of hard promises. Failure to keep these promises, as it turned out, made the Democratic triumph of 1844 into a Pyrrhic victory.

5. Into the Vineyard

DURING THE NIGHT of November 8, 1844, John Quincy Adams, asleep in his Quincy home, was awakened by the boom of cannon. Polk and Dallas, he learned, had clinched the election by carrying New York State. The jubilant Democrats were busy with the task of distributing rewards. The defeated Whigs indulged in post-mortems.

Theodore Frelinghuysen, the defeated vice presidential candidate, insisted that "the alliance of the foreign vote and the most impractical of all organizations, the Abolitionists, have defeated the strongest national vote ever given to a Presidential candidate." [1] Millard Fillmore, who lost the New York governorship to Silas Wright, seconded these views and mourned, "all is gone, and I must confess that nothing has happened to shake my confidence in our ability to sustain free government so much as this. . . ." [2] With aristocratic detachment, Philip Hone thought the evidence proved conclusively that,

The party leaders, the men who make Presidents, will never consent to elevate one greatly their superior; they suffer too much by contrast. . . . Moreover, a (prominent) statesman, . . . must have been identified with all the leading measures affecting the interests of the people, and those interests are frequently different in the several parts of our widely extended country. What is meat in one section is poison in another. Give me, therefore, a candidate of an inferior grade, one whose talents, patriotism and public services have never been so conspicuous as to force him into the first ranks. He will get all the votes which the best and wisest man could secure, and some, which for the reasons I have stated, he could not. [3]

The flagrantly sectional appeals which Walker had made during the final weeks of the campaign amply supported Hone's
conclusions. For late in September, under the watchful eye of
the energetic Senator, thousands of pamphlets entitled *The
South in Danger* had been mailed into the South. They appealed to southern fears of the Whiggery by accusing northern
Whigs of possessing views "identical with those of the abolitionists." To elect Clay, who had denounced slavery as "a curse, *a
wrong, a grevious wrong, to the slave,* no possible contingency
can make it right," meant that the South invited the abolition of
slavery. Once again Walker had resorted to waving the black
flag of abolition.[4]

Willis Green, chairman of the Whig campaign, after obtaining a copy of the pamphlet, arranged for the Washington *National Intelligencer* to print forty thousand copies for distribution in the North, compelling the Washington *Globe* to warn its
northern readers against this effort of Whig "Munchausens." An
irate Green charged Walker with authorship of the pamphlet.
The Mississippian, shrewdly calculating the situation, admitted
authorship in a letter to the *Globe.* He reasoned that Democrats
under Whig attack as a result of the pamphlet need only cite
that issue of the *Globe* enabling them to either disprove the
charges or to take advantage of the pamphlet. And ultra southern
Democrats now had further reason to support his cabinet aspirations.[5]

As the Whigs bemoaned their defeat, Democrats wrangled
over the division of spoils. To some it seemed that Polk had
"come into office less transmutted by pledges, or having less influence from party association to force upon him the retention
of those who he may find already occupying places," than any
previous president.[6] This hardly describes the predicament of
the President-elect. As the leader of a specific faction, he would
have been expected to deliver the choicest plums to his supporters. As a supposedly uncommitted dark horse, every faction

looked to him for an abundant reward. Their disappointment threatened bitterness and intensified division.

Nor did the character of Polk mitigate this possibility. Methodical, jealous of his prerogatives, an instinctive moderate, he brought to the Presidency an excellent, watchful, dutiful, but unimaginative management. His pervasive control led naturally to the conclusion that adverse decisions originated in the Presidential office. A touchy pride prevented him from allowing subordinates to assume responsibility for controversial decisions. These characteristics found full expression in Polk's determination to manipulate patronage so as to insure support of Presidential policies and to secure the dominance of moderate Democrats.

By the middle of December of 1844, politicians and public were speculating on the future cabinet, but Polk revealed to the nation an ability to use "much discretion in keeping his own counsel." [7] He later asserted that at this time there had been "but one individual about whom my mind was definitely made up, without consultation with anyone, . . . and that individual was Silas Wright of New York." [8] He had offered him the Treasury, which he described as "the most important of the Departments," but Wright, who felt bound to retain the New York gubernatorial chair, declined the position.[9] Jackson, even as Polk negotiated with Wright, thought his protégé "wide awake to cabinet problems" with "only Mason certain." [10] This conflict in testimony suggests that the offer to Wright, one which it was known he would not accept, aimed to free Polk from pledges to give the State and Treasury posts to supporters of Van Buren.[11]

While Polk maneuvered his way through the feuding New York democracy, supporters of Walker carefully campaigned to place him in a top cabinet post. Uncle George Dallas, never reluctant to advance family fortunes, claimed the State Department for his nephew's services as the "moving impulse . . . of the late canvass." Anxious to replace the whole of Tyler's cabinet, the Vice President insisted, "the country expects an entire and undiscriminating change. It wants a Cabinet at the hands of James K. Polk." [12] Subsequently, the "uncommon linguistic ability" of Walker "to speak French, German, and Spanish" were set forth as "expedient" in the State Department.[13] This family connection prompted Cave Johnson to warn Polk of the close ties Walker had with "that family in Pennsylvania." [14] A blunter protest came from a group of Pennsylvania Democrats who charged that the political influence of both Dallas and William Wilkins, the retiring Secretary of War, resulted from their "being the centre of a large family . . . with branches all over the State and union." Though they did not wish to impugn Walker's loyalty to the Democratic party, the Pennsylvanians deemed it wise for Polk to remember that Walker "is a member of that great 'Family' whose overshadowing influence Pennsylvania Democrats dread so much." [15]

By the middle of February, Polk squelched the State Department agitation by offering the post to Buchanan who promptly accepted it. The offer carried with it conditions that left no doubt who would be chief. "In the making of my cabinet," Polk noted, "I desire to select gentlemen who agree with me in opinion, and who will cordially cooperate with me in carrying out my principles and policy." And, as if to accentuate the subordinate relationship, he insisted that all cabinet officers agree in writing to resign should they become active candidates for the Presidency.[16]

Protests followed swiftly upon the Buchanan appointment. Shortly before Polk left for Washington, Jackson warned him that "he had no confidence in Buchanan, and . . . would not . . . invite him to the cabinet." [17] An embarrassed President-elect regretted that "he had already invited him to be Secretary of State." [18] Reaction outside Buchanan's camp in Pennsylvania expressed dismay at the appointment. Henry Simpson, a disgruntled supporter of Van Buren, complained sourly: "Frazer, Forney, Hutter, *the Camerons*, and a host of small politicians from Pennsylvania are at Washington pushing Buchanan for

Secretary of State." [19] His old friend Dallas angrily denounced
the appointment as "grotesque and humiliating." To Walker he
sent the prompt warning that though he had become Vice President "willy-nilly," he did not intend "to be considered a
cypher." [20] Further hostile appointments from Pennsylvania, he
implied, would precipitate an open break within the administration.

Walker did not ignore the devious maneuvers within Pennsylvania. When Simon Cameron, already rumored to have
backed Buchanan in expectation of a senate seat, offered to use
his influence within the Pennsylvania democracy on behalf of
Walker, the Mississippian eagerly grasped the offer. In February, Polk offered the Attorney-generalship to the Senator, but
"explosions" greeted the offer. Dallas insisted that he press for
the State Department, while an old friend from Pennsylvania
reminded him of the obscurity of the Attorney-generalship. Unless he obtained appointment to either the State or Treasury Department, the consensus of his supporters felt that "the Senate is
the field for your operations." Only in a post of prestige could he
aid "the gentlemen who were so active and efficient in the Baltimore convention in establishing the two-thirds rule . . . to prevent the nomination in '48 from falling upon . . . the Van
Buren dynasty." To assuage his disappointment should he not get
a suitable cabinet appointment, his friends reminded him that
"the nomination for the Presidency in 1852 must come from the
South." [21]

Polk reached Washington to find that the city seethed with
claimants for office. He hastened to placate Van Buren with the
assurance that he "was still anxious to select a citizen of New
York for the Treasury and came to Washington with that intention." But the President-elect soon learned that "The South
had in advance of [his] arrival . . . united on a distinguished
gentleman from that section of the union for the office." [22] When
Polk proposed to Van Buren that they agree upon Bancroft to
check the southern move, the wily New Yorker, aware that Wil-

liam Marcy whose Hunker sentiments made him suspect had urged the Bancroft appointment, parried with the notice that every President-elect faced such pressures. Polk needed only to avoid "just cause for dissatisfaction" to prevent "threats of disunion in the ranks of your party." Van Buren had made it evident that he thought he had ample reason to feel dissatisfied.[23]

By the end of February, Polk had opened a permanent breech with his predecessor. Not only did Van Buren not receive the cabinet posts he expected but the Hunker opposition had received the choice New York patronage. To a certain extent Polk had ample justification for his behavior. While the opposition to Van Buren had fought openly for their reward, the Van Burenites carried themselves with aloof disdain, hardly condescending to join the fight. Butler refused the War Department and Flagg considered the New York collectorship beneath his dignity. Pure frustration drove the proud Tennessean to ignore meeting the New York radical's expectations. Even before the new administration commenced operations a yawning gap within the party existed.[24]

As New York claims disrupted the party, the "distinguished gentleman" from the South, sensing opportunity, renewed his claims with vigor. The Democratic Congressmen from Indiana announced that "the appointment of Robert J. Walker of Mississippi, as Secretary of the Treasury, would meet with the universal approbation of the Democratic party in Indiana." [25] All but a handful of the Democratic members of the Ohio legislature petitioned for a Walker cabinet appointment. Fernando Wood, already well entrenched in Tammany, and harboring a marked distaste for Van Buren, offered to use his influence to secure support for Walker in New York.[26] Any question about the extent to which Walker gave an orthodox interpretation of southern rights halted with the publication of the letter by eccentric old Justice Henry Baldwin to the theologian Congressman William H. Hammett of Mississippi. In it Baldwin affirmed that in 1819 Walker had, despite his eighteen years, loyally supported him during the Missouri controversy in his insistence that Missouri enter as a slave state.[27]

Walker early abandoned his claim upon the State Department, anticipating the retention of Calhoun. The accession of Buchanan to the State Department strengthened Walker's claims on the Treasury for Polk knew he would have to placate the irate Dallas. The prospect of settling the currency and tariff questions now stirred Walker's imagination.[28] Nor could Polk ignore Calhoun's indication that he "would give place more willingly to Walker." On the long trip from Tennessee to Washington, Gwin, longing to replace Walker in the Senate, pressed upon Polk the qualifications of his old friend for the Treasury. Lewis Cass, fearing that the appointment of Flagg, a known Van Buren supporter, to the Treasury would result in its patronage being used to advance the Presidential aspirations of Wright, and feeling called upon to repay the seemingly solid support Walker had given him at the convention, added his voice to the growing clamor. When the Mississippi Congressmen added their support, Polk had little choice but to accept the vivacious Mississippian.[29]

As friends and interested spectators advanced his case before the President-elect, Walker energetically boosted his own future. Three days after the 2nd Session of the 28th Congress had convened, Walker appeared in his seat. He left Washington the following day for a hasty trip to Nashville. Returning two weeks later, he observed gloomily that "so far as fortune is concerned, many severe lessons in the school of adversity" had rendered him "both wiser and better for the future." [30] It seems that Polk had informed him that only the Attorney-generalship would be offered him.

Though he had contemplated accepting the Attorney-generalship, Walker decided against it as a political deadend. He meant to have the Treasury or nothing. On March 2, Polk, confronted with Walker's thoroughly mobilized support, accepted him as his Treasury chief, an appointment which provided Smith Van

Buren with the opportunity to conclude bitterly, "the Treasury arrangement tells the whole story for New York." [31] Having made his decision, Polk felt uneasy over his total disregard of the Van Buren faction. To a dismayed Van Buren, he lamely protested, "the change of position of the members of the Cabinet seems to be imperative upon me." [32] His plaintive plea only accentuated the grievance of Old Martin who agreed with his son that "he (Polk) has sold out to Buchanan, Cass, and Walker, and . . . all that we can do, 'will only make him unhappy.' " [33]

The announcement of the cabinet by Polk permitted the Washington *Globe* to describe them as "men of Talent—of fine business aptitudes—of unblemished and exalted characters." Greeley's *Tribune* graded the cabinet as average with Walker unquestionably "the weakest choice." [34] John Quincy Adams thought he detected in the prevalence of expansionists "a radical change of measures." He predicted an end of the old Jacksonian coalition with the removal of Blair from editorship of the party organ; the dismissal of Calhoun and his replacement by "an apostate federalist from Pennsylvania"; the degrading of a "Virginian Secretary of the Navy . . . to make way for another apostate federalist from Massachusetts"; and the appointment to the Treasury of "a speculator in Texan stock, a refugee from Pennsylvania to the repudiatory region of Mississippi." As if to confirm these expectations, Jackson himself questioned the appointment of Walker whom he dismissed as surrounded by too "many broken speculators." [35] A single appointment had managed to unite the two great protagonists of 1828 in mutual distaste.

Dislike of the Treasury chief entered into the cabinet itself. William M. Marcy did not expect Walker "to sustain himself in the Treasury"; nor did he expect the appointment to meet "with very general favor except in the extreme South and Pennsylvania." [36] The war chief found confirmation of his beliefs in G. A. Worth, soon to achieve fame as a General in the Mexican War, who thought, "My friend Walker should have gone to

War—and sought for reputation in the cannon's mouth." With a prophetic touch, he added, "He was for Texas and will probably be for Mexico." [37] Dallas accepted Walker's advance as balm for the appointment of Buchanan, though Jackson anticipated cabinet rifts would occur in the absence of "that cordial good feeling between Walker and Mr. Buchanan as ought to exist." Only among southerners did there exist a general enthusiasm for the appointment, some treating it as the first step toward "preparing him for still higher honors." [38]

But southern enthusiasm, especially Mississippi's, received an unexpected jolt. Walker had hardly assumed the Treasury helm when rumors circulated in Washington about the strange maneuvers used to fill the now vacant Mississippi seat in the Senate. C. C. Cambreling explained to Van Buren that the failure of Polk to meet his promises to the radical New Yorkers resulted from dishonest councils in Washington before the President-elect's arrival. The core of the conspiracy, Buchanan, Walker, Cave Johnson, and Thompson "who wants Walker's seat in the Senate" had masterminded the State and Treasury appointments. Though Cambreling had his details twisted, he had correctly suggested a close and intimate relationship between Walker and Thompson.[39]

Throughout the tangled maneuvers to displace Van Buren as the party candidate, the calculating, brash, and grossly ambitious Thompson had diligently supported the schemes of Walker. "We all knew that unless we could defeat Mr. Van Buren's nomination," one Mississippian recollected, "this movement would prove our political defeat." [40] Thompson naturally expected his risk warranted a suitable reward. He anticipated a promotion from House to Senate, but misjudged, for Walker lobbied vigorously to persuade Governor Albert G. Brown to appoint William Gwin. He urged the selection of Gwin as necessary to assure the presence of a loyal Democrat in the Senate ready to vote for a Democratic printer should an executive session meet for that purpose. The appointment, he assured Brown, would be made "only to prevent the defeat of Colonel Polk's administration in the election of a printer." [41] Brown, well aware of Gwin's unsavory reputation as a gross speculator and of his unpopularity in the state organization, forwarded to Walker a senatorial commission for Thompson with the request that Walker deliver it to Thompson if the "contingency" that Walker feared arose.[42] Before the commission reached Walker, the Senate in executive session, declined to elect a printer. When the commission finally reached him, Walker assumed that he had the right to withhold it.[43] Moreover, he failed to inform Thompson of its existence, allowing him to return to Mississippi, where to his consternation he learned about the commission from Governor Brown.

A justly outraged Thompson immediately returned to Washington to learn why Walker had concealed the commission. Despite protestations from Walker that he had no malicious intent, the affair became a major topic of Washington gossip, especially in anti-administration circles. Having denied any evil intent, Walker kept an aloof silence during the subsequent controversy. When the gossip reached Mississippi, it had the dimensions of a roaring brawl. Gwin began to actively campaign for the vacant Senate seat and, in passing, managed to convince many Mississippians that Walker had deliberately withheld the commission for his own benefit. Governor Brown advised Walker that the controversy "beggars description." As he sought to share Walker's aloofness, Brown could not help warning him that "the war between Gwin and Thompson is waxing hot." The latter in his politicking constantly alluded to the commission. When the Vicksburg *Sentinel* threatened to publish the correspondence between Walker and Brown on the commission, the Governor lost his composure and advised the editor to "go to Hell." When Brown learned that Walker held him responsible for the difficulty, the irate Governor reminded Walker he ran the risk of being the "sufferer" in any question of veracity.[44]

On June 16, 1845, Walker publicly protested against the con-

tinuing attacks, contending that Brown had left to his discretion
whether to deliver the commission. Since he believed the commission was contingent on the appointment of the printer, it had
not been delivered.[45] With considerable candor, the Secretary
admitted his debt to Thompson who had "exerted himself more
warmly and more efficiently" than any other man "to place me
in my present position." However, Thompson momentarily
tempered the controversy when he flatly declared he would not
accept the commission if it were offered him.[46]

The retreat of Thompson indicated his sensible acknowledgement of Walker's immense new power. Still ambitious, he did
not choose to risk losing the patronage and favors the Treasury
had at its disposal. Nor was the former Senator's political power
in Mississippi negligible. Privately, however, the Congressman
vented his spleen. He recalled for Claiborne the strong expression of gratitude with which Walker had acknowledged his efforts
to get him appointed to the Treasury. Thompson contended that
he alone had urged Walker to press for larger recognition than
the Attorney-generalship. In a midnight visit to the President-
elect on March 3, 1845, Thompson claimed he had persuaded
Polk to "re-cast the cabinet, and assign Walker to the Treasury."
With genuine indignation, he described the emotional response
of the little Senator who seized him "with both hands, and said,
'Oh Thompson, you are my best friend . . . I can never, never
forget you.' " One can hardly blame Thompson for concluding
that he had been dealing with a "man devoid of fixed principles,
controlled by any man who had decision and will," a man whose
"fertile genius" could be "as readily employed on one side of
a question as another." Public protestations of friendship hardly
disguised Thompson's conviction that Walker remained "true to
a friend, so far only as that friend could serve him." [47]

Unfortunately, indignation provokes exaggeration, and
Thompson's accuracy is suspect. His melodramatic description
of his interview with Polk is nowhere supported by other evidence. And the Treasury appointment had been made at least

two days before the supposed midnight meeting. Furthermore, he avoided explaining Walker's motives in opposing his appointment.

William Gwin, who had been the new Secretary's choice to replace him as Senator, had actively lobbied during the autumn of 1844 for a bill to enable some Chicksaw Indians to sue the Federal Government for $112,000, which they were supposed to have received when they accepted removal from Mississippi.[48] Walker had worked to have the Senate approve the Gwin bill, but his efforts had come to naught when Thompson personally blocked the bill's passage. If the Congressman cautiously avoided suggesting the motive, Mississippi's press, both Whig and Democratic, did not hesitate to accuse the former Senator of having been adversely influenced by Thompson's opposition to the Chicksaw claims. There the issue bubbled until the Mississippi House of Representatives on January 23, 1845, requested Governor Brown to reveal his correspondence on the subject. The Governor presented a vigorous defense of Walker's behavior, arguing "that Mr. Walker has not acted from any unworthy motive." [49] So far as he was concerned the issue was one he would prefer to leave in the limbo of history.[50]

Thompson, who had muted the controversy by repeating he would not have accepted the commission had it reached him, sought his revenge in a manner which Polk characterized as "mean and vindictive." [51] Early in February 1846, he launched a strong personal attack in the House against a man named Tate, a Mississippian, whose nomination to the Consulship at Buenos Aires was before the Senate. He charged Tate with involvement in illicit speculations which had also attracted Walker's attention. The Secretary of the Treasury promptly went to Polk and requested that Tate's nomination be withdrawn until he could return from Buenos Aires to defend his character. Polk declined the request since the Senators from Mississippi, Chalmers, who had filled Walker's seat, and Speight, had urged the nomination. The urgent pleas of Walker finally persuaded the President to

offer compliance if the Mississippi Senators so requested. Walker
quickly received the necessary requests and upon delivering
them to Polk told him that "he was the person whom Mr. Thompson intended to assail." The President cryptically noted in his
diary that "with this controversy I have nothing to do, and do
not . . . deem it . . . necessary to record Mr. Walker's statement concerning it, further than to remark that according to
Mr. Walker's statement there is not in his conduct or in that of
Dr. Tate anything to censure." [52]

It was evident that the little Secretary had made a political
blunder of major magnitude. Uneasy about its effect upon his
future, he engaged the President in "a very solemn and earnest
conversation in relation to his position in the administration."
Walker protested that rumors hinting at his presidential aspirations were part of an effort by certain Democratic senators to
discredit him. Fully aware of Polk's insistence that his cabinet
hold itself aloof from presidential campaigning, he offered to
write a letter in which he again disavowed presidential aspirations. The President heard with pleasure his Treasury chief avow
that "no member of the Cabinet could, without prejudice to the
administration by impairing his own usefulness, be regarded as
an aspirant to that station." [53] The Tate difficulty came to an end
when Walker wrote Polk a letter in the winter of 1846 which
the solemn Tennessean pronounced "a full and triumphant vindication of Walker and Dr. Tate." [54] When the President made
this pronouncement, Walker had proved himself an esteemed
and valuable cabinet officer.

The commission seemed to have been forgotten. The chief
actors appeared to agree with Gwin that no useful purpose was
served in opening "old sores that are healed over." However, in
Mississippi, the affair had done irretrievable damage to Walker's
political prestige. The Vicksburg *Sentinel*, although Democratic,
denounced Walker for having behaved in a manner which "wears
an aspect of most barefaced usurpation, if not corruption." The
newspaper questioned whether the continued presence of Walker

in the cabinet was justified.[55] The severity of the attacks brought
a vigorous defense of the Secretary's behavior from Jefferson
Davis. That aloof southerner acknowledged that "the public has
a right to know all that their agent had done in relation to a
transaction so important as the appointment of an United States
Senator," but he reminded the Mississippi democracy that "*their*
Secretary" was now directing "all his energies . . . to 'the
divorce of Bank and State,' and 'the repeal of the protective
Tariff of 1842.' " [56]

It remained, however, for an embittered Van Burenite to
estimate most accurately the consequences of the commission
dispute. "Walker is . . . politically dead in Mississippi," John
Van Buren read, "patronage will give him a little power while
Polk's administration lasts, but his influence is gone, lost forever." But for the moment the warning was to "beware of the
Talleyrand of the Treasury Department." [57] Walker's undoubted
success in the Treasury Department and the enormous patronage
power he wielded blotted out the commission issue. Yet, this
trivial incident proved to be a turning point in his political
career. It deprived him of a state basis for his future efforts to
advance his political career and it implanted a seed of mistrust
that would flower into a constant suspicion of his motives. And,
one day, Thompson, as Secretary of the Interior, would be called
upon to support a beset Walker as he struggled to govern the
Kansas Territory. He would abandon him to his fate. However,
that day was far distant, and for the present no one doubted that
the Treasury had a formidable chief.

6. Talleyrand of the Treasury

ANDREW JACKSON, dying a slow death in *The Hermitage*, viewed Walker's appointment with undisguised dismay. Polk's reassurances that his cabinet had a "united and harmonious" composition failed to convince the old man. It stirred in him the valid fear that Walker, encumbered with debt and surrounded by "broken speculators" seeking to redeem depreciated Choctaw Indian script, would assist their effort by restoring the script to par through the issuance of a Treasury order. Old Hickory denounced such a maneuver as a corrupt effort to "get hold of the cash." Unless the executive squelched the plot, he feared the new administration would be "blown sky high." [1] A taciturn Polk heard the warning and redoubled his strict surveillance of the executive department.

The dour Tennessean never allowed anyone to forget who governed as chief executive. His cabinet, no matter how reluctantly, followed his lead and learned to expect a vigorous and commanding reprimand when their political conduct offended his sensibilities. The Treasury chief, though head of a semi-autonomous department, quickly understood that Polk expected from him the same deference given by the other cabinet members. If anything, an uneasy President, disturbed by rumors of Walker's involved financial difficulties, paid especial heed to Treasury operations.[2]

The care with which Polk supervised his administration probably saved Walker from serious charges of corrupt conduct in office. In a major lapse of his normal circumspection, the Treasury chief permitted his speculator friends to persuade him to support the efforts of William M. Gwin to redeem the $112,000 of Choctaw script that he held. Once made aware of the decision, the President promptly forbade payment until a full investigation established the legality of the Gwin holdings. Walker meekly accepted the presidential directive. Usually, however, the two men worked in harmony. Upon general economic policy, they possessed a rapport, though on occasion Polk disagreed with the intensity at which Walker preached free trade doctrine. But, most important, the Treasury chief subscribed wholeheartedly to Polk's desire to establish moderate domination within the Democratic party.[3]

Upon no subject did the President evidence a more telling determination than in his intention to strengthen the Democratic coalition through the elimination of both divisive issues and personalities. One of the latter, Francis Preston Blair, the rambunctious editor of the semi-official Party organ the *Globe*, had alienated Polk by his subdued support of the 1844 ticket. Walker had felt that the old Jacksonian had complicated the Democratic campaign with his biting attacks upon John Tyler. Nor had the stubborn loyalty of Blair toward Van Buren escaped the notice of the two men. They agreed that continuation of the *Globe* as the party organ endangered a united party support for the administration.[4] "The press," Polk asserted, "must have no connection with, nor be under the influence or control of any clique or portion of the party which is making war upon any other portion of the party—with a view to the succession and not with a view to the success of my administration." [5] This decision sealed the fate of Blair.

An effort, however, to replace the *Globe* as party organ required a large sum of money with which to purchase Blair's publishing plant. While dispatching the offending journal, Polk revealed a lively interest in creating a friendly replacement. Blair, resigned to his displacement, agreed to sell his interest for $50,000. By late March, 1845, with all necessary payments made and the conversion of the *Globe* into the *Union* complete,

rumors about the source of the payment flitted through the cor-
ridors and salons of Washington. Jackson, whose distance from
the capital did not prevent him from being privy to its secrets,
angrily and correctly charged that Simon P. Cameron, "a rene-
gade politician and a bankrupt in politics," had engineered the
whole arrangement. Thomas Hart Benton, the belligerent Missouri bullionist, refusing to discount the responsibility of the
administration, indicted Walker with complicity in permitting
Cameron, the cashier of a deposit bank in Middletown, Pennsylvania, to use government funds in making the purchase.[6]

Most Washingtonians, believing that Walker was "the chief
agent in the intrigue," neglected the critical role of the President, who had used his Secretary to achieve his intention. Ritchie,
editor of the *Union*, later recalled he had accepted the post after
he had learned of "the wish of the president and some of his
friends that we should remove to Washington and conduct a
journal which might become the organ of the administration."
Walker stood among those friends prepared to serve his chief.
After holding private conversations with Cameron on the purchase of the *Globe*, he permitted the wily Pennsylvanian to use a
government deposit of $50,000 to meet the purchase price of the
Globe, and refrained from any effort to reclaim the deposit
until November, 1847. But at all times he followed rather than
inaugurated presidential policy.[7]

Even the distribution of patronage in the Treasury Department involved Walker's deference to the wishes of Polk. The
Secretary quickly discovered that the President meant to use his
appointive power as a means to exclude from office disruptive
individuals or factions. In New York, as Walker subsequently
realized, the prime targets were the supporters of Van Buren.
Yet, Polk took exceptional care not to offend the Old Magician
and his supporters. This was particularly manifest in the New
York customs house appointments. The normal feuding between
conservative and radical factions of the Empire State democracy reached bitter proportions over the Port of New York col-

lectorship. Everyone agreed that C. P. Van Ness, the incumbent collector, had to go; both factions insisted, however, that their man receive the appointment. Polk, detesting factionalism and favoring the conservative faction, but determined to maintain a united Democracy, directed Walker to appoint Cornelius Lawrence, a conservative banker, who, despite his identification with the conservative faction, had loyally supported Democratic candidates in New York no matter which faction they supported. Radical dissent had been effectively spiked.

William Marcy assured Walker that the choice "takes like a charm—everybody speaks well of it." Disgruntled radicals, he added, "dare not show how they feel." The Treasury chief, betraying his ignorance of the vindictive temper of New York Democrats, concluded "that the administration had now passed safely through all the whirlpools of New York politics." Actually, the radicals, ominously silent, detected in their treatment Walker as a candidate "for the next Presidency," a prospect which they rejected, declaring, "He can never be the president . . . he never ought to be." [8]

As the administration worked to pacify the turbulent New Yorkers, Walker discovered that Democratic politicians across the nation, anticipating either largess or political direction, expected a full hearing at the Treasury. David Levy, who chose to change his surname to Yulee when elected Senator from a newly admitted Florida, pledged unswerving support to the administration in return for Treasury patronage to keep the peninsula "democratic." The Floridian set the southern tone, for every pledge of support from beneath the Mason-Dixon line carried with it the pre-emptory demand for reward.[9] Northerners proved no less expectant. Elijah Haywood, basking in the knowledge that his efforts had mobilized the Democratic members of Ohio's legislature behind Walker's Treasury aspirations, submitted a list of "appointments and removals in . . . Ohio." From Connecticut, Gideon Welles prepared to give the Secretary "safe and profitable" advice "upon all subjects." The insatiable demands for office, far in excess of available places, finally drove Walker to pledge offices should the incumbent vacate it. One irate critic, watching the devious maneuverings of both Polk and Walker, concluded, "These men are playing cards very loosely indeed." [10]

However, despite the pressures of patronage, Walker devoted increasing attention to reducing the tariff "to the revenue standard." [11] It proved almost impossible during the autumn of 1845 to obtain an interview with the Secretary. After eight visits to the Treasury, one visitor complained, "Mr. Walker . . . has always been 'so busy in making out his report' that I have not yet seen him." The resultant proposals on the tariff, when first revealed to the cabinet in early November, so unnerved Buchanan that he denounced them as "a strong free trade document . . . opposed to his whole course on the subject during his whole life." [12]

The Secretary of State expressed sentiments common to most Pennsylvanians. As the distribution of patronage made enemies for the administration in New York, so the tariff proposals threatened to make them in the Keystone State. But all prospect of open dispute in the cabinet ended when Polk supported Walker. The President privately thought the tariff sentiments of his Treasury chief "speculative, and perhaps too highly wrought," but he subscribed to the idea of a revenue tariff.[13] The prospective alienation of Pennsylvania democrats seemed not to enter his thoughts.

No sooner had Congress heard Polk's first annual message than Dallas, always the skeptical patrician, reported, "Polk's message has produced a strong sensation, but whether, on the whole and durably, it will be beneficial . . . remains in doubt." Members of the Pennsylvania congressional delegation, "struck with despair," left the Vice President wondering whether they would "survive the free trade battery which Walker will assail them with in his annual report tomorrow." They survived, and resolved never to support the presidential aspirations of the ex-patriated Pennsylvanian.[14]

The 1845 Treasury report explicitly defined the program of economic reform to which Polk had committed his administration. Walker left no doubt that the administration wanted a revenue tariff able to provide for the wants of an economically administered government. He explicitly stated his preference for a tariff that would permit the United States to experiment with a modified free trade. It was evident that tariff revision constituted the keystone of the whole program.

An advocate of free trade in the 1840's had to admit that dangers existed in removing or lessening tariff barriers without reciprocal agreements. Walker chose to present it as a challenge to American patriotism. "Let our commerce be as free as our political institutions," he pleaded, "and nation after nation will . . . follow our example." Balancing patriotism with self-interest, he charged that the farmer and planter paid a heavy price since they lost the chance to buy cheap foreign goods with money earned from their agricultural exports. Only the domestic manufacturer profited through "profits and dividends extracted from the many, by taxes upon them, for the benefit of the few." Unless thwarted, Walker believed that the industrial capitalist, already preoccupied with profits, intended to depress wages until an outraged working class, driven to desperation, rebelled, only to meet subjugation from an alliance between government and capital. The Secretary drew a grim sketch of impending class struggle.[15]

He also defended the established order. The American future depended upon its agrarian population. Industriously farming the "fertile lands" of the United States, they had within their grasp the chance to "feed and clothe the people of nearly all the world." Already, burgeoning crops threatened to swamp them with surpluses they could not hope to sell. Free trade by opening up the markets of the world to American produce would relieve their distress. The vast inheritance of unused lands protected the working man from too crass an exploitation. Congress by allowing him to buy "320 acres of land for $80" or "160 acres for $40" provided a permanent safety valve for social discontent. But deny the farmer a decent livelihood from his land and both he and the escaping worker would share a common fate— exploitation from industrial capital. In supporting free trade, Walker believed that he defended the Jeffersonian inheritance of a free agrarian republic.[16]

By vigorously advocating Jeffersonian dogma and free trade, Walker achieved national stature and an international reputation. Abroad, especially in Great Britain, news of his defense of free trade created a sensation. The British Parliament, preoccupied with the decision of the Peel Ministry to venture into free trade, ordered the printing of several thousand copies of Walker's report for distribution among Members of Parliament. When news of this almost unprecedented honor reached the United States, a disgruntled Greeley promptly knighted Walker, "Sir Robert." [17]

British reaction reflected the considerable attention which their own free traders had given the 1844 campaign in America. The English free trade organ, *The League*, had distributed, at home and in the United States, large numbers of pamphlets supporting Polk which had excited "growlings" among Whigs.[18] Whig journals carried frequent reports during the campaign of efforts among English free traders to raise money to publish such propaganda.[19] The danger that these charges might stimulate American chauvinism moved journals supporting Polk to describe as "political humbug" reports of the British supplying money for "the purpose of putting down the American tariff." [20] Despite such denials, the free trade movement in England, according to the London *Times*, had in 1844 raised $2,129,000 to finance the circulation of free trade tracts in foreign countries, much of it in the United States.[21]

The English, however, hardly viewed the election of Polk

without misgivings. "His (Polk's) success has been mainly secured by the annexation cry," one journal editorialized, "an unpopular cry on this side of the Atlantic, as it is associated with slavery and its evils." Polk's inaugural address accentuated English misgivings as they read his belligerent references to the Oregon territory, though his support of tariff reduction mitigated their expectations of a hostile administration. Peel's decision, in March of 1845, to reduce or repeal duties on many important trade items, especially farm products, stimulated American cotton and grain trade. The influential *Journal of Commerce* predicted, "it will be impossible to maintain our present high tariff in the face of the bald and extensive Free Trade movement in England."[22]

The British experiment in free trade led its proponents to stress the interdependence of the Oregon and tariff issues. The *London Economist,* a vigorous proponent of free trade, made no effort to hide its belief that an American subscription to free trade would more than justify British surrender of Oregon. London speculated that Louis McLane, the new American minister to London, brought a pledge to reduce substantially the American tariff in return for a satisfactory settlement of the Oregon question.[23]

Though McLane carried no such proposal, numerous northwestern congressmen reiterated their demand for all of Oregon even if it meant war. Lewis Cass, a fire-eating proponent of an aggressive stand, obtained Polk's private reassurance that his administration did not intend to surrender northwestern interests. Walker assumed an ambiguous posture; an aggressive expansionist but a passionate exponent of free trade, he had to accept that war with Britain meant the abandonment of free trade. Upon him fastened the suspicion, of those who advocated all of Oregon, as the member of the administration most likely to seek a compromise settlement.[24]

The *Union* flatly denied rumors that Walker had entered into conversations with the British minister to negotiate a compromise

settlement of the Oregon issue. All it admitted was that the
Secretary had conveyed "the hope" to the envoy "that Great
Britain would repeal her duties upon our agricultural products
and provisions, and especially upon Indian Corn." In fact, however, the Secretary had resolved upon an Oregon compromise,
fearing a war with Great Britain would tie up the "whole energy
of the government" to the detriment of the tariff.[25]

The decision of the Senate on April 16, 1846, authorizing
Polk to terminate joint occupation of Oregon assured a major
crisis. The imminence of war with Mexico raised the spectre of
a two front war. The President, however, had long since decided
to reach a compromise settlement with Britain, and he hoped
to achieve his purpose without dividing the party. He dismissed
the belligerence of "many Democratic Senators" as an expression
of their presidential politicking. The British, alarmed by threatening war, offered to settle the dispute by dividing the territory
along the 49th parallel, thereby reviving a settlement that Polk
had contemplated as early as July of 1845.[26]

The President, intent upon making any decision a collective
responsibility, polled his cabinet and found that Walker, Marcy,
Bancroft, and Johnson favored the submission of the British
proposal to the Senate. Buchanan refused to commit himself
until pressed by Polk and, even then, declined comment until he
had read the presidential message that accompanied the submission. An irate Walker, suspicious of "Old Buck's" presidential
ambitions, emphatically declared for submission so long as the
entire cabinet gave its undivided support. On this demand he
had Polk's wholehearted support. Capital gossip soon had
"Buck" ready to abandon "political paradise" as he chafed
under "the ruling spirit in that council"—the obvious rapport
between the Chief Executive and his Secretary of the Treasury.[27]

The Senate promptly approved a compromise settlement along
the 49th parallel. It possessed no other alternative unless a
collective madness were to convince them that war with both
Mexico and Britain had advantages. The Whigs, though viewing

the prospect of a reduced tariff without relish, joined southern Calhoun men in seeking to force compromise. A President who never seriously entertained war with Great Britain had won a compromise with the assistance of the political opposition. Polk, as Robert Toombs, the sardonic Georgian, noted, "would be as much surprised and astonished and frightened at getting into war with England as if the Devil were to rise up before him at his bidding." And he had managed a settlement without seriously dividing the party.[28]

The settlement permitted Walker to concentrate upon his major concern: the construction of a new tariff law. He had admitted before a Washington Day dinner his wish to settle the Oregon controversy on reasonable terms, for without a settlement all tariff reform was impossible. Alex Gardiner, a guest at the dinner, observed, "Walker would naturally desire to see the dispute arranged for he is engrossed with the tariff, and of course jealous . . . of any other question." He realized that support of an Oregon compromise involved a calculated political risk, since the 54-40 diehards were certain to harbor strong resentments. There always existed the chance that they would withhold their votes from a tariff reform. But Walker gambled that since most of the diehards represented northwestern agricultural interests they would hardly approve "a vote for the support of a system [protectionism] so inimical to those interests." [29]

Furthermore, the Secretary had energetically marshalled facts to support a tariff change. A broadside of forms requesting information about the economic state of the union had poured out of the Treasury. A properly awed *Union* reported, "Walker is actually engaged in collecting from all parts of the country every information . . . necessary to assist him in the management of our finances." The Whigs exploded with charges of unconstitutionality when the Secretary sent out a circular seeking to elicit extensive information about the scope and profit of American manufacturing. "If the Secretary is acting for Congress," they complained, "then he is acting beyond the general duty presented to him by law, . . . and . . . it . . . must . . . be considered as the work of a mere party or personal purpose." [30] Horace Greeley, always the Whig partisan, charged "that these circulars are mainly transmitted to postmasters, and by them handed out to those manufacturers . . . who are likely to return such answers as Mr. Walker desires." The fiery editor added his expectation that tariff reduction insured "a financial disaster." [31]

Administration supporters energetically defended the circulars. "What more thorough method of distributing them," challenged the *Union*, "could have been adopted than to send a number of them to all the postmasters?" Slyly, it added, "the great body of these officers will undoubtedly make a fair circulation of them among the leading and most intelligent manufacturers in their neighborhood." [32] William Cullen Bryant, a determined foe of the "black tariff" of 1842, expected after Mr. Walker had completed his survey that it would be revealed "in all its depravity." "If glaring incontrovertible black facts will do the deed," Bryant believed, "this execrable relic of Whiggery is doomed." [33] The sparse response to his circular secured the Secretary in his conviction that only the manufacturer drew benefit from the 1842 tariff. He had always thought of it as "unfortunate," and nothing arose to alter his opinion.[34]

"At present my chief occupation is with the details of the tariff," Walker assured Mississippians. "It must be reduced to the revenue standard." [35] Whigs and Democrats who represented industrial constituencies protested against his intention. Moreover, among the Pennsylvania delegation, opposition transcended party labels. Heeding the advice of Pennsylvania Congressmen, both Whig and Democrat, threatened Keystone manufacturers formed "an iron and coal association" which issued a circular to request statistical information about the iron and coal industry. The Pennsylvanians made no effort to disguise their intention—they meant to match Treasury statistics with an opposing set of figures. They also worked to organize protest rallies in both Philadelphia and Pittsburgh. To their aid came Louisiana sugar producers declaring their readiness to defend "the present protective duty." [36]

Those opposed to tariff reform faced an almost impossible task. Southern and Western agricultural interests genuinely believed the prevailing rates discriminated against them. Headstrong South Carolinians expressed the most vehement dissent. It was doubtful whether anything short of tariff abandonment would gratify them for long. Already, Congressman Rhett, eternally discontented, had protested, "All we can expect on the Tariff, is a modified Protective Tariff Act." For Joel Poinsett, an anti-Calhoun Carolinian, Rhett's attitude was not unexpected; gloomily, he predicted, "once the tariff issue is settled favorably, the Calhoun group will find something else to complain about." Other southerners feared that "The course pursued by the Southern democracy about Oregon has had the effect of alienating the good feelings of many of our northern and western democrats . . . rendering the harmonious and united action of the party (on the tariff) more difficult." [37] Somehow, the tariff would be reduced, but there existed the real threat that in the process a permanent rupture within the party might occur. Walker had to accomplish this reduction without rupture.

Shortly after the delivery of the Treasury Report, the Committee on Ways and Means invited the Secretary of the Treasury to prepare a tariff bill for congressional consideration. On February 17, 1846, the proposed bill reached the heavy hand of its Chairman, James Iver McKay. A correspondent present when it reached the Committee reported that he had "conversed for a few minutes with one of the Gentlemen who had been engaged in the laborious task of preparing the bill. He informs me that the changes are to come in at the rate of 20% ad valorem. All specific duties are abolished. The price or the cost is only the basis of impost recognized in the bill." [38] Many years later, Grover Cleveland, eager to institute his own tariff reforms, inquired about the preparation of the 1846 tariff bill, and received the information that "it was framed 'from personal examination of experts taken from every prominent customs house in the country. The labor was immense but Walker successfully performed it, and gave us the best Tariff we have ever had.' " [39]

Long and tedious hours of work went into the making of the tariff. A regular stream of economic advisors visited the Treasury. One or two officers from each of the customs houses at New York, New Orleans, Philadelphia, and Boston came to discuss the practical effects of the changes upon their respective ports. For nearly two months, Walker devoted several hours a day to gathering the material necessary for formulating a proper plan.[40] The tariff which finally emerged advocated a modified free trade. The shift from a specific to an *ad valorem* tariff had unusual significance for a government which derived more than 75 percent of its revenue from tariffs, for the income of the federal government under the *ad valorem* principle would expand or contract as the price of imports rose or fell. The belief existed that a lowering of import duties would stimulate the importation of goods, thereby making up any deficit through the expansion of trade. Nevertheless, fearing the opposite might occur, Walker proposed to empower the President to proclaim a duty of 10 percent on tea and coffee.[41]

As a supplement to the new tariff, the Secretary urged Congress to authorize a system of reciprocal trade agreements. If this were done, any nation which agreed to lower its duties on American agricultural products would receive special rates on their exports to the United States. Particularly pressing in Walker's estimation was such an agreement with Canada. He expected it to encourage a diversion of Canadian export trade through New York City, thereby increasing the American carrying trade. Privately, he anticipated that economic ties would provide the cement for a political union between the United States and Canada. This expectation explains why Walker, ordinarily an aggressive expansionist, agreed to the Oregon compromise. The remaining territory would enter the Union along with all of Canada; for him, the result of the Oregon settlement was temporary rather than permanent.[42]

The tariff proposals finally reached the House of Representatives on June 15, 1846. Within nineteen days, the Congressmen had exhausted all debate and sent on, by a vote of 114 to 95, the approved bill to the Senate. Passage had not, however, been accomplished without a serious party split. An almost solid Whiggery had been joined by nineteen defecting Democrats, mainly from the Northeast. Particularly vehement opposition had come from Pennsylvania where Whig and Democrat stood united. Even David Wilmot, the only Pennsylvanian to vote for the bill, admitted his vote had been determined by the sentiments of his district rather than by his own feelings. Though House protest had been beaten down, an invidious issue remained to plague the Democracy. As Horace Greeley observed, the administration had posed a new question, "genuine Free Trade or a frank, open Protective and Revenue Tariff." And, he might have added, the tariff had yet to hurdle the almost evenly divided Senate.[43]

There a combination of Whigs and Pennsylvanians threatened a tie vote. For George Mifflin Dallas, who would have to break a tie, the debate provoked the weary protest that "these Tariff speeches are as vapid as they are inexhaustible; but they must have their say." These were bearable, but he added, "All sorts of ridiculous efforts are making, by letter, newspaper-paragraphs, and personal visits, to affect the Vice's casting vote by persuasion or threat." The angry insistence of Senator Cameron that Pennsylvania would not have supported candidates committed to "any alteration of the tariff of 1842" left the discomfited Vice President wishing the Keystone electorate had known and had rejected the Democratic slate.[44]

While the verbal battle continued in the Senate chamber, a less conspicuous but, nonetheless telling battle raged in the capital lobbies. Bryant angrily charged, "there are Whigs in this city who boastfully declare that sufficient money has been sent to Washington to defeat the new tariff bill." The Whigs retorted that "the only persons to be bought over at this moment are the Democratic Senators"—a charge hardly supported by the final and nearly solid Democratic vote. Dallas, wearily awaiting his day of decision, wryly commented, "The Tariff and its fate keep all the restless mortals on earth in perpetual movement." [45]

Unexpected complications developed during the last week of July. Senator Haywood of North Carolina resigned his seat rather than follow instructions from his state's legislature to vote for the measure. His action left the bill's fate up to two men: Senator Jarnagin of Tennessee and Dallas. Jarnagin had been instructed by his legislature to support the bill. If he were to follow his instructions, the bill would pass by a twenty-eight to twenty-seven vote, but if he were to refrain from casting a vote, the final decision would rest with Dallas. Jarnagin, however, did not intend to defy openly the legislature that he hoped would re-elect him the following year.[46]

The Tennessean was, however, ready to aid in efforts to delay a vote on the tariff until adjournment. On the 27th of July, after some unusual parliamentary proceedings, the bill seemed irretrievably lost after a one vote margin referred it back to the Finance Committee. All during the night of the 27th the administration strove to regain control. In desperation, Walker, before daybreak of the 28th, hastened to the Capitol where he promised to sponsor an amendment aiding Pennsylvania iron and coal interests in return for a switch in her vote. The promise was never redeemed, for, as Walker labored to salvage his tariff, administration supporters within the Senate successfully forced the bill out of committee. Quickly the measure was put to a vote. Jarnagin, attempting to reconcile his beliefs and his instructions, refrained from casting a vote which thus resulted in a tie. Dallas, who forgot his Pennsylvania sentiment and cast the tie-breaking vote, had subsequent reason to rue his decision. "Especially has my casting vote for the Tariff of '46 embittered against me the monopolists everywhere, and the miners and manufacturers of Pennsylvania in particular," he mourned, "but my convictions were sincere." The tariff had become law. "The bill was then ordered to a third reading by the vote of the Vice-President, and was thereupon forthwith read the third time and passed, by 28 yeas to 27 nays—Mr. Jarnagin coming in and voting for the passage of the bill"—so did the Washington Whig organ report the crushing defeat of their party.[47]

Once the Bill had become law, second thoughts found expression. Dallas, uneasily instructed his wife that "if there be the slightest indication of a disposition to riot in the city of Philadelphia, owing to the passage of the Tariff Bill, pack up and bring the whole brood to Washington." Subsequent tranquillity in Pennsylvania proved these fears unfounded. One suspects that the fire and thunder of senatorial debate had clouded the Vice President's good sense. Buchanan who had been distinctly disenchanted by the tariff viewed the issue with equanimity. To his supporter, John Forney, went the advice that chances for a tariff alteration were best if "the State adheres to its Democratic faith." "A protective tariff," Buchanan warned, "is not the word." His political sagacity dominated as he warned Forney not to identify him with this point "too distinctly." Perhaps, his sanguine view had its origin in the assurance of a Pennsylvania lieutenant that "there is little excitement here on the Tariff bill." [48]

As for the Treasury chief, Gideon Welles informed Van Buren, already disturbed about suspected administration attacks upon his supporters, that "Walker is the master spirit in all that relates to this matter, and the President I apprehend, and all the members of the cabinet have not only given in to him but support and sustain him." The implication was obvious: the man who many Van Burenites believed had alone defeated their leader in 1844 was not to be trusted.[49] Friendlier sources rejoiced, "Heaven be thanked that the dawn of the political millennium is faintly streaking the skies and that the first blow of Free Trade has been struck and by *you*." Others worried lest their triumphant Secretary endanger his delicate health. They pleaded, "For Heaven's Sake take a little relaxation after Congress adjourns, or your system may be irreparably injured." [50] But for "a man of great originality, somewhat speculative in his views, and willing to experiment on questions of revenue to the point of rashness," the prospect of total victory meant only fuller application until the whole program had been enacted.[51]

Horace Greeley grimly endured as the anathemas of his life became legislative realities. Perhaps he thought the lost ground might be recovered. At best, the Democracy was a haphazard coalition torn by scarcely concealed dissensions. Why not exploit a few of the more obvious discords? As the divided New York democracy approached the November elections, the *Tribune* dutifully informed the public that "Sir Robert Walker, it is thought, has no objections to being made a Free Trade candidate for the Presidency in opposition to Silas Wright." A sore spot had been touched. Even as the Polk administration achieved its program, there existed ample evidence that it had so done at the price of party disintegration. But before the full consequences became evident, Mr. Walker had other projects to complete.[52]

7. Bull of the Woods

FROM THE MOMENT he assumed charge of the Treasury Department, Walker set out to restore the Independent Treasury. He
prefaced that intention by cautiously undermining the system of
district banks established under the Act of June 17, 1844. The
program of withdrawals from these banks instituted by his
predecessor, George M. Bibb, continued under the new regime.
The informed few knew that the administration intended to assure the "speedy realization of our means, in case the Banks
make a difficulty in December." [1] Congress heard in December of
1845 a call for the restoration of the Independent Treasury, an
institution that had provided "a secure depository for the public
money, without any power to make loans or discounts, or to issue
any paper whatever as currency."

To justify the proposal an array of traditional Jacksonian
arguments against private bankers using government funds
deluged the Congressmen. "The money of the people," Walker
insisted, "should be kept in the treasury of the people created by
law, and be in the custody of agents of the people. . . ." A
prospective opponent found he risked indictment as antidemo-
cratic, since "to say that the people or their government are incompetent, or not to be trusted with the custody of their own
money, in their own treasury . . . would be to concede that they
are incompetent for self-government." [2] If any congressman
thought as much, he did not betray the fact.

Well before the tariff bill reached Congress, Representative
Dromgoole of Virginia, fatally ill but determined with his last
strength to restore the Independent Treasury, introduced a res-

toration bill on December 19, 1845. The debate and vote followed party lines. A hopelessly outnumbered Whiggery delayed a House vote until April 2, 1846, when a united Democracy swamped with their one hundred twenty-two votes the sixty-six Whigs.[3] The real struggle, as everyone knew, would occur in the more evenly divided Senate.

New York bankers promptly expressed their concern. "There is a real panic in the street [Wall] today on account of the Sub-Treasury," one journal reported. "Even the Oregon war has lost its terror in comparison to this monster with his iron chests." [4] The stock market responded with a general decline as financiers warned that the instability of the national economy, perpetually afflicted with inadequate capital, faced accentuation with the removal of government deposits from circulation.

Bankers, refusing to accept the House decision as final, concentrated their protests upon the Senate. A memorial from the New York Chamber of Commerce warned, "the Sub-Treasury Bill, now before the Senate, if passed into law in its present shape is calculated to produce evil far greater than it designs to remedy—one which will be found extremely difficult if not impossible to carry out." [5]

Despite such pessimistic warnings, Alabama's massive Senator Dixon H. Lewis, liquid with sweat, guided the bill through a Senate made short-tempered by the torrid July heat of Washington. At the periphery of the Senate chamber, a nervous Walker cajoled, threatened, and pleaded with doubtful Democrats against all but minor amendments in order to insure solid Democratic support for the proposal. On the first day of August the Senate approved; seven days later a jubilant Secretary witnessed the Presidential signature. Among suspicious Whigs there lingered the belief that Dixon Lewis, upon the urging of Walker, had deliberately held back the Independent Treasury bill, a measure commanding greater enthusiasm among Democrats, to add a further incentive for pushing through the new tariff.[6]

A bill which established government depositories at the

Philadelphia mint and its branches, the New York customs house, and the Boston customs house seemed a hard money measure. But Walker, who no one thought met the specifications of a Loco Foco, had provided for the payment of government dues either in specie or in Treasury notes. Nor did the bill limit the use of these notes as currency. "Bullion" Benton mixed suspicion and enthusiasm as he scrutinized the continuance of paper issues.[7]

If the Missourian had known how carefully Walker had cultivated the New York business community, his suspicions would have flamed into open denunciation. While reducing the deposits at other depository banks, the Secretary had reversed the process in New York City. Only after mid-year of 1846 did withdrawals start in the national fiscal center. The Secretary had revealed a tender spot for the New York financial and commercial community, a feeling which continued throughout his career.[8]

Those banks and businesses which possessed ample supplies of specie benefited from the restoration of the Independent Treasury. Ready access by American bankers to foreign capital also proved advantageous. Usually the two situations existed only in eastern commercial centers. Western and southern banks, however, obtained a measure of independence as long as they possessed government deposits, but the removal of these made them almost wholly dependent upon eastern financial resources. Periodic withdrawals of specie from circulation to meet government obligations accentuated this dependence. This tendency alarmed the eastern business community who feared that periodic tight money conditions would seriously hamper commercial activity. And the government also discovered it had seriously damaged its ability to raise large sums to finance extraordinary expenses.

The passage of the Warehousing Act on August 6, 1846, qualified the most immediate danger of the Independent Treasury to eastern commercial interests. They no longer had to tie up large sums in tariff payments on imports not intended for

immediate consumption. Instead, the government agreed to hold
such imports in bonded warehouses until needed, thereby re-
leasing money that might otherwise have been trapped in the
Treasury. When pressured by businessmen to determine whether
duties would be assessed "upon the *first cost* which is shown by
the *invoice,* or upon the value as including and covering *first cost,
insurance, commissions, freight & exchange,*" Walker agreed
to the latter interpretation with its obvious protectionist implications. The assurance of a prominent Philadelphia editor
that such a decision would assure "the future political com-
plexion" of Pennsylvania and of "all *Sound* Manufacturers" no
doubt partially determined his decision.[9]

Walker consistently endeavored to interpret liberally all
measures which affected business. The vehemence with which he
defended free trade tended to obscure his actual practice: he
worked toward a free trade policy without permanently damaging any substantial segment of the domestic economy. Only the
manufacturer had genuine cause to fear his intentions, but even
they received a more severe verbal punishment than one instituted into law. The Secretary always allowed for a future
adjustment in his plans should political circumstances so dictate.[10]

When Congress adjourned in August it had completed a major
program of domestic reform. An irate Whiggery, defeated at
every turn, turned its wrath upon the suspected architect of its
humiliation. They scathingly denounced "the Little Secretary's
destitution of every honorable political principal (sic)." His
"imps" were suspected of seeking to "secure him the nomination
for the next presidency or vice-presidency." He was castigated
as "the little arch fiend" and indicted "as the greatest political
intriguer . . . of the age and as the most cunning and corrupt
of his class." [11]

As the Whigs vented their wrath, the administration increasingly concerned itself with the task of defeating Mexico. The
war, launched when American troops under Zachary Taylor

advanced into the disputed territory between the Nueces River and the Rio Grande, raged unabated. Jefferson Davis gloomily complained, "Though we pick the millstone we can't see through it," and promised, "if ever I find a hole it will give me pleasure to communicate . . . the wonders found within." [12] But Walker had no time for gloom; he anticipated only a triumphant result enabling the United States to annex the whole southern republic. His energy concentrated itself upon the task of financing the war effort.

Congress, before its adjournment, had authorized the floating of loans amounting to twenty-three million dollars. Early in September, the Secretary, well aware of their political implications, issued a call for five million dollars, noting:

. . . it had been usual heretofore with my predecessors, in advertising for loans, to emit no sum to any individual under $25,000, but with a view to insure the largest possible subscription, and at best rates, and to diffuse the loan as far as practicable throughout all classes of the community, bids were authorized . . . as low as the lowest denomination of Treasury Note . . . fifty dollars.[13]

No one had less intention than Walker to institute a broad base loan but his propensity for democratic rhetoric, and his past appeals to class antagonisms, made it certain that he would try to create the illusion that he had democratized federal borrowing.

A previous issuance of $965,750 in Treasury notes at 5.4 percent had already established the pattern of subscription to government loans. The banking firms of Corcoran and Riggs; Beebe, Ludlow and Company; Washington Hunt; and W. W. Woodworth had taken up the entire loan. Even as Walker declared for a popular subscription, he prepared to visit Wall Street in the hope it would take the whole $5,000,000 loan at 5 percent interest. Upon his arrival at New York, however, he discovered the bankers insisted upon a 6 percent interest.[14]

An angry Secretary, orating at Tammany festivities, announced he would "get along without the banks." The banking community mockingly retorted: "He cannot; for the Treasury notes have been discredited by Banks, bankers, and business men." The banks, moreover, charged the redemption method of Treasury notes rendered "it impossible to recover anything from the Government." [15] Nor did the Independent Treasury system simplify the government's dilemma. Even before it went into operation there had occurred a sharp credit contraction which severely affected the government. "While new systems of finance are coming into operation," a distraught Secretary learned, "it is especially necessary that our moneyed institutions should maintain a strong position, and they do not perceive how an Administration, which has proclaimed that its fundamental policy is separation from banks and the rejection of bank bills, should so immediately come back asking for loans from these rejected institutions of their currency." Wall Street could not perceive "why the Administration should not try its own policy as well as the people; and certainly none why the people should be made sick to save the Administration from its own medicine." [16]

A chastened Walker reported back to an angered Polk that he did not expect to raise the subscription. The President unsettled the Secretary with his demand to know why he had not been informed beforehand of his plan to visit New York. Walker told him only that he wished to avoid unnecessary speculation about his actions, precisely the result he had achieved with the touchy Polk. The chief executive, concerned to know that disbursements during the previous month had exceeded Treasury receipts by $800,000, refused to accept his pessimistic conclusions on the subscription and prodded him into issuing a call for bids on the $5,000,000 loan at 5.4 percent interest. By the end of October both men realized that the subscription effort had failed. They then decided to advertise Treasury notes yielding a 6 percent interest and "receivable for all public dues, both in the land office and customs house, as well before as after maturity." The administration journal accurately described them as "specie bearing interest." [17]

The Treasury now actively courted the financial community. The new notes actually provided a new medium of currency that circumvented the restrictive provisions of the Independent Treasury Act. Walker, incapable of half-way measures and determined to unite the self-interest of the banker to that of the administration, delegated to the nation's bankers the task of transferring funds from New York to New Orleans and, subsequently, to Mexico. Until the completion of the transferrals the money remained on deposit with the banks earning short-term interest, often encouraging bankers who wished to collect additional interest to inordinately delay completion of the transferrals. The system had all the earmarks of a scandal before the war ended, but Walker intent upon successfully financing the war turned a blind eye to the abuse.[18]

Allowing the bankers their reward disposed them favorably toward the government loan, and within a few weeks it had been entirely subscribed. Wall Street bankers glowed over reports of profits exceeding $200,000, but defended their endeavor with the protest, "This is a trifle compared with what the South makes by the Mexican War." [19] Walker warily avoided involvement in any estimate of the advantages which each section derived from the war.

Rather he concerned himself with improving his ability to bargain for better terms in floating loans. When Congress reconvened he requested it provide the Treasury with an additional $4,500,000 by authorizing an *ad valorem* tax of 25 percent on tea and coffee, establishing the graduated pricing system on public lands, and extending the pre-emption principle to settlers on unsurveyed lands. The request for the tea and coffee tax reached the Committee on Ways and Means on January 2, 1847, with the injunction from Walker that "these duties were suggested in view of the necessity of obtaining the loan . . . proposed, and this department feels . . . that, in the absence of these duties, it will probably be wholly impracticable to negotiate the loan on . . . terms as would be permitted by Congress." The House, torn by Democratic intraparty feuding, ignored Walker's plea and rejected the proposed tax.[20]

Rejection forced the Secretary to consider alternative sources of revenue. None seemed more attractive than the proposal that the Mexicans help finance the American war effort. Congress received information that "the President of the United States has . . . directed contributions to be levied in Mexico in every form that many be sanctioned by the law of nations." These included "diminishing the estimated expenditures by obtaining so far as practicable supplies for the army in Mexico; by duties upon [Mexican] imports, as a military contribution; by enforcing the Mexican duty upon exports; and by . . . the seizure and appropriation to the support of the war and the Army of all the internal revenues of Mexico, . . . whether assessed by the General Government of Mexico, or by any department, city, or town." [21]

It is expected that a victor will compel the defeated to pay reparations, but the novelty of these proposals consisted of their seeking reparations from a still undefeated enemy. Those Mexicans already defeated faced the prospect of helping to supply the means to subdue their still unconquered brethren.

Walker and "competent persons from New York and Pennsylvania" worked to draw up tariff lists for occupied Mexican ports. The plan had a cleverness which provoked James Gordon Bennett to comment, "There is not a Yankee in all New England but that would consider himself immortalized by being the originator of such a measure." Less enthusiasm, and, ultimately, the more accurate prophecy, characterized the antiwar Horace Greeley, who complained, "to render this tariff decidedly productive, we must conquer not 'a piece' merely, but substantially the whole of Mexico—the bulk of her population as well as territory." The former Vermonter, revealing his rural origin, concluded, "And then the horse is only pulled and pushed to water—his drinking is still to be provided for." The Mexican, hardly in a mood to finance his own subjugation, proved a reluctant consumer. As late as October 20, 1847, only one small cargo from Europe had entered the harbor of Vera Cruz, leaving Walker to reflect sadly that Mexicans generally revealed little inclination to support the enemy war effort.[22]

Assiduous cultivation of bankers and investors gradually produced the looked for result. George W. Snow, commercial editor of the *Tribune,* expected an eager market for the whole $23,000,000 loan at 6 percent redeemable in twenty years. A provision in the Loan Act of 1847, included by Walker upon the advice of W. W. Corcoran, permitted the conversion of Treasury notes into twenty-year stock. The appearance of this gilt-edged currency encouraged eastern financiers to purchase outstanding Treasury notes. Wall Street buzzed with rumors that large shipments of specie were being shipped into the South and to the army camps along the Rio Grande for the purpose of purchasing available notes. The Secretary, though he labored hard to persuade Democrats to support the provision, and had ample opportunity to observe the enthusiasm among Whig senators and representatives, failed to estimate accurately the unusual attractiveness of convertibility. A deluge of complaints inundated the Treasury as it floundered about without a suitable policy for facilitating conversion.[23]

To recoup his failure in anticipating public response, Walker promptly issued a call for bids upon an $18,000,000 loan secured by 6 percent Treasury notes redeemable within two years. The public demand permitted the Secretary to specify stringent restrictions, including unconditional bids with distinctly stated premiums, with no bid under par accepted, and, ultimately of greatest significance, the Treasury specified the period within which the money must be paid. The power to regulate payments also gave the government the power to regulate the money market as long as there existed outstanding payments. In spite of these conditions, bids upon the loan came in rapidly. An unusual prosperity resulting from a heavy increase in grain exports supported the public purchases of government obligations. As Snow of the *Tribune* asked, "Money is, and is to be, plenty— and who can find better opportunities of investment than in United States funds, bearing an interest of six per cent?" [24]

In early April, after the deposit of all bids at the Treasury department, a gleeful Dallas chortled, "Mr. Walker has been eminently successful in obtaining his loan of 18 millions." He drew the conclusion, "This is proof of his success in the Tariff and of the general confidence in the government. He was offered 58 millions." [25] The spectacular success of Walker's loan converted the "business in Treasury notes" into "one of the most important and extensive branches of Wall Street operations." The heavy demand for notes created a standing premium of 3 percent. Those who had taken the loan expected to "make fortunes." [26]

This latter expectation accounts for the continuing success of Treasury operations. No matter what Walker said about bankers publicly, he never hesitated to cooperate with them privately. He enlisted the services of the government banker, W. W. Corcoran, to insure a free flow of communications between the government and private bankers. Corcoran, fully aware of the substantial profits awaiting the financier of government obligations, obtained the support of his brokerage partner, George Washington Riggs; of the latter's father, Elisha Riggs; of George M. Peabody, head of the great Anglo-American investment house; and of Baring Brothers, the British financiers, to take most of the announced loans. Walker collaborated fully, even permitting Corcoran to examine competing bids, thereby enabling him to offer a higher bid. The Secretary rationalized his behavior with the thought that he had earned the government more money as a result of Corcoran's higher offer. [27]

There existed ample evidence of the intimacy between Corcoran and Walker. During a period of speculative fever over

Treasury notes, Corcoran and Riggs announced the sale of $600,000 in notes at a 4 percent premium in Boston alone. Rumors circulated that New York and Washington investment houses had divided the entire loan with "the latter feeling some uneasiness at being the holders of the enormous shares they have taken." [28] All pretense at a wide distribution of the loan had been abandoned; the overwhelming majority of Treasury Notes had been placed with established banking firms.

Of the $15,469,800 in Treasury notes accounted for in the 1847 Treasury Report, $11,713,850 had either been taken directly by the Corcoran and Riggs firm, or by Elisha Riggs as an individual. An additional $1,987,500 had been bid on successfully by M. Morgan and Company, a firm closely associated with the Corcoran and Riggs interest.[29] The large assignments to the Corcoran firms persuaded the *Union* to deny that partiality had been shown Corcoran and Riggs. Since they had bid an 8 percent premium, Walker, they argued, had merely accepted the highest bid. He had judiciously given the full amount of their bid to all who had bid more than the 8 percent premium, something he could hardly have avoided, but he had also granted to the other 8 percent bidders the full amount of their bid rather than divide the loan among all the bidders proportional to the size of their bid.[30] Nevertheless, Corcoran and Riggs bagged over 80 percent of the loan. The intimate cooperation between Corcoran and Walker, lasting until the death of the latter, was cemented by the lucrative profits that came from floating government loans. So close had their friendship become during the first years of the Polk administration that Robert Winthrop, Whig Speaker of the House during the 30th Congress, eager to learn whether the administration planned to call a special session in the spring of 1847, asked Corcoran if he knew its intentions, adding significantly, "You [Corcoran] have a golden key for unlocking the mysteries of Walkerdom, if not of Polk-dom." [31]

By May 15, 1847, all doubt about the success of Walker's fiscal policy had been dispelled. Treasury notes sold at a 5 percent premium. The New York press reported "the business streets now present an appearance of activity which speaks well for the prosperity of our City. The narrow streets appropriated to the sale of dry goods . . . have seldom been so active and busy." The assertion by one of his long time friends that *"Walker is Bull of the Woods"* seemed irrefutable. Within a few months, August Belmont, proud agent of the haughty Rothschilds, bent to Walker's inflexible demand that Belmont's agent, Davidson, in Mexico City, pay the American army of occupation their wages with "no expense" to the government "but the interest rate from the date of payment to the date of reimbursement." Candor illuminates the manner in which Belmont accepted the agreement: he did it in anticipation of favors to come.[32]

8. The Price of Success

SUCCESS IN FULFILLING its pledges undermined the Polk administration. Each step forward had only served to disenchant some portion of the coalition which had elected the President. The tariff had secured the loyalty of the commercial East and of the staple crop South, but it had alienated the Pennsylvania industrialists. The Independent Treasury which ought to have convinced Van Buren of administrative orthodoxy seemed only to heighten the grievances of the Old Magician, smarting from patronage neglect. The Oregon settlement reminded Northern expansionists that their interest earned compromise while Southern expansionism warranted war. The impending defeat of Mexico stirred again the question of how far the Union was committed to sustain the South's *peculiar institution.* Triumph in Mexico rebounded to the benefit of the Whigs since both commanding generals, Taylor and Scott, belonged to the Whiggery. And as always, no matter how conscientious the administration was, as Walker knew, it never had sufficient patronage to reward the faithful.[1]

Polk unwittingly complicated the political situation at the outset of his administration. Not only did he pledge himself to a single term, but he also demanded from his cabinet members pledges that they not seek the nomination while serving in the cabinet.[2] Obviously, with the most prominent Polk supporters eliminated, the 1848 presidential nomination promised to attract increasing attention from those politicians *not* attached to the administration. This certainty threatened particularly dangerous implications for party unity, since both Van Buren and Cass, still bitter rivals, intended to seek the nomination in 1848.

Democratic prospects were aggravated by Van Buren's mistaken conviction that Polk intended his destruction. Denied nomination, patronage, and repelled by the chilly behavior of Polk, the chief of the New York radicals had decided he had but one recourse.[3] He groomed his protégé, Governor Silas Wright, for an 1848 bid. All that remained to complete his preliminary plans was the re-election of Wright in 1846. As election year dawned, rumors circulated through New York State that the administration intended to defeat Wright. By early autumn of 1846 Van Buren and Wright no longer doubted that the administration was hostile. When the collector of the port of Rochester announced his opposition to Wright and insinuated he did so in response to administration directions, Walker, seeking to prevent a complete rupture, assured Wright the administration hoped for his re-election. Wright angrily accused the whole administration, "with a few elevated exceptions such as Butler and Hoffman," of plotting his defeat. The Treasury chief, at the direction of Polk, gave Wright a "carte blanche to have these rumors corrected if deemed advisable, thro' the *Atlas* in any form you think best." [4]

As an additional reassurance, Walker notified Wright that he considered himself an indirect target of attacks upon the Governor. Sibly, the Rochester collector, had been appointed at Marcy's behest and had no fondness for the Treasury chief. Nevertheless Walker made no effort to exonerate the whole cabinet of enmity toward the Governor. He knew only that neither he nor the President wished Wright's defeat. Appointments in New York had been made in response to local political pressure, and Wright received numerous reminders from the cabinet that he had been notoriously coy about pressing his own demands. Finally, Walker appealed to Wright's sense of proportion, arguing, "I can hardly suppose that my humble opinions could have any influence upon the elections of New York."

Wright and Van Buren were left to mull over the possibility that their difficulties arose from the hostility of Marcy and the Hunker faction.[5]

The appearance on the eve of the New York election of a letter in the New York *Ledger* which stated Buchanan's opposition to the Tariff of 1846 convinced Walker and Dallas that their fellow Pennsylvanian pursued a devious course. Simultaneously, Buchanan reassured Wright of his friendship while informing the Hunker faction that he supported their opposition to administration tariff policies. Dallas pressed for a showdown with Buchanan "at once and with an open brow." But he no longer believed that anything could save New York. Walker agreed.[6]

The disaster that overcame Wright at the polls convinced his supporters that their betrayal had been complete. A defeated House candidate bluntly charged that Wright's defeat had resulted from the "secret direction of the administration." The Customs House employees, following the directions of their Hunker chief, were guilty of "desertion and ingratitude." [7] But for Walker the most stunning result of all was in Pennsylvania. The Democrats lost half their twelve House seats. His unease was not lessened when incautious southern Democrats, still rankling over the Keystone stand on the tariff, rejoiced that "Whigs have superseded such Democrats," and expressed a preference for being "in the minority" rather "than . . . in the majority controlled by such men." [8] A winter of discontent enveloped the Democracy, as factionalism ran rampant.

Nowhere did greater dismay exist than in the Van Buren ranks. It hardly mattered that Polk no longer intended to grant the Hunkers "favors"; Van Buren's estrangement from the administration could hardly have been more complete. All that remained for him was to await the 1848 convention, there to press his claims for recognition. Van Buren, moreover, made ready to exploit free soil as an issue. This question had taken shape as American armies pressed deeper into Mexico. Sagacious Democrats feared that intervention in Mexico threatened disruption for their party. Before the war came, Henry Gilpin, who had an amateur interest in the activities of the Philadelphia democracy, read uneasily that Polk was increasingly called "the Hangman of the Confederacy." A surprising prescience infused his warning: "Take notice of that first act of hostility on the part of Mr. Polk against Mexico . . . from that moment the Confederacy falls to pieces, like an old Barrel after the hoops have been eaten . . . by Worms." [9]

But the Polk administration seemed oblivious to the dangers implicit in the Mexican venture. The disputes that agitated its membership were largely over the scope of the war aims. These found their most expansive exponent in Walker. At a Pennsylvania rally, early in the war, he proposed: "We have already more than doubled the area and the States of the Union, and no combination of Foreign Powers can say, upon our own continent, thus far shalt thou go and no farther." As the armies probed deeper into Mexico, the Secretary of the Treasury militantly defined the national war aims. On June 29, 1846, Polk recorded in his diary that "a discussion arose between Mr. Buchanan and Mr. Walker in regard to the objects of the war with Mexico, in the course of which Buchanan expressed himself in favor of acquiring the Rio Grande as our western boundary as high up as the Passo in about 32 degrees of North Latitude and thence West to the Pacific. He expressed himself as being opposed to acquiring any large slave territory. Walker argued for the 26 degree of North Latitude. In order to obtain this territory, he was willing to fight the world." [10] The laconic Polk made no comment.

As the war progressed, old friends from Mississippi kept Walker fully informed of developments at the front. Jefferson Davis, who had been sent to Taylor's headquarters at the Secretary's request, communicated regularly about the deficiencies of quartermaster service. The fall of Monterey brought the notification that "our Mississippians have been in a situation which tried both the men and the new rifles, and the experiment has proved them equal to my highest expectations." Any inclination Walker had to settle for limited gains dissolved with the assurance of J. A. Quitman, now a major general, that the whole of Mexico lay "entirely in our power." If anything, these reports stimulated his preoccupation with making the Mexican defeat even more complete. The Secretary evidenced a growing interest in experiments with military equipment. The more devastating a weapon promised to be, the more enthusiastic did his response become.[11]

Simple annexation of northern Mexican territories no longer sufficed for the increasingly belligerent Walker. A perplexed Polk heard with alarm that his Treasury chief "attached greater importance to the free passage across the Isthmus of Tehuantepec than to the cession of New Mexico and the Californias." To obtain a canal route and the northern territories, he would agree to pay the Mexicans $30,000,000. Furthermore, he "insisted that the free passage across the Isthmus . . . should be a sine qua non to the making of any Treaty." Polk soberly commented: "To this I objected." Lest the Mexicans fail to make preparations for a Tehuantepec canal, Walker suggested that $5,000,000 of the sum "to be paid to Mexico should be retained in our Treasury, and not paid to Mexico until that Government should have constructed a canal or a railroad over the Isthmus." During the 1850's Walker's insistence upon the Tehuantepec project foreshadowed his preoccupation with the construction of a transcontinental railroad.[12]

Before Scott's army occupied Mexico City, Walker had resolved upon the total annexation of Mexico. Bancroft sent assurances from London that a "grievously tried" England would do nothing to prevent the United States from conquering and holding "the whole of Mexico." A spokesman for the Mexican party advocating total annexation, Carlos Landa, lobbied his case with Van Buren, Dix, Calhoun, Benton, Buchanan, and Walker. The enthusiasm expressed by the latter convinced Landa that "Walker knew Mexico best." Extreme expansionists accepted without question "that Walker's opinion 'almost always prevails in the Cabinet.' " The "fertile imagination" that had persuaded a nation to annex Texas now contended that annexation would be to "the immense reciprocal advantage [of] the two Republics." When the question arose on how to convince the two peoples of the wisdom of a prospective union, Walker dismissed it as a task of "making the public opinion conform to the sentiments of the government by agitation." Only Polk needed persuading that total annexation made sense. As events turned out, however, his more conservative temperament overrode his Secretary's overwhelming desire for expansionism.[13]

When Polk informed Walker that he intended to settle the war on the basis of the Treaty of Guadalupe Hidalgo, the Secretary announced his intention to resign and lobby for the defeat of the Treaty in the Senate. Nothing less than total annexation would satisfy him. As a step toward the fulfillment of the American continental destiny; as part of the necessary justification for the sacrifice of American lives, both in the war and before; and as a monument to the memory of his beloved brother, Duncan, the act was imperative. Polk, already beset with party antagonisms, and unwilling to precipitate a major rift in his administration, agreed to allow Walker to remain within the cabinet while he lobbied for complete annexation. Both men agreed on the need to keep new political disputes in the family kitchen. The growing demand in the Whig press for the nomination of a war hero in 1848 convinced them that the Democracy faced a major crisis. Gloomily Walker complained that his own political future was endangered by "too many new generals, seeking a reputation in other political spheres." Success had gone too frequently in this pursuit to Whig generals. As he attempted to create an authentic Democratic war hero and mend his Mississippi political fences, Walker pressed successfully upon Polk the urgency of appointing Jefferson Davis a brigadier general.[14] Without realizing it, he encouraged in Davis an esteem for his military prowess that would have disastrous consequences for the Confederacy.

But the circumstances which led to this unforeseen result, though subsequently understood fully by Walker, mirrored the perplexity of a party about to win a war and lose the Presidency. The confusion over war aims convinced some Democrats that Walker led "a large Party growing up in the United States, who are for taking the whole of Mexico." Senator John M. Niles of Connecticut notified his former chief, Van Buren, that Walker made "no secret of advocating the acquisition of all Mexico." Misjudging the true temper of administration decision-making, he concluded, "the President is believed to favour the views of Walker, but is of course more cautious in expressing his opinions." Efforts to clarify administration policy became more difficult as Polk grew more suspicious of Buchanan whom he thought "selfishly trying to do things best calculated to aid him in getting the nomination for presidency." [15]

As debate over war aims increased, northern Democrats added their contentiousness to an already floundering policy. No matter what happened—if only minimum demands on Mexico were met —American territory would increase by more than one-third. Division of this land into states threatened to affect profoundly party lines and the functioning of federal authority. Since the defeat of Van Buren in 1844, many northern Democrats viewed with skepticism an expansion which seemed mostly to benefit an overweening South. Bitterness permeated the words of Gideon Welles, writing to Van Buren:

It has appeared to me for several years that a derangement of parties was inevitable . . . that the party organization was perverted, and . . . we must sooner or later be involved in difficulty. The aggressive spirit of the southern democrats . . . their arrogance which has led them to believe that they alone are qualified to direct the democratic party . . . their patronizing airs to *their* "allies" the northern democrats, some errors and too great concessions on the part of the north, could not otherwise than cause a reaction if there is a salutary corrective in the public mind. Matters have come to an issue on the free territory question, but there are others that will be interwoven with it, and constitute a part of the platform on which the democratic party is to be reconstructed.[16]

Northern enmity had its parallel in the willingness of southern Democrats to equate northern antagonism to new slave states with northern determination "to crush Slavery." [17]

As success engulfed the Polk administration, it threatened the very foundations of the party. Superficially, the major issues dividing the party had been resolved. The result ought to have been a greater party solidarity. Actually, the reverse condition prevailed. Northern free traders had joined with Southerners of similar persuasion to institute a free trade policy. But once the goal had been gained, there existed no compelling reason for a northern free trader to display an enthusiasm for territorial expansion that might result in more slave states. Even Walker felt uneasy about the consequences of his insistence for a war of total conquest, especially one that was drawn out. "Though others may be more clamorous," he conceded privately, "probably none are so truly anxious to obtain an early and cheap peace, as the *free trade Democrats.* If our State Dept. were filled with the trophies of war and we left free to extend our boundaries wherever we chose, I should think the acquisitions dearly purchased if it cost us what we have gained in progress to free trade." [18]

Torn between his aggressive instinct for expansion and a firm intention to conserve free trade advances, Walker's uneasiness intensified as evidence accumulated showing that the war had become identified with sectional aspirations, most specifically, with those of the southern yeomanry. Reports reached Washington that a flood of volunteers were pouring into New Orleans. The War had hardly been declared when some 4,000 backwoodsmen came forth from Louisiana alone. One joyous correspondent informed Walker that the popular cry had become, "still they come." From Georgia he received assurance that "a volunteer company could be raised in every county." Even Kentucky, which had not cast its electoral majority for Polk, halted debate upon "the necessity of war" and acknowledged that "a sufficient claim" had been made upon "her patriotism." [19]

Unanimity, however, even in the South, did not exist. New

Orleans expressed a mixed response to patriotic appeals. "Private bickerings and jealousies among the military men of the City" complicated efforts to mobilize a substantial force of men. The "lukewarm and indifferent" response of the "French and Spanish Creole population" convinced the American Hotspurs "that when we have American democratic Presidents to elect, and Battles to fight, the American population are the only reliable troops that can be depended upon." The obviously nativist sentiments did not fall upon deaf ears. Walker had expressed his own suspicions of "Papists, . . ." many of whom were transcendent in villainy—robbers, murderers, aye even infidels and deists." [20] Yet, for him, these sentiments never justified disruption of the Democracy. In time, he even came to believe that the salvation of his party depended upon its ability to win the support of the immigrant. But for the moment, he gave pungent expression to pugnacious nativism.

Abruptly, the sectional discords over war aims erupted into national attention. A small roguish man arose in the House and proposed an amendment prohibiting slavery in the Mexican cession to the bill which authorized the establishment of an executive fund to aid the administration in negotiating a Mexican peace. The amendment achieved a solitary notoriety. David Wilmot, its proponent, had obtained a signal distinction as the lone member of the Pennsylvania delegation to vote for the 1846 tariff. This he had done despite his own disinclination for low tariffs. His home district had wished it, and so he had complied. Subscribing to the Jacksonian doctrine that a congressman should represent the views of his constituents, Wilmot had articulated his "burnt-over" district's antipathy toward slavery, a sentiment he shared.[21]

That the Wilmot proposal struck a respondent chord in the North could not be doubted; the House membership, reflecting northern dominance, voted heavily for the proviso. Faced with the prospect of having to face an electorate biennially, congressmen expressed in their votes an acute sensitivity to popular

attitudes. The six year term of the Senate permitted statesmanship and often provided an accurate index of informed opinion;
but the House reflected the opinion of the public. Much of that
opinion can be dismissed but instances occur that adumbrate an
abiding theme—such as free soil. In time, the Senate followed
in the wake of the House, subscribing or opposing "free soilism"
as each section dictated. The politics of the succeeding decade
proved little more than a sustained effort to achieve a settlement
over this troublesome issue. In the end, it fatally disrupted political communications and attained resolution not through words
but bullets.

Van Buren, nursing his resentment, recognized the potency
of the issue. Unlike abolitionism which made its appeal to humanitarian sentiment, free soil couched its plea in terms of self-
interest. Whereas the former expected a donation of spirit, the
latter held forth the promise that the landed heritage would be
made available to all. Not only would it be free from slavery,
but also free from cost. The culminating act of free soil would
be the Homestead legislation. The Old Magician, well versed in
the political necessity of judiciously disposing patronage, realized that the politician who made free soil his central issue
offered the voter nearly half a continent. When called upon by
the New York democracy to define his position on the proviso,
he declared with alacrity his irrevocable support of the free soil
movement. Though the issue, as yet, could not bring victory in a
presidential election, it could be used to threaten a major defection from party ranks if the Democratic candidate were objectionable. It also posed a puzzle for Southerners. "If the
hostility to Slavery," a planter wondered, "has become so extended as to tempt Martin Van Buren to bow low and worship
at its shrine for the highest office in the gift of the people, how
long will it be before our own security will require that we withdraw from those who deem themselves contaminated by our
touch?" [22]

Consternation stirred the ranks of the Democracy. Former

President Tyler who remembered too well the result of his own defection in 1840 dubbed the proviso "nothing less than a gratuitous insult on the Slave States." Elsewhere, he denounced it as seeking "to stamp upon the records of the country an anathema and an edict which is unnecessary and wanton." Angrily he continued,

No man doubts but that California and New Mexico will be free-States whenever the proper time arrives, if it has not already arrived, for them to form State constitutions. Their territory is already parcelled out to a great extent under Spanish and Mexican grants to those who do not and never will hold slaves; and the flow of the population from the free-States outnumbers that from the slave-States fully ten for one. What Southern man, then, would be so reckless of his own good as to carry thither his domestics with the positive certainty that at an early day he would be deprived of them by the legitimate action of the people of the Territory? . . . The Wilmot Proviso then is to the free States an abstraction, while to the South it is a reproach and an insult of the deepest dye. . . . The slave-holding States either stand on a footing of equality with the non-slave-holding, or they are inferior and degraded. Better by far the language of the Abolitionists, in their demand for secession, than that of the Free-soilers for exclusion and absolutism. The first admits by fair inference that equality of the States, the last denies that equality, and adds gratuitous insult to aggression.[23]

Polk agreed with his predecessor; the proviso appeared to him both "foolish and mischevious." Moderation governed his own estimate of the situation. He rejected the prospect of an addition to the Union of "another foot of Slave Territory." Attempts to extend slavery could not be accomplished "without endangering the harmony and stability of the Union." Though in agreement with the proviso's major premise: the need to terminate the further expansion of slavery, Polk realized southern politicians considered it a deliberate affront. He pressed for a face saving extension of the Missouri Compromise line to the Pacific, convinced that the territory so opened to slavery would never support the institution. Dallas believed, however, that if the proviso were to pass, Polk would "not veto it." His presumption may have been conditioned by his own passionate espousal of the proviso. Shortly after Van Buren had publicly endorsed it, Dallas offered to support him at the 1848 convention. No one, least of all Walker, failed to recognize that Dallas's decision was in response to Buchanan's rejection of the proviso. The Philadelphia aristocrat also had grudging admiration for its bumptious author.[24]

Walker maintained silence during the early stages of the developing controversy. His presidential aspirations dictated that he avoid becoming involved in "all the excitement that the 'Free-Soilers' and the factionists of the South have been able to get up about 'Niggers.' "[25] As internecine warfare tore the Democracy, it appeared more than ever that a stalemate would impend at the 1848 convention. Only those who remained aloof from faction, Walker believed, could hope to profit from a stalemate. His wracking illness conveniently justified both his prolonged silence and his absence during cabinet debates when the dispute waxed fiercest.[26]

Throughout 1847, there appeared increasingly favorable comments about Walker's prospective candidacy. Even Whigs conceded that "Mr. Walker has certainly financed this administration through some very tight places, and it must be conceded that he has done it in a manner which not only greatly benefited the government but bore as gently as possible on the monied interest of the government." The Philadelphia *Ledger* proposed a ticket with Walker as President and General Worth of New York as Vice President. This influential journal believed that "Walker more than any other man is identified with all the leading measures of the Democratic Party," and that "he would come into the Convention as the second choice of Pennsylvania, Delaware, New Jersey, and several other Northern States."[27] All these expectations terminated when precarious health forced the Secretary, "in the most uniform, decisive, and unequivocal manner, to reject all propositions and efforts to conduct him to the Presidency."[28]

Despite his withdrawal, Walker did not intend to play a

passive role at the convention. Senator Niles of Connecticut warned that "Walker and his friends are at work for Polk," despite the President's announced unwillingness to seek a second term. Though such an eventuality seemed remote, Van Buren intended to make even its least possibility distasteful to the convention. He instructed his son, John, "to withdraw from the convention," rather than submit to a second term for Polk.[29] Refusing even to allow his name to appear before the convention, Old Martin insisted that a free soiler receive the nomination. When the convention attempted to resolve the tangled New York dispute about the seating of the Hunker and *Barnburner* factions, requesting only that both agree to support the party candidates, the Barnburner supporters of Van Buren deserted the convention. The subsequent convention voting revealed that only Buchanan and Cass had much chance to secure the nomination. Walker and Dallas chose to support Cass, helping to insure his nomination.[30]

At long last, Van Buren had the reason and political means to impress upon the Democracy that to ignore him would mean defeat. It also meant that he could vent his spleen upon the "despicable" Cass. The bolting Barnburners, following the direction of their leader, reassembled in Utica in late June to nominate Van Buren. His unabashed intention was to run on a free soil platform. Van Buren had triggered a demand throughout the upper North for a convention that would unite all antislavery forces within a single party. John Hale, who had disrupted the New Hampshire democracy rather than support its espousal of the annexation of Texas, arrived in Buffalo to organize a free soil party. Convinced that his earlier "work of emancipating New Hampshire from pro-slavery Democracy" had reached its culmination, he meant to break the back of "a bastard Democracy." A jubilant convention endorsed Van Buren and Charles Francis Adams. The candidates announced their intention to run on the principles of the proviso.[31]

The nearly three hundred thousand free soil votes cast in

1848, drawn from both Democracy and Whiggery, though enough to defeat the Democrat Cass, revealed that a dry rot infected both parties. Politicos quickly noted that regiments of voters had defected from their traditional allegiance. Walker anticipated that a new party, appealing to a northern vote, would emerge from the debacle that had shattered the Democracy. Uncertain about his own political future, he contemplated the need for a political debate, no matter how disguised, on the further expansion and continued existence of slavery. His ill health had precluded his active participation in the convention and the campaign of 1848, but his known intimacy with the Polk administration exposed him to attacks from disgruntled Democrats. Shrewdly, he conceded before a convention audience that the nomination of a member of the cabinet would insure that the overweening issue would be the administration record. Though convinced that the record needed no apologies, Walker privately concluded that an interlude of four years would provide a perspective with which to make a fair and favorable judgment. The *Mississippian,* one of Walker's firmest newspaper supporters, accepted philosophically his being passed over in 1848. "After all," it commented, "Mr. Walker is comparatively a young man —the youngest in the catalogue of distinguished Democratic names who have yet been brought into view for the office. He is willing to bide his time. His reputation is one that he can repose upon." [32]

Walker admitted there was no undue haste in reaching the Presidency. He contended that in entering the Polk cabinet he had relinquished his right to recognition in 1848. Nothing remained but to sit out four years of Whig control. The squabbling Democracy, deprived of patronage, must submerge its differences and work to win in 1852. Furthermore, he did not intend to "go to war" with Taylor, victorious hero of Buena Vista. Patience had brought its reward in the past, it could do so again. What he did not immediately recognize was the possibility that the issue raised by Van Buren had precipitated a sectional strife which would eliminate or qualify the chances of a man with pronounced Union sentiments. An uncertain rather than a militant posture was proving the mark of political success in the 1850's.[33]

Slowly, but irrevocably, the Secretary moved away from a proslavery position. As long as he had been the Senator from Mississippi, or thought his political prospects depended on that state, he had judiciously avoided action that might suggest antagonism to the *peculiar institution*. Privately, in 1847, he had arranged to emancipate a slave girl who had served his wife. Shortly before he left the Treasury Department, Dallas recorded that he had visited Mr. Walker one evening. "He tells me," the Vice President noted, "that he attended a meeting of the Colonization Society last night, at which a Resolution of his was adopted complementary to the objects and achievements of the Society, particularly as to Liberia, for which he expects to be assailed by the South Carolinians." As rumors spread about the former Mississippian's apostasy, Howell Cobb, a Georgia aristocrat demanded to know Walker's stand on slavery. Several days later, Francis Preston Blair, hardly able to suppress his astonishment, informed Van Buren that Walker now expressed regret at having opposed the former President in favor of the southern *oligarchs*. Walker maintained that free soil was as necessary for the survival of the Democracy as for the nation. The task of the future would be to translate it from an issue of divisive debate into one guided toward solution by legislative action.[34]

9. The Business Constituency

AS WALKER SEVERED his bonds with the extreme proponents of slavery, he worked to secure his tie with the eastern business constituency. Candidly he admitted that during his administration of the Treasury he had labored "to advance [the] interests . . . of the business man, and especially the merchants." [1] The Mexican War had stimulated the economy, creating new wealth, but it had also obliged the government to float new loans to meet its cost. As that need increased, the government found its bargaining position compromised. Confronted in 1848 with a worsening fiscal condition, Walker, who had worked to persuade "Father" Ritchie and the *Union* to editorialize in the autumn of 1847 "against the practability of an immediate peace," actively pushed for quick peace negotiations. Reduced to a choice between all of Mexico and a stable Treasury, he settled for secure finances.[2]

Hoping that news of the Peace Treaty would stimulate the purchase of subsequent government bond issuances, the Secretary refrained from announcing a new loan. From London came the depressing news that the Barings and Rothschilds, though prepared to bid upon a future loan, did not intend to permit the government to escape the consequences of its adverse bargaining position. Furthermore, W. W. Corcoran, the government banker, did not encourage the Secretary to think that the American market would meet his needs "without creating the most serious embarrassment in the money—of the country." Instead he pressed Walker to float a loan in London and alleviate the tight domestic money market with foreign coin.[3]

Stubbornly, Walker continued to procrastinate, only to have Congress force his hand by passing heavy and unexpected appropriations. Since the Treaty of Guadalupe Hidalgo obliged the federal government to assume Mexican debts to Americans, Congress, at the behest of interested creditors, directed the Treasury to commence a prompt liquidation of the debt. Moreover, the fast approaching presidential election convinced both parties that a bounty to the returning veterans would be both patriotic and rewarding at the polls. No longer able to delay, Walker turned in desperation to Corcoran in the hope that he might advance the needed funds. The banker instead offered to travel to London in an effort to persuade British financiers to provide the necessary sixteen million dollars. To increase the prospect of Corcoran's success, Bancroft, the American ambassador, received urgent instructions to assure any London banking firm with which Corcoran might deal that the Treasury notes he offered would carry interest from the date of purchase.[4]

Corcoran, who had assumed the same role in fiscal politics that Nicholas Biddle had once played, provided the critical link in negotiations between the administration and both domestic and foreign bankers. Intimate ties bound the firm of *Corcoran and Riggs* with the British investment house of *Baring Brothers*. Advance information on prospective administration money policy flowed to the British firm from Corcoran's office. When the question developed over the rate of interest to be paid by the government on the assumed Mexican debt, Corcoran blithely assured F. W. Ward, Baring's Boston agent, that "the Secty is disposed to meet the views of Messrs. B. B. & Co." With admirable agility, he mobilized the New York banking community to support his retention as government banker despite the change in administration. Even as he conducted business with the outgoing administration, he kept Baring Brothers aware of impending political changes, assuring them "that Clayton is to come into either the State or Treasury Dept." As Corcoran traveled to London, he knew that his government had no alternative but to rely upon his influence with foreign bankers. The Treasury chief struggled to avoid "an impression in Europe that we were greatly in want of money . . . that we have not sufficient capital of our own to be invested in our own loans, but must ask the aid of foreign capital," but only the word of this private banker carried the necessary conviction. Walker resented American dependence upon Corcoran, but he knew of no alternative. The man whose word could persuade the European financier of the wisdom of American fiscal policy would inevitably exercise inordinate power. Corcoran delighted in the experience.[5]

The triumphant conclusion of the war and Corcoran's glib persuasiveness enabled Walker to conclude successfully his fiscal policies. The $16,000,000 loan sold at par and slightly above par on the London market. At home, sales continued well above par. The strength of government obligations complicated the Treasury's efforts to retire half a million of both five percent Treasury stock due in 1853 and the six percents due in 1862. Exerting considerable caution and working through C. W. Lawrence, the eminently respectable Hunker Collector of the Port of New York, the Treasury managed to withdraw over half a million of its stock "without paying advanced rates." The two men acted with such secrecy that William C. Bouck, "arch-Hunker" and receiver of the public money at New York, knew nothing of the transactions. Though never explicitly stated, Walker harbored a growing distaste for the extreme Hunkerism that had disrupted a united New York democracy. Though sympathetic to the conservative fiscal policies of Hunkerism, he preferred the moderate stance of Lawrence to the no-compromise stand of the extreme Hunkers. Disclaiming any doubt about the "integrity" of Governor Bouck, the Secretary refrained from putting it to the test. In the remaining months of his tenure, Walker struggled to liquidate, whenever possible at favorable rates, outstanding war debts. He meant to convince the public that he put its interest above all.[6]

At the same time, the proud Secretary continued his efforts

to improve the Warehousing System. The beaming approval of the mercantile community convinced the little man that the system deserved his devoted care. The slightest protest over its operation brought a prompt investigation. Among businessmen, Walker gained a reputation for tactful understanding of their problems. As so often in his career, he presaged the politician of four decades later who gave to business that assistance for which others would have exacted a price. In return, he gained the cordial and sustained support of the business constituency during the remainder of his political career.[7]

Once he had surrendered his hope for the total annexation of Mexico, Walker managed an enthusiastic evaluation of the War's result. With boundless faith in the future, he described the Treaty of Guadelupe Hidalgo as presaging a new surge of American power. Confidently, he predicted to John Forney:

You must not think the boast extravagant—altho its fulfillment is distant —it is quite certain. The advance towards it is rapid—Here Louisiana, Florida—Texas & large portions of Mexico added to the *United States*— with one Commerce, language and Confederacy—England extended over nearly the balance of North America, much of Europe & large portions of Asia . . . progressing—with one commerce— . . . and government becoming more & more republican every day. In time with the advancing knowledge & improvements of age as . . . the electric Telegraph, the Press, the free schools, what shall prevent this destiny? See with no foreign relations, treaties, ministers or diplomacy because of one nation—No fortifications, no tariffs, no standing armies or navies, no Secy of State, War, or the Navy, the power of the general government but few and simple—A vast majority . . . will speak the English language, the general convenience will in the end make it universal. . . . The expense of such a govt. would be about one twentieth of the aggregate expenditure of the several governments of the world. To what a pitch of glory, of happiness, of freedom, of knowledge & goodness would not *man* advance under such a system.[8]

"Common language . . . kindred race, and . . . mutually beneficial . . . commerce and intercourse," pointed the way to a rich and triumphant future for the Anglo-Saxon peoples. Soon he would pronounce the inevitable reunion of the British and

American nations. Manifest destiny, he believed, existed as a racial rather than as a national phenomenon. It ultimately permitted Walker to convert the tragedy of civil war into a necessary step toward racial fulfillment. News of the Revolutions of 1848 confirmed his expectations. "The bugle notes of freedom . . . sounding . . . across the glad Atlantic" proved the coming triumph of the principles which underlay the Declaration of Independence. Tyranny could not long prevail against "the Christian doctrine of *liberty, equality* and *fraternity.*" The day would come when the world would celebrate American independence "as the dawn of freedom . . . throughout the world." To doubt that the French would succeed in their new revolution "is treason to liberty and the rights of man." The manifest triumph of democracy defied timidity. "There is an overruling Providence," he asserted, "which directs and controls the destiny of men and nations . . . and . . . will break the chains of his oppressors and give him everywhere, even upon this earth through universal freedom, millennial foretaste of the still greater blessings prepared . . . in the mansions of heavenly and eternal joys." [9] The belief of countless Americans that upon their virgin continent the City of God had been foreglimpsed captivated the Secretary's imagination.

But the world insisted upon intruding into his reverie of prophecy. The war hero Taylor had given the Whigs a formidable candidate; the defection of Van Buren threatened to undermine the New York democracy. Continuously through the year preceding the election, Walker worked to induce favorable British free trade policies. Bancroft received instructions to urge upon the radical free traders Joseph Hume and John MacGregor, both Members of Parliament, the critical import of a reduction in the duty on tobacco. "If he wants to keep us democratic," the Secretary bluntly observed, "he had better reduce the duty." Unless a tariff reduction occurred, the Presidential election of 1848 would be lost, "and with that must rise or fall democracy & free Trade or Whiggery & ultra protection." [10]

British and American free traders actively collaborated to guide reciprocal legislation through Parliament and Congress. When Congress passed the Passenger Acts of 1846, both free trade shippers and the House of Baring were threatened with loss through a too literal interpretation of its provisions. Bancroft assured both of them that Walker was "very friendly to the commercial interest, and would impose no hardships. . . ." Assiduous cultivation of British business interests also included the use of London insurance firms to secure the Warehousing System against loss. Time and again Bancroft exerted his influence among "friends in [P]arliament" to obtain more liberal terms for American trade. At home, Walker promised the retiring British Minister Pakenham that such action would further cement the already extensive "ties of common language and of kindred race." [11]

Underlying his continuing effort to exploit free trade sentiment, Walker clung to the abiding conviction that at stake was the destiny of the United States as a democratic beacon. To praise the revolutionists of 1848 without giving substantial aid would provide small comfort. At the behest of Bancroft, Walker agreed that "it would be a signal service to liberty, & a most politic movement in the way of the expression of national friendship, if the sale of French articles could at this time meet with encouragement in the United States by a temporary or permanent reduction of duty." Working within the framework of the tariff laws, the Secretary manipulated the duties to benefit the new French revolutionary government.[12]

Though British free traders achieved a substantial reduction in the tobacco duty, notwithstanding Walker's prediction, the Democrats lost the Presidency. The defeat had one saving feature: Congress remained Democratic. Walker, possessed of intimate and extensive business ties, prepared to return to the law. Public life had brought him prominence without wealth. Unwilling any longer to deny his family the security which had until now eluded him, he proposed to exploit his knowledge of government affairs for his own benefit. In the months remaining to him as Secretary, he was determined to secure his connections with the business community. Fully aware of the popularity of the Warehousing System, he labored to strengthen it further through the appointment of a committee to investigate the operation of the parallel British system. The findings of the committee confirmed what Walker had claimed: American warehouses were the equal of their British counterparts. Minor suggestions for improvement were promptly instituted. Once again, the business community received assurance that the Secretary had its interest at heart.[13]

Concurrently, Walker activated a campaign to establish an Interior Department which it hoped would relieve the Treasury of its General Land Office and of supervision over federal court expenses. The State Department announced its willingness to surrender the Pension Office to a new department. Under proposals formulated by Walker, Congress also agreed to organize an Indian Affairs Office. Though not explicitly stated, the implicit purpose of the new cabinet post was to provide a single office which would administer the results of the Mexican War.[14]

Walker revealed the purpose of the Interior Department when he urged Congress to consider that the

business of the Land Office which occupied a very large portion of the time of the Secretary of the Treasury each day, . . . must . . . greatly increase . . . by the accession of our immense domain in Oregon, New Mexico, and California, especially in connection with their valuable mineral lands, their private land claims and conflicting titles. For all decisions of the commissioner—and appeal lies to the Secretary of the Treasury.

Four years of experience had convinced the incumbent Secretary that failure to relieve the Treasury of this responsibility would seriously hamper its operations. "I have pronounced judgment in upward of five thousand cases, involving land titles, since the 10th of March, 1845," he observed. "These are generally judicial questions . . . requiring often great labor and research, and having no necessary connection with the duties of the Treasury Department." [15]

The vast Mexican Cession would inevitably attract speculation. The Treasury, already heavily burdened with administering federal revenues, could ill afford to permit its primary function to be impeded by inescapable hordes of self-seeking lobbyists and scheming politicians. Suspicious of an overweening concentration of power in any department and acutely aware of the disastrous result to public credit should corruption touch the Treasury, Walker insisted that the task of administering national finances be divorced from the disposition of public lands. Significantly, he acknowledged that the vast increase of public lands made it inescapable that the federal government would become a major focal point of speculative investment in land. Thinly disguised, Walker hinted that the administration of public lands invited actions of tenuous legality. Such actions, though hardly laudable, would not entertain the same grievous consequences if located outside the Treasury.

Too often Walker had discovered that efforts to resolve land disputes made the Secretary of the Treasury an object of considerable political pressure. One particularly exasperating and illuminating experience involved Charles Sibbald, a Philadelphian and, distressingly, a friend of George M. Dallas. In 1816, the Spanish government had granted Sibbald three parcels of land in Florida. To maintain these grants, Sibbald agreed to erect a sawmill on the land. He complied with the stipulation and when Florida came under American control the grants were reconfirmed. However, in 1836, the government, charging that Sibbald had failed to operate the saw mill, challenged the legality of his claim. Sibbald promptly appealed to the federal courts. Finally, in 1838, after lower courts had rejected his appeal, the Supreme Court agreed to hear his claim and found in his favor.

Subsequently, Sibbald received $18,000 from Congress to compensate for the period he had been denied the use of his land. Being a true Philadelphian, he rejected the compensation as inadequate and filed a claim with the Treasury department for $1,700,000. A regular galaxy of lawyers argued in his behalf. Webster, Berrien, Gilpin, Thomas L. Smith, and Dallas joined their legal talents in one consummate effort. The claim reached Walker in April, 1846. Dallas cautioned his wife when she complained of his continued absence from home:

It is wholly useless to grumble and pine about the time consumed in Sibbald's business. It can't be helped. I regard it as one of the most important and interesting cases of the professional practice I have ever engaged in; and, unless Mr. Walker has lost his intelligence and fairness, it will be the most lucrative one.

As his nephew dawdled over a final decision, the Vice President's patience wore thin. "It is impossible," he insisted, "for me to leave the matter before I bag what has been earned." At the end of April, Dallas scarcely suppressed his rage as he fumed, "We rest on our oars, waiting for a wink, a nod, or a sigh of any sort from Mr. Walker . . . he seems to care about our waiting as little as he does about the stock transactions of Tahiti. *I* am rebellious, and would not stand it another hour—but my colleagues will permit no outbreaks." Dallas, having endured his nephew's reticence for more than a year, finally received notification that the Secretary had concluded that the original offer had been fair. Walker blithely notified Mr. Sibbald that it remained a matter of indifference to him whether he sought relief elsewhere. For several months after the decision a noticeable coolness persisted between the Vice President and the Secretary.[16]

On March 2, 1849, Polk, swallowing his constitutional scruples, signed into law the Bill creating the Interior Department. The relationship between Walker and his chief that many had predicted in 1845 would be of short duration closed with an eloquent testimony of presidential faith in the Secretary's acumen. To erase any doubt whether his appointment had been made willingly, Polk wrote Walker, reminding him both of the pleasure that his appointment had given him and of a signal honor: "I submitted to you for examination the inaugural address." All

public doubt about their relationship ceased with the announcement that Walker had been invited to accompany Polk on his
return to Nashville. In this way the former President chose to
indicate to his fellow southerners that the Secretary shared with
him the achievements of his administration. A worn and profoundly weary Polk left an ailing Walker at Columbus, Georgia,
to continue alone his journey homeward. Before the summer
solstice, death had claimed the former President. Wearily,
Walker returned to Washington to inaugurate a new career.[17]

While others would align themselves with state or section, the
former Secretary would declare himself a nationalist. With
symbolic appropriateness he took up permanent residence in the
federal seat—Washington, D.C. Within the Democracy he chose
to speak for the constituency that knew no boundaryline in its
search for profit—the businessman. Between Walker and business there existed an unyielding tie: unflinching loyalty to the
Union.[18]

10. Private Interlude

FOURTEEN YEARS of public service had given Walker much public glory but slight material reward. The needs of his growing family had convinced him that a private legal practice would insure adequate physical comfort for them. He did not misjudge the situation since his legal talents brought him an abundance of clients, especially when their cases appeared on the Supreme Court calendar. His intimate knowledge of the Washington world enabled him to exploit contacts denied to less favored lawyers. To him came the affluent, able to afford the fat fee.[1] Within months after his departure from the Treasury office, Walker could hardly contain his delight with the pleasures of private life: "My practice in the Supreme Court," he told Stephen Douglas, "is becoming of great value, & . . . I am resolved never again to become a candidate for any public office." Any doubt about the wisdom of his choice dissolved when his arguments in the Wheeling Bridge Case excited considerable comment. Arguing for the state of Pennsylvania, Walker challenged, under the interstate commerce clause, the right of Virginia to charter construction of an Ohio River bridge which would obstruct river transportation. The Virginia counsel, though not challenging Walker's contention, insisted the federal government lacked jurisdiction, since the Virginia charter came under the reserved powers clause. The case raised anew the right of federal authority to regulate commerce on internal waterways. A committee headed by Reuben Hyde Walworth, a prominent New York jurist, confirmed that the bridge obstructed commerce. Happily, Walker heard the Court uphold his argu-

ment, but the vehemence of his arguments supporting federal
supremacy had stirred the suspicions of states' rights Southerners. They questioned not only his nationalist sentiments but
his attitude toward slavery.[2]

Walker soon received notification of these doubts. John A.
Quitman, newly elected governor of Mississippi, not only forwarded his inaugural address to the former Secretary, but also
took the opportunity to warn him that though he might "think it
too strong on the slavery question," it was "mild for this atmosphere." The continued assaults in the North upon the South,
which Quitman characterized as "outrageous and unprovoked,"
had led other southerners to question "The many professions of
Northern men and Northern states of their attachment to the
Union while they seek to rob us of our rights." Howell Cobb of
Georgia demanded to know the thoughts of the once Mississippian on the *peculiar institution*. It contained the blunt invitation
for Walker, if his sentiments were right, to redeem the party
from the "hopeless . . . leadership of Mr. Calhoun." These
efforts failed to provoke a response, for Walker did not intend
to admit to any southerner that he thought "Slavery as a domestic institution . . . worse than monarchy as a political
one." [3]

But Walker's thinly disguised hostility toward slavery did
not mean that he now accepted the Negro as an equal. Indeed,
so long as the South remained burdened with its institution, he
opposed any federal regulation of slavery where it already
existed. This stand permitted him an unbending hostility to any
further extension of slavery. Even its permanence in the South
he accepted only with reluctance. Both the funnel theory and
"colonization" commanded his support. When Horace Greeley
advocated similar policies, he pleaded with "Father Ritchie"
to publish an article in the *Union* favoring these programs "lest
Greeley's advocacy of it cause Southern papers to take the opposite ground." [4]

Slavery became doubly objectionable when its continued

existence precluded fulfillment of the national Manifest Destiny. "Slavery in the South and SW," Walker insisted, "was England's security in Canada." Once the pernicious institution had perished, Canada would join the Union. Despite the growing controversy over the disposition of the Mexican Cession, Walker felt a sanguine confidence that "the present panic about new territory is destined to pass away." Sooner or later, "the onward march of the American people over the North American continent" assured the domination of "the Constitution and the flag of the Union, and free trade between the states," from the Andes to the North Pole. Anything that stood in the way must ultimately perish.[5]

Against this uncompromising vision of a transcendent Union, there remained the "magnetic influence" which permeated the South. If, as Quitman had insisted, "the North must back out from her position and do it with kindness, or we shall begin to feel degraded by a connection with them," then it followed that the cotton kingdom might feel twice degraded by continued association with a Southern apostate.[6]

Walker, convinced that time worked to relieve the tension of a divided nation, labored among his congressional friends to secure their support for the Compromise of 1850. After it had been enacted, he unhesitatingly defended its wisdom publicly. Before a Philadelphia audience he asked that the North uphold the Fugitive-slave Act as necessary assurance to the South of its continued safety in the Union. "The doctrines of nullification or secession," he repeatedly denounced as "revolutionary in their character, and leading to the overthrow of the Constitution and of the Union." So long as the Union kept intact, "interest" and "affection" insured a peaceful resolution of dividing differences. Otherwise, he feared a "blood-drenched civil war" that would, no matter who emerged victorious, forever alter the Union. With such a prospect the survival of the Constitutional Republic transcended any particular interest or peculiar institution.[7]

James Buchanan questioned the wisdom of his former colleague's vehement statements. "Members of Congress," he noted skeptically, "must have changed very much since I knew them if they are not jealous of written addresses from distinguished men for the purpose of influencing their votes." [8] The future President evidently did not seriously contemplate the vigor of Walker's nationalism, a failure which would play havoc with his administration.

The role of elder statesman, however, remained subordinate to Walker as he continued to be preoccupied with the accumulation of wealth. Some of the intensity with which he met threats to the stability of the Union resulted from his fear that sectional strife would delay exploitation of western wealth. He had not needed Greeley to enjoin him to turn his thoughts westward. Two western assets—mineral wealth and land—and a promised technological development—the transcontinental railroad—received his undivided attention.

Rumors, which he assiduously fostered, associated him with California's fabulous *New Almaden Quicksilver Mine,* whose prospective profits exceeded a million dollars a year. Actually, a welter of litigation left possession of the mine unsettled until 1863. A multitude of conflicting claims based on Mexican land grants compelled American courts to resolve the respective legality of each. This judicial effort had been complicated by the laxity of the Mexican government which had permitted unscrupulous speculators to deposit forged land grants in the Mexico City archives. Many American judges withdrew disheartened from the New Almaden case as they boggled at the seemingly endless task of determining whether a particular grant had been misdated by a century or two. [9]

Doubt about Walker's interest in the mine ended during the spring of 1851 when he openly negotiated the purchase of a claim from Knowles Taylor and John B. Gray. The "most glowing accounts" of a Lt. W. Patterson "of the U.S. Navy" had convinced Walker "that the mine is worth millions." After originally seeking to persuade the two men "to work the mine on a *large scale*," which neither Taylor nor Gray could afford, he organized a syndicate to buy their claim. After the purchase price had been agreed upon, Walker discovered he had not bought a mine, but merely a claim to one. Rather than risk a major loss, the syndicate chose to cooperate with the equally strong *Los Capitancillo Ranch* claim. In the resulting merger Walker came into contact with a Mr. Fossatt whose name remained identified with the complicated legal maneuvers the new syndicate followed as it fought for full control of the mine. Fossatt, however, scenting an interminable legal battle, promptly sold his interest to James and Lawrence Eldridge, with whom Walker subsequently organized *The Quicksilver Mining Company*.

A judicious distribution of stock interested Jeremiah Black, Frederick P. Stanton, Reverdy Johnson, Henry S. Foote, who took up residence in California to direct the legal fight from there, and William Gwin, now senior senator from California, in the syndicate's success. When Justice Curtis, outraged by the Dred Scott decision, resigned his seat on the Supreme Court, Walker persuaded him to devote his legal talents to pushing the Fossatt claim. By the summer of 1855, having interested a galaxy of influential politicians in the mine, Walker decided "to fight up to the Supreme Court for rights to work mines in California." He heartily subscribed to the conclusion of his California agent that "The chance of making something out of the Almaden mine is too tempting not to be prosecuted with eagerness." [10]

The wealth of the mine excited not only private speculators but also the General Land Office. Ultimately, the federal government's interest profoundly affected the behavior of Walker during the Kansas controversy, but he seems not to have felt at the time that it posed a genuine difficulty. The presence temporarily of W. W. Corcoran in his syndicate seemed to assure him of ample means with which to meet any challenge. Fortune and California had become synonymous for Walker.[11]

Even as he busied himself with the Almaden mine, he pushed a scheme for the construction of a transcontinental railroad. The intensity of this interest compelled Janin, his California agent, to observe dryly, "I ought not to disguise to you that—people consider your connection with the Pacific Railroad Company as interfering with your regular prosecution of your practice of the law in Washington City." Walker dismissed the complaint as picayune when compared to the importance of the railroad. No one denied its worth, but in the strained congressional atmosphere, transcontinental railroads threatened to revivify sectional strife. Each section urged its peculiar route, forestalling any one's authorization. But delays only wetted entrepreneurial appetites, for whoever received final authorization to construct a route knew that the congressional land grants ensured profits, at least for the managers.[12]

Dilatory tactics failed to discourage Walker, who joined with Levi S. Chatfield, past attorney general of New York State, in offering to build a southern transcontinental route. They expected Congress, in return, to permit them to select a route which would justify a liberal extension of the boundary southward at the expense of Mexico, to make requisite land grants with which to attract investors, and to loan them $30,000,000 of congressional bonds upon which the government would pay the interest until completion of the railroad. Walker seemed content with nothing less than a gilt-edged risk. Upon the advice of Major W. H. Emory, his brother-in-law, who had thoroughly explored the southern route, Walker pressed for the purchase of Mexican territory. Not content with exerting influence solely in Washington, Walker persuaded the compliant New York legislature at Albany to grant him a charter for construction of the Atlantic and Pacific Railroad with authorization to issue $100,000,000 in capital stock.

The project immediately attracted an avalanche of subscribers who rapidly took up the whole stock issue. As often happened with Walker speculations, few subscriptions were accompanied by hard cash. But this defect seemed trivial to the optimistic entrepreneur. The lure of vast wealth stimulated his efforts. Texas, whose affection for him seemed unbounded, temporarily bailed out his plans. Governor Pease of the Lone Star State awarded a charter to build the Mississippi and Pacific Railroad to Walker and Thomas Butler King, a Georgia Whig whose speculative enthusiasm proved that speculation had no political limits. Walker reasoned that once the new route reached El Paso, the completion of the southern route would be assured. The languishing Atlantic and Pacific stirred again with new promise. Walker and King now worked with remarkable energy to secure as many Texas railroad charters as possible. Within a short time, they had achieved complete control of all potential Texas routes.[13]

As prospects brightened, Walker and King, eager to consolidate their control, forced the resignation of the Atlantic and Pacific officers. The two men had no sooner assumed the post of President and Vice President than the ousted officers exposed the precarious fiscal condition of the company. Once again Atlantic and Pacific prospects underwent a rapid deterioration as its subscribers took heed and withdrew. Matters worsened when the Pierce administration cooled toward the project, accentuating the already chilly relations between Walker and the administration, a rapport which did not improve when the Gadsden Purchase superseded his efforts to purchase from Mexico a railroad right of way through the disputed region.[14]

Unwilling to relinquish its Texas gains, the now floundering syndicate permitted Walker to attempt to raise the $300,000 deposit needed to retain the Mississippi and Texas charter. Time had finally run out. Governor Pease, suspecting that continued association with "the one hundred million company" would damage his political career, accepted only $2,000 in New York

State bonds, while rejecting as of dubious value the remaining
$298,000 in New Jersey Iron Company and Memphis Bank
stock. Walker, now desperate, relinquished the Mississippi and
Texas charter to concentrate upon exploitation of the recently
obtained Texas and Western charter. This grant permitted the
construction of a railroad from any point on the eastern Texas
boundary to El Paso. Texas had guaranteed that for every mile
of line constructed it would give the company sixteen sections
of land. Once again the syndicate reorganized. Early in January,
1855, the remaining stockholders of the now defunct Atlantic
and Pacific joined the new company, transferring to it the old
company's debts.[15]

The prospects of the Texas and Western would have led a less
optimistic man to despair, and, obviously, a more sensible man to
withdraw. Thomas Hart Benton did not improve matters when
he bluntly accused Walker on the House floor of being "a mere
speculator." But the object of his denunciation contemplated
obtaining some 12,800 square miles of Texas real estate upon
completion of his eight hundred mile railroad. Doggedly he
sought out new stockholders, a task which proved impossible.
Even as the search for investors led nowhere, Walker prepared
contracts for the job of grading and furnishing cross ties for the
first twenty-five miles of road.

As other congressmen, taking their cue from Benton, increased
their attacks upon the speculative nature of the project, Walker
indignantly denied accepting "any stock for my services," and
insisted, "I shall hold no stock but as I pay for it in cash at
par." The suggestion that his inability to meet the terms of the
Mississippi and Pacific charter foreshadowed like failure for
the Texas and Pacific railroad brought the quick rejoinder that
"it is quite certain that if our deposits had not been rejected by
the Governor, we should have completed the first fifty miles in
the time prescribed . . . , either under the provisional arrangement made last fall with foreign capitalists, or with American
contractors who stood ready to do that part of the work for bonds

of the company." Stung to the quick, he pressed his construction program. "Our railroad through Texas to [the] Pacific," Buchanan read in the spring of 1856, "has succeeded." His fellow Pennsylvanian had bought and paid for the first iron to begin construction of the road in "our native state." [16]

With construction started, Walker evidenced a habit which led many to suspect his reliability, among them Corcoran. He now actively lobbied for an extension of his proposed railroad from El Paso to San Francisco. The route as planned passed through the Gila Valley, then a part of Mexico. To purchase a right of way for the proposed route he entered into negotiations with the Mexican government. Subsequently, he contended, as he was about to conclude the negotiations for $6,500 in cash and $500,000 in Texas railroad stock, the federal government bought the valley for $10,000,000. Thomas Hart Benton promptly indicted the purchase as a complete fraud designed to promote Walker's "one hundred million company . . . to enable them to sell lots and railroad shares in New York and London." The irate Missourian, in a freewheeling attack, charged that several army officers associated with Walker fostered San Diego as the transcontinental terminus. He gave especial attention to Major W. H. Emory "who was of the Boundary Commission, and is in charge of the Pacific route surveys, and who is the brother-in-law of the president of the one hundred million company." [17]

Walker dismissed the charge as without foundation. But among his friends and business associates the perpetual activity which surrounded Walker led many to think that he spent too much time dwelling upon the projects of tomorrow while neglecting those of today. Janin complained gloomily of the lack of information from his peripatetic employer. The New Almaden seemed forgotten and Walker now ignored the Louisiana properties which had once held his interest.[18] Corcoran, anxious over Walker's indebtedness, insisted he make a settlement. Not only were his numerous enterprises in great disorder, but his personal investments revealed an equal confusion. Western railroads and eastern iron works commanded equal attention. With the former came the lure of land subsidies which Walker hoped to increase by influencing Congress to increase the grant. Corcoran irately complained that Walker continually failed to keep appointments: a moment of explosion threatened when the railroad magnate kept the banker waiting in New York as Corcoran tried to get the necessary powers of attorney. Yet, Walker had shrewdly envisioned, though prematurely, the profits present in railroad investments. Two decades later others reaped abundant reward from the western wealth that had eluded him. All that came of his many schemes was a stretch of twenty-seven miles of railroad that started in the middle of a Texas prairie and went nowhere. Rarely has a business failure had a more appropriate monument.[19]

If his activities on behalf of the Pacific railroad constituted his most spectacular fiscal endeavor, then his efforts for the Illinois Central proved his most prestigious. Late in September, 1850, the retired Secretary asked Douglas for advice on "the propriety of my becoming President of the great Illinois Rail Road." He expressed particular interest in negotiating the necessary construction loans. Whatever the advice of the Little Giant, the following summer Walker told Corcoran, hoping that he would assist, that he had decided "to take the whole loan of the Illinois Central R.R. [of] . . . not . . . less than 15 nor more than 17 millions of dollars." Never prone to underestimate costs, Walker calculated the construction costs of 670 miles of road "at $20,000 to the mile." The banker received an arch reminder that the figure of $20,000 had the merit of convenience, though both knew the average western road cost considerably less to construct. There would result an attractive surplus for division among the promoters.

Should that prove an insufficient inducement, the proposed company prepared to issue $17,000,000 in bonds, to meet all expenses in excess of that amount, and to pay in $2,000,000 of the outstanding capital stock. To whet Corcoran's appetite further, Walker reminded him, "The land granted to build the road by Congress amounts to 2,572,000 acres—which at $6 per acre would build the road, & who can doubt it will reach this price, when the *road is finished*." No investor could wish for more than that. "This loan is in fact *secured by Congress*, by a grant from Congress of public lands sufficient to build the road." Railroad construction had the virtue of involving a subsidized risk.[20]

The attraction of the enterprise proved irresistible to Walker. He agreed to negotiate the proposed loan in New York and London. As his salary, he accepted all interest on deposits made to the Illinois Central account. But he also planned to reserve between five and seven millions as his own share in the expectation of placing it on the European market. The knowledge that "money never was so abundant in England and in France" led to his decision to go abroad. Beside the participation of Corcoran, Walker wished his "sound judgement" and, if possible, his company on the voyage to England to "join in the *negotiations*." The banker declined to share in the enterprise with the cryptic advice that "the amount to be borrowed is too large." Nevertheless, he did not stint in supplying Walker with every aid to assure a friendly English reception.[21]

Walker finally sailed for Europe on August 31, 1851, armed with letters of introduction to the House of Baring and the Peabody Banking House, a credit account of $20,000 drawn upon the Illinois Central Railroad, and a £500 letter of credit from Corcoran, which Walker believed "will help me more than a dozen introductory letters." The railroad with its 2,572,000 acres, he privately declared, would attract "John Bull" who "loves *real estate* security." [22]

The trip, unexpectedly, turned into a triumphal tour, as Free Traders lionized the former Treasury chief who had given yeoman service to the cause.[23] Gladstone, Bright, Cobden, Russell, and Monckton-Milne hastened to make him welcome. The aloof Barings displayed unexpected friendliness by tendering him a

testimonial banquet. His agreeable disposition excited favorable
comment, and it appeared that Walker would never settle his
business as he made the rounds of the great English country
houses. "A general free trade demonstration" marked his visit
to Manchester. "There is something extremely racy and piquant,"
all agreed, "about Mr. Walker's oratory." Since his speeches
combined a belligerent plea for free trade and "a still more
fraternal intercourse for England and America," his natural
ebullience and the warm reception of his audience combined to
encourage an Anglophilism that provoked Anglophobes at home
to growls of protest.[24]

When Arthur Davies, a Member of Parliament, approached
Walker on the possible "Union . . . of the United States with
the British Empire," the American declared "that a time shall
come when the human race shall become as one family, and that
the predominance of our Anglo-Celt-Sax-Norman stock shall
guide the nations to that result." The prospect of an economic
union between the United States and the Empire, for the purpose of creating "a perfect cosmopolitan state of fusion, a unity
of thought and action on all the great questions of dominion,
trade, the education of the people, and the amelioration of the
industrial classes," led Walker to invite Britain and her colonies
to join the Union as states, enabling them to use the Constitution
which provided for "free trade between all the States of the
Union." As a preface to this union, he advocated that the British
extend the right of representation in Parliament "to those races
who are fit for self-government," lest as soon as the "colonies
. . . become strong and powerful, . . . they . . . become independent nations." Anglo-Saxon Union, though only a distant
prospect, intoxicated Walker with its power, surely certain to
sway the world. But he conceded there existed a barrier; the
pernicious institution of slavery which threatened the Union. A
new strand had been woven into the web of suspicion among
southern extremists of the erstwhile Mississippian's reliability.[25]

As Walker expressed his dreams of the future in soaring

rhetoric, the Illinois Central project languished. George W. Billings, who had accompanied Walker abroad, expressed dismay at the endless time the British took in entertaining his companion. However, British admiration for the energetic American ended at the pocketbook. "John Bull," a gloomy Billings notified the home office, "is a slow coach until you get him started." As far as he could determine, "Mr. Walker has not succeeded in obtaining the loan for the railroad." Such a triviality hardly disturbed the unsuccessful negotiator as he revelled in his designation as the greatest of American free traders. The prestige fed his boundless ego; the wealth would come later.[26]

Upon his return to the United States, Walker's fertile imagination considered construction of a canal between the Bay of Honduras and the Pacific Ocean. The presidential election of 1852 momentarily distracted him. A disturbing recurrence of his old lung affliction prevented him from being present at the convention which nominated Pierce; however, no Democrat dared ignore him. He expressed no interest in a cabinet appointment but took a lively interest in the distribution of patronage. If Walker had had his choice, he would have placed Caleb Cushing in the Treasury where the lively New Englander would "carry on the commercial policy" Walker had inaugurated under Polk. While Pierce worked to achieve a balanced cabinet, Walker, recuperating from his illness, drew up plans for his Central American canal. Among its grandiose touches, he planned to name either the Pacific canal terminus or the railroad that would be built if a canal proved impracticable, "Walker." As his enthusiasm for the project grew, he initiated negotiations with the President of San Salvador for a route through that tiny country. He simultaneously pressured Pierce to appoint a full minister to Honduras to aid in obtaining a suitable right of way through that land. This effort ended abruptly when Walker fell into a dispute with the President that poisoned their relations for the remainder of Pierce's term.[27]

These difficulties had begun when Pierce decided to appoint

Walker to the China Mission. His known interest in the Pacific and its trade coincided with that of the administration, but there occurred considerable surprise when Walker accepted the appointment, his ill health being frequently cited. The State Department made available an allotment of $9,000 to cover his immediate expenses and promised to provide a naval craft to convey him to the Celestial Kingdom. Mary Walker, whose own health had been undermined by a grueling trip across the Atlantic, forced a drastic revision of these plans when she decided to accompany her husband. Walker soon resigned the appointment, explaining, "She never would have reached China alive." Some skeptics thought the administration's decision to press the construction of a transcontinental railroad had governed his decision. When tendering his resignation, he offered to return the expense account, which Marcy accepted in the early autumn of 1853. On February 2, 1854, an outraged Walker learned of a rumor implying he had not repaid the money. He urgently requested the Secretary of State to publicly confirm payment and to explain the delay in its return as resulting from the government not being "ready to receive it." When Marcy ignored his request, adding a new dimension to the rumor, Walker, thoroughly enraged, severed relations with the President and his cabinet chief. At the bottom of the disagreement there existed the smoldering resentment of Marcy toward his former cabinet-mate who he believed had worked with Van Buren and his supporters to damage his political influence. When Walker protested that he had wished only to reunite the New York democracy, Marcy halted all further communications. The Pierce administration had made certain that an embittered Walker would seek its replacement in 1856.[28]

Grand schemes had kept Walker busy; it hardly fazed him to think that for all his effort, he could not in 1856 redeem an $11,000 note held by Corcoran. He deemed it more important that the Illinois Central stockholders wanted him "to organize the Board of Directors & become president." With obvious relish, he heard out Amos Kendall who, proposing that Walker join him in constructing a telegraph line to California, had mused:

I doubt not you feel as I do, more comfortable in promoting great schemes of improvement in your individual exertions & enterprise than you did in the harness of the Government, where every pseudo patriot and ignorant upstart assumed to be your teacher & driver.[29]

But events were rapidly propelling the former Secretary back into politics. Within a short time, he would have ample reason to rue that return.

11. Within a Budding Tragedy

THOUGH WALKER evinced no further desire to participate directly in politics, he had continued to cultivate his established contacts. When Zachary Taylor entered the Presidency, he had not hesitated to call upon the rugged old General. Subsequently, he recalled jocularly those days at the "White Sepulchre" when "primitive simplicity" marked the presidential entertainment. Within the Democracy, he shared both the prestige that had descended upon the Polk cabinet and the hostile suspicions that focused upon it. The latter he shrugged off, but for James Buchanan, who greedily sought the Presidency, the political backwaters brought only painful discontent.

The death of Taylor had convinced the once Secretary of State that "a regular old fashioned Whig administration under Mr. Fillmore with Mr. Clay as dictator and Mr. Webster as Secretary of State" impended. The prospect moved him to lament "it is a melancholy spectacle to witness men of three score and ten and upwards still struggling on the political arena with all the ardor of youthful ambition as though this earth was destined to be their eternal home." Prayerfully, he concluded, "I trust in Heaven that I may never present such a spectacle in my own person." [1] His prayer was destined to go unanswered.

The Pierce inauguration left Buchanan uncertain of his reward. "Much has been said about the offer of the English mission to me"; he complained, "but it has never been offered, nor do I believe it will be." It might be added that he had mixed emotions about the appointment, fearing it would injure his supporters and his prospects. When the offer finally came, before accepting it, he reconnoitered its implications from the household of Mr. Walker. There he had an opportunity to talk with his old cabinetmate "on the past, the present & the *future*." What that discussion implied is concealed behind the veil that descends upon unrecorded conversation. Suffice it to note that Buchanan and Walker had little taste for Marcy and neither felt any particular affection for the incumbent President. One pursued the Presidency; the other had a score to settle with Messrs. Pierce and Marcy. Common cause would unite them in a single camp when the 1856 Democratic convention convened in Cincinnati.[2]

April, 1856 found Buchanan, lately returned from London, energetically seeking the nomination that had thrice before eluded him. A less persistent man might have despaired, but endurance ranks high among the major virtues of a perennial candidate. More so as Buchanan suspected that his age would preclude a fifth chance. Seeking to mend his political fences along the back streets of Washington, he had prevailed upon Walker to permit him to use his residence as the Buchanan campaign headquarters. Walker, ever hospitable, prefaced his welcome with a warning. He realized that if Buchanan hoped to inherit the executive mantle, he could ill-afford to offend any major political figure, least of all the incumbent President. For Buchanan to choose to reside with him might "be displeasing to the President, and a *small* portion of his Cabinet." To illuminate Buchanan further, he added, "It is now two years since I have called on the President, or met him, and altho he has urged me, thro my friends, and thro Mrs. Walker, to meet him and with superabounding professions of love and affection, has assured them, that he could explain all satisfactorily to me, yet I will not go." [3] The affair of the China Mission, and the abuse he had sustained from Marcy rankled too deeply for him either to forgive or to forget. The ever cautious Buchanan, certain of Walker support, reflected upon this warning and chose to dwell elsewhere.

Nor did the shrewd little politician encourage the recently

retired Minister to St. James to believe he would obtain the
nomination easily. Despite the ovations and public outpourings
that greeted his return and which seemed to promise easy election if he were nominated, Buchanan had to overcome the ob-
stacle of what Walker happily described as "my old two-thirds
rule." Without its modification, he doubted whether the Pennsylvanian would achieve nomination. Little Bob suggested a bit
smugly, "I have, as the author of the rule, a modification to suggest, that after the 1st day's balloting, (as under the constitution
in an election by the House) the voting shall be limited to the
highest. This will secure the choice of some of the distinguished
men designated by the people." Otherwise, he warned, "The contrary rule, will now and forever suppress the voice of the people,
lead to the abandonment of conventions, the consequent extinc-
tion of the Unity and Success of the Democratic Party, and as
a consequence, I fear, the overthrow of the constitution and the
Union." [4] Walker seemed oblivious to the fact that if these dire
results were to flow from the "old two-thirds rule," then he
would be the author of a national catastrophe. But he had never
been marked by either a logical or profound consistency in his
political thinking. His politics were invariably conditioned by
the circumstance of the moment. Once Buchanan was nominated,
Walker explored the problem of assuring the Pennsylvanian's
election. His trained eye told him that Democratic chances depended upon its pointing out that it alone possessed a national
scope as opposed to the "sectional and geographical party, composed exclusively of the States of the North," which called itself
Republican. [5]

The appeal to Union sentiment came naturally to Walker. The
single consistent strand which existed in all his political preach-
ments was the inviolability of the Union. But it was a Union
which embraced a "confederate" rather than "a *central* Republic" principle. The election of Buchanan he made synonymous
with the preservation of the traditional Republic. "The truth
is," he insisted in a campaign pamphlet, "the Black 'Republican'

party is revolutionary and agrarian." In its unswerving attacks upon the property institution of slavery it revealed its intention to establish "an elective despotism, by which a majority of the people may abolish, divide, or confiscate all property." If one species of property were so endangered, then "lands, houses, rents, vessels, railroads, debts, stocks, and all other property" would be subject "to division or confiscation . . . at the ballot-box." [6]

Agitation over the institution of slavery only delayed its doom. So long as northern attacks continued, southern opinion normally hostile to slavery defended the institution. Permitted to render a decision without pressure from without, "several of the slave States" would have terminated the institution. The Kansas-Nebraska Act, which permitted territorial residents to settle the issue, spared southern pride, while assuring northern dominance in the remaining territories. Even in Kansas, the only one in which there existed an effort to establish slavery, the northern cause would triumph. Quietly, almost as an afterthought, Walker remarked, "I do not believe Kansas will become a slave State." [7]

Since a great dispute broke out subsequently over whether the Buchanan administration properly understood Walker's position on the future status of Kansas, it is worth noting that no less than a million pamphlets containing this statement were broadcast across the nation. Not only were there hundreds of thousands of copies printed in English, but copies were also printed in Welsh, German, French, Spanish, and Italian. An eager Walker sent off a final draft of the pamphlet to Buchanan with the comment, "now that I have got my hand in and my heart also, I may try a speech." Buchanan read with "true" gratification that the solution for the slavery issue existed in a fusion of the "Texas funnel" theory and "the true safety valve of abolition—Colonization." An atmosphere of unworldliness permeates Walker's assurance to Buchanan that "we shall commence operations in . . . Colonization's favour here on a large scale after the election and hope to establish a regular steamer to Liberia, by individual subscription." [8]

In this superficial solution of the slavery problem, one sees the essential defect of moderate thinking. By treating the survival of the *peculiar institution* as beyond compromise, the radicals of both North and South had left no doubt about their expectations. Moderates thought to assign the problem to time, the great healer of all wounds. Delay rather than solution preoccupied their thoughts. Few moderates felt comfortable about slavery; they felt even less comfortable about the prospect of Negro equality. The only release from their dilemma remained to return the slave to his source, or at least to continue the pretense that it could be done.

While the Walker plea reverberated, its sponsor labored in New York to advance the Buchanan cause. The presidential candidate read his optimistic forecast, "We shall carry this city and neighbourhood by Storm, and leave the Hudson River with an overwhelming majority. Whether we can pass the infected district with our flag flying remains to be seen." [9] The city and its environs performed according to the prognostication, but upstate New York crushed the city under a massive vote. But when the vote counting elsewhere had ended, Buchanan had received a plurality of the vote and an electoral majority. The long quest had finally been rewarded, and an administration with a tragic history had been launched.

No sooner was the result known than there opened a strong effort to secure the State Department for Walker. His intimate connections within the New York financial and commercial community made their support of him known. A galaxy of southern senators pressed for his appointment. Old Pennsylvania friends urged Buchanan to disregard opposition from within the Keystone State, opposition, which, coming from the state's many other cabinet applicants, cried, "Take Walker and we are done —for he is a Pennsylvanian." [10]

Despite the heavy pressure, Buchanan remained hesitant. The near solid support he had obtained from the South obliged him to move carefully lest he antagonize one of the many southern factions that united provided a sectional buttress for the Democracy. The outspoken distaste with which Walker viewed nullification had done little to aid his reputation in South Carolina. It hardly interested southern extremists to know that he denounced with equal vigor "the sectional interference of the propagandist nullifying Legislature of Massachusetts." Nor had his oft-repeated belief that slavery represented a national hindrance gone unnoticed. Some even suspected that he held "free soil" views beneath his public expressions of sympathy with the South. The enmity of Jacob Thompson, soon to be Secretary of the Interior, recalled uncomfortable memories of the Lost Commission. Innuendoes appeared, charging that the intimacy between Corcoran and Walker could be traced to the ample reward the banker had received when the Treasury chief had released to him the fourteen million dollar Mexican War loan.[11]

As February, 1857, wore on, the pleas in behalf of Walker grew more urgent. A round robin calling for his appointment circulated in the Senate. A petition signed by Senator Rusk of Texas and Senator Clay of Alabama drew from Buchanan the admission that he felt kindly toward Walker and did not credit the charges of corruption made against him. But the President-elect questioned why the "portion of the South" which supposedly "stood ready to interpose in his behalf" had not done so sooner. The unfriendly New York *Tribune*, which recognized both the weakness and strength of Walker, supplied a quick answer. His long residence in Washington had made him thoroughly familiar with the ebb and flow of national politics but it had also raised questions as ". . . to which region or State Walker really belongs." It continued, "He hails from Mississippi, is a housekeeper in Washington within sight of the executive mansion, splurges in New York, and, like spilled milk, lies loose around generally." The *Tribune* concluded solemnly, "He will not turn up this time in office." [12]

Walker, an eminently practical politician, soon recognized that his failure to obtain solid backing from any single region or state made it unlikely that he would be chosen to head the State Department. The only consistent southern support he received came from single senators from the states of Florida, Alabama, Mississippi and Arkansas. Support from the Pennsylvania democracy dissipated quickly when it learned that Buchanan did not intend to offer the post to Robert M. T. Hunter whose radical *Calhounite* sentiments made him objectionable to conservative northerners. John Forney, the Pennsylvania firebrand, who had thrown his mercurial vivacity behind Walker, quickly abandoned the cause, lest it harm his own expectations. He assured Howell Cobb that "we ran to Walker as our only harbor, but this only when we are (sic) assured that you would not object—indeed that you were with him and his friends at the National and gave Walker public credit for ability, statesmanship and versatility of Talent." [13]

Faced finally with the prospect of either Lewis Cass or Cobb in the State Department, Walker threw his support behind Cass. This action had its crass aspect since there was a strong belief that an almost senile Cass could hardly expect to remain in office long. During Cass's anticipated brief tenure, Walker expected to mend his political fences and, thereby, secure his claim upon the office when it became vacant. To permit Cobb to enter the office precluded its ever being obtained since the Georgian possessed a vigorous intelligence. It also repaid the future Treasury chief for his earlier stubborn refusal to serve in a cabinet which gave Walker "the premiership." [14]

A cabinet without Walker led automatically to speculation about how Buchanan intended to employ the valuable talents of his old friend. No single problem demanded more immediate attention from the newly inaugurated President than the appli-

cation of Kansas for statehood. Nowhere was the stark determination of northern and southern radicals to advance their
cause more nakedly revealed. Buchanan knew that if an adequate solution were achieved during the first months of his
administration, the prestige of both the Democracy and its chief
would be enhanced. Combined with the impending Dred Scott
decision, which both defined the property nature of slavery and
confirmed the abrogation of the Missouri Compromise, Buchanan expected to settle finally the omnipresent slave issue.
Certain subtle considerations entered into his thinking. The obvious past failures to resolve the Kansas issue could be eliminated if the new governor of Kansas were a man of national
prominence and prestige. More important, if a final decision on
Kansas were to come under a governor known as a friend of
the South and with strong northern ties, the question of ob-
jectivity would not be raised. The solution had the charm of
simplicity; the legal minded Chief Executive assumed a ready
obedience to judicial decision and a national desire for a reasonable Kansas settlement. It ignored a blunt fact: the extremists of
both North and South would never accept anything less than
complete victory for their cause, since their very existence hung
on the outcome.

Momentarily the social whirl that accompanies the inauguration of a new administration submerged thoughts of a crisis.
Walker joyfully passed his time sleighing with the hordes of
children whose presence was an accepted condition in his household. One niece cheerfully described to her brother how at the
inaugural ball, besides fearsome heat and crowds, "the members
of Congress got so overexcited with wine that they had to be
locked up in the supper room lest they should reappear in the
ballroom in no very enviable situation." [15] Even as the festivities
went on, the much maligned Governor Geary disgustedly resigned the thankless governorship of the Kansas Territory. His
resignation permitted Buchanan to offer the post to Walker who
immediately recognized its political promises and hazards.[16]

Caution became his byword. The haggard and careworn features of Geary had sufficiently warned him against accepting the task without suitable guarantees. The President received the alternative of either granting Walker complete discretion to meet the problem as he deemed necessary or of looking elsewhere. Buchanan promptly guaranteed that he and his cabinet would support any decisions that the new governor might make in Kansas. The Walker family quickly expressed its dissent with Buchanan's proposal, questioning whether life on the distant prairie would be dangerous to a man of Walker's delicate and often precarious health. Only a direct appeal from the President shook the determination of Mary Walker to oppose acceptance by her husband. Subsequently, Walker wrote his sister, Martha, that he had accepted only after being subjected to severe pressure from "the constituted authority" who had made the danger from Kansas to the Union "clearly visible." The administration heard an emphatic assertion from Walker that the Kansas problem was "reduced to the simple question of slave or free state, and must be decided by a *full* and *fair* vote of a *majority* of the people of Kansas." An incorrigible optimism led him to predict that Kansas would be resolved peaceably as had all other disputes between the North and South. He sanguinely expected to settle the issue before October and to return the hero of "a successful mission." [17]

There seemed hardly any reason for doubt. The administration had pledged its unswerving support. Equally encouraging were the beguiling hints that a successful mission to Kansas might prove a stepping stone to the Presidency. The latter best explains why Walker, who had only a short time previously insisted that "chains could not drag him back into the public arena," had chosen to accept a post with an unenviable record of having wrecked the political aspirations of every previous incumbent. There also existed the more immediate lure that "his promotion to the Department of State" would attend "any reasonable success." [18]

Judgment on the appointment was temporarily suspended, although many Republicans privately expressed concern over his rumored policies as the new governor bustled about preparatory to departure. They could hardly criticize Walker's announced intention to aid the Kansans in achieving a free state status. But they felt that there existed a concealed purpose which time would reveal. A future Vice President of ill-repute, Schuyler Colfax, protested to the free soil Governor Robinson of Kansas, "The plot at Washington seems to me a transparent one." He detailed its particulars to the grim prairie free soiler:

Mr. Walker is appointed Governor, with authority said to be almost unlimited. He declares, if report is true, that he thinks Kansas will be a Free State, and is going there to appeal to *all* her people to participate in the decision of that vital question; but he, purposely postpones his arrival in your midst until after the Bogus officers shall have completed their packed Census Returns. *Then*, he expects you to decline participating in the election in spite of his appeals and he will return with the Border Ruffian Constitution declaring that he went there expecting Kansas would be free, but that the Free State people would not vote, and consequently a slave state constitution was inevitable.[19]

The actions of Walker in Kansas belied the Colfax predictions, but the fears they expressed made it imperative that Walker conduct himself circumspectly. The least sign of a sellout and the resulting roar of protest would wreck his expectations of political reward. Ugly rumors reminded many that he had "for several years past, . . . been the center of a whole brood of kindred spirits of the land jobbing tribe," who now contemplated "what a glorious field Kansas now affords for speculative operations in her public lands." A mitigating factor was the devious operations of the Auburn Kansas Company under the leadership of the no less illustrious William Seward. One thing had become apparent; the slightest promise that Kansas would be pacified and free had sufficed to stir Wall Street speculations in prairie lands. As tales of profit spread, William Gwin, Senator from California, renewed the fight for the Pacific Railroad Bill.

The association of land and railroad profits set heads nodding knowingly.[20]

A friendlier source protested that for a "timid, vacillating, hesitating and pliable man, it were better now to undertake the Government of the Fiji Islanders than the management of the Border Ruffians." As events revealed, the policy followed by Walker proved anything but timid. He believed that Kansas would be free if it were given a chance to choose its fate without interference. Unlike previous territorial governors, he possessed the happy knowledge that Buchanan, with an explicitness unique to a man made wary by long efforts to dodge the explicit, had plainly warned the more ultra of southern politicians "that the Democratic Party of the North cannot safely stand the violent pro-slavery policy heretofore pursued in Kansas." The persistent Pennsylvanian had implied he understood that any policy other than that suggested by Walker would threaten the destruction of the Democratic Party in the North.[21] Momentarily, at least, Buchanan had indicated that he did not intend to preside at the liquidation of the Northern Democratic Party. The question remained whether his determination would persist under challenge.

12. A Pigmy on the Prairie

BLEAK DESCRIBES the spring of 1857. Gale winds, heavy rains and, inauspiciously, snow with midwinter temperatures combined to take from April its classic tenderness. Commuting between Washington and New York, Walker had ample chance to observe the desolate landscape still denuded of vegetation. It was as if the fates were determined to give him a foretaste of the raw prairie.

Meanwhile, the myriad details of his tangled finances demanded careful attention. Corcoran insisted upon bringing their accounts into some order. Large transfers of stock were made to Riggs and Company so that suitable management of Walker's affairs could continue once the new Governor had departed. He lingered so long in the east that editorials began to speculate whether Frederick Stanton, his Secretary and long time business associate, who had preceded him west, was in fact if not under law the Governor of Kansas.[1]

Political reporters commented increasingly upon the significance of the decision by Walker to go to Kansas. E. L. Godkin attempting to describe its implications to an English audience wrote:

Mr. Robert J. Walker, one of the truly great men still left among us, in these poorhouse days of the statesmanship of the Republic, has consented to go and rule Kansas. He appears to stoop in taking this office, but he rises to meet an exigency. It is as if your Lord Elgin should go to achieve honours in the most distant and troublesome province of India instead of Pekin. Mr. Walker's appointment has been hailed with satisfaction by the whole country, and he is in the enjoyment of too much fame to be wrecked on so stupendous a failure.[2]

A Kansas journal confessed that "this appointment gives us exquisite satisfaction . . . For the first time since the origin of the Territory has a first class statesman been appointed to this post." The unfriendly New York *Tribune* admitted its inability to understand "what possible motive can Mr. Walker have in accepting the office of Governor of Kansas, only to be used as a catspaw to rake other people's chestnuts out of the fire, with no promise whatever of advantage, but, on the contrary, of pain, misery, and mortification." The puzzlement felt by Greeley suggests where the Buchanan administration had erred when formulating its Kansas policy. It had been fully informed of the strong sentiment among Kansans, whether proslavery or profreesoil, to have done with internecine warfare. The natural assumption was that Kansas needed only a forceful Governor to achieve an acceptable solution. It tended, therefore, to treat Kansas as a local problem, while Greeley in the *Tribune* treated it as a national problem with ramifications far beyond the confines of the Kansas prairie. Upon the shoals of national sentiment, the well-laid administration plans were to founder.[3]

In mid-May Walker departed from Washington for the west. His trip proceeded at a leisurely pace. At New York, exuding confidence, he pledged his Wall Street friends "the utmost exercise of his official power and his personal influence . . . to secure . . . the people of Kansas . . . an opportunity for a full, free and solemn expression . . . upon the adoption of any Constitution." This pledge moved hostile observers to suspect that his true motive in going to Kansas was "to make money." Once he had indulged in the purchase of real estate, it was expected that he would do everything to protect its value. Walker did not deign to reply.[4]

As the Governor moved west from New York, it became increasingly evident that the nation had decided to suspend a lengthy discussion of his prospective acts. From Kansas came reports that everyone there asked "What will Walker do?" It seemed that frequent disappointment had made Kansans skepti-

cal of pledges promising free and fair elections. The tranquillity
which greeted his appointment elsewhere assured Walker that
he would shortly return to Washington a national hero, the father
of a free Kansas. Only an occasional somber note flawed his
westward progress. His sister, Martha, bedecked in yards of lace
and furbelows, delivered an original poem, the triumphantly un-
cadenced notes of which called upon him to drape about his
slender frame the flag, for "if they dye [it] in thy blood,
'Twere a fitting shroud to wind thee in, O Patriot, true and
good!' " As mourning poetry echoed out of the east, a disgruntled reporter, awaiting Walker at Lecompton, gave bitter-
sweet sympathy to the seeming reluctance with which Walker
journied west when he warned, "he will see enough of this hole
after he gets here." [5]

Walker, upon reaching Chicago, met with Stephen A. Douglas
to inform him of the policies agreed upon by the administration.
As the Little Giant already knew that the Governor supported
popular sovereignty, the proposed policies seemed to commit
the administration to accepting the doctrine with unqualified
enthusiasm. A basis for future collaboration between the two
men was reached when the Illinoisan read and approved
Walker's proposed inaugural address. Since it was to prove the
provocation for a storm of southern protest, Douglas, having
given his approval, could hardly avoid defending Walker. Nonetheless, the immediate result of the meeting was to confirm the
impression that the Democracy had united upon a single Kansas
policy.[6]

The final stage of the journey was made on the Missouri River
steamer, the *New Lucy*. At every stop the townsfolk besieged
Walker with pleas for a speech. His response reiterated with
regular monotony his intention to have every Kansan vote on the
constitution. He had scarcely set foot in Quindaro, Kansas, when
the first of the local politicos arrived to greet him. That dignitary
was Governor Robinson who combined his activities as representative of the New England Aid Company with wholesale

speculations in land adjacent to Quindaro. Conversation between the two men dealt mainly with the state of Corcoran's numerous interests in Quindaro. Senator Henry Wilson of Massachusetts, who had appeared mysteriously on the *New Lucy*, arrived to open his own investigation of Kansas. Some wags thought that he had been delegated by the "Black Republicans" to keep a check upon the Governor.[7]

The journey had ended at Leavenworth when General Lane chose to attend the new Governor. The known violence with which the General expressed his free soil views led some to expect an unpleasant exchange when the two men met. Again all was sweetness and light. Amid cordial handclasps, smiles, back slappings, and winks, Walker sharply and clearly stated, "General Lane, you cannot tell how happy I am to meet you upon the soil of Kansas." He had deliberately launched a campaign to secure the confidence of the free soil leaders. Everyone familiar with the Kansas situation knew that a meaningful election could be held only if these men were persuaded that they could expect a fair election. Should they continue their previous boycotts of elections, the pacification of Kansas would fail.[8]

A less subtle effort endeared the Governor to the male population of Leavenworth when he treated them to $210 worth of wine and whiskey. This, one observer commented, indicated that for the moment, Walker preferred "drinking to speaking." He had balanced this appeal to the baser instincts when on the previous Sunday he attended services at the Lawrence Unitarian Church in the company of Senator Wilson and Governor Robinson. The three men used the service each to deliver a speech; Walker pledged fairness in the forthcoming elections, Senator Wilson called upon Kansas to give herself to freedom, while Governor Robinson demanded a guarantee that the proslavery elements would be compelled to accept the election results if they should lose. The minister, the Rev. John Pierpont, not to be outdone, delivered a resounding political sermon denouncing the evils of a bogus legislature, ending his ringing peroration with the declaration, "No taxation without representation." The first days had provided some *opéra bouffe* touches, not the least of which had been the distinct impression that the Governor meant to drink one half of the population into submission while praying the other half into it.[9]

The inaugural address came as something of an anticlimax. At the "bogus metropolis" of Lecompton, Walker swiftly delivered his sentiments upon the prospects of Kansas. He immediately set forth the crucial issue when he emphasized, "The law has performed its entire appropriate function when it extends to the people the right to suffrage, but it cannot compel the performance of that duty." Again he made it evident that he believed a permanent solution would never occur unless the free soilers agreed to register. He insisted that he could do little to aid them in making Kansas a free state until they exercised their suffrage rights. Lest there develop doubts of his sincerity, he flatly pledged to use the full power of the Governorship to fight a fraudulent election.[10]

The remainder of the address consisted of a determined effort to justify placing the slavery issue under the jurisdiction of the States. "What possible good has been accomplished by agitating in Congress and in presidential conflicts the slavery question?" he asked. "Has it emancipated a single slave, or improved their condition?" Warming to the subject, he challenged, "Has it made a single state free . . . or accomplished any practical good whatever?" His own reply was an abrupt "No, my fellow citizens, nothing but unmitigated evil has already ensued, with disasters still more fearful impending . . . as a consequence of these agitations." [11]

Once again, his thinking revealed a blind spot. He understood that the growing agitation over slavery threatened fearful consequences, but he could only offer a solution of cease and desist. The difficulty in such a course derived from the existence of an uneasy northern conscience which prided itself upon its democracy but assailed itself constantly with doubts over the internal contradiction of slavery in the South and its own negro-phobia. A nation founded upon a commitment to equality could not ignore for long, no matter how hard it tried, the insistence within a third of the nation that almost four million black human beings were forever bound to slavery. The issue in Kansas might be resolved as Walker claimed by "a law more powerful than the legislation of man, more potent than passion or prejudice, that must ultimately determine the location of slavery in this country; it is the isothermal line, it is the law of thermometer, of latitude or altitude, regulating climate, labor, and productions, and, as a consequence of profit and loss." But beyond the borders of Kansas a far more potent and aggressive force was at work on the problem, not only of Kansas but of the nation. It was described in the argument that claimed slavery was being denied Kansas by "the spirit which puts Justice before Expediency, and demands for all men, 'the rights of life, liberty, and pursuit of happiness.'" It was not as Walker contended "the influence of climate, but of conscience" which assured Kansas would be made free.[12]

The suspicion with which the northern radicals greeted the inaugural address compared as naught to the open contempt with which the proslavery cabal treated Walker in Kansas. The territorial legislature, then dominated by the proslavery minority, tendered the newly inaugurated Governor a dinner. The toastmaster, John Calhoun, then federal surveyor and the acknowledged proslavery spokesman, opened the festivities with an innocuous toast. The good feelings dissolved abruptly when L. A. McLean, Calhoun's chief clerk, called upon to render a toast, turned against the tiny Governor and spat forth: "And do you come here to rule over us?—you, a miserable pigmy like you? You come here with ears erect, but you will leave with your tail between your legs. Walker, we have unmade governors before; and by God, I tell you, sir, we can unmake them again!"[13]

Walker revealed little emotion during the outburst. He had

not fully comprehended the nature of the men with whom he dealt. It is equally certain that few who witnessed the vicious scene understood the fiery determination that smouldered within the "pigmy." Walker realized the true state of affairs a few days later when a delegation of "slave democrats" appeared at his office with a demand that he cease preaching the gospel of free elections. The gubernatorial memory raced back to a day in early April when Calhoun, McLean, and other proslavery Kansans waited upon him at his Washington residence. There had been an inkling of what was to come when one of his visitors had demanded whether he proposed to administer the affair of Kansas in the interest "of Democracy or that of Abolition." Then he had replied, "In that of the whole people." Now the challenge had become more explicit. The men before him knew as well as he did that sharp southern criticisms had followed the Lecompton Inaugural. Walker knew, however, that to bow to intimidation could end only with disastrous consequences for his future career. Surrender to the demand would make his name synonymous with coward throughout the North, while the South would treat it as an acknowledgement that he had been justly castigated. It was no longer his political reputation that was at stake, but his honor as a man when he blazed forth, "Gentlemen, today, . . . I have learned what is your real course and policy . . . you cannot force me into that policy." McLean warned, "Walker do you come here expressly to balk us always? Has Buchanan sent you to Lecompton to defy us? Are these your instructions? Look out! And let your master at Washington look out, too. Remember!" But the issue had been joined; Walker had committed himself irrevocably to insuring Kansas would be free. One month on the brooding prairie had convinced him that, "The permanent existence of slavery here is preposterous." [14]

To assure the free soilers of his constancy, Walker stumped the territory. He meant to persuade the voters to cast their votes in the forthcoming territorial elections. A democratic solution existed once the mass of the free soilers voted, for they out-

numbered the proslavery voters by more than two to one. The
contemptuous treatment accorded Walker by Calhoun and his
retainers reflected only a small portion of Kansan sentiment. Indeed, his prestige vitally encouraged the mobilization of free
soil sentiment. General Lane, an ardent free soiler, gave vivid
testimony to the growing importance of this factor, when he recalled that "Walker" had been a household word during his
youth, and that his father and the Governor had served together
in Congress, which together convinced him that fairness alone
would govern the forthcoming election. But Walker also learned
from Lane that the National Democracy had paid a heavy price
in Kansas for its identification with the proslavery element.
Never again would Lane or his followers return to the party
which held their allegiance when they first came to Kansas. The
Governor realized that his hope of establishing a dominant
Democratic party in Kansas had little chance of success. He
planned, therefore, to mitigate the damage.[15]

The strategy with which he hoped to recoup the party fortunes
involved the divorce of the National Democracy from the Kansas
minority of slave Democrats, otherwise the free soil Democrats
would join the Republican camp as their only hope to escape dis-
enfranchisement. But Walker noted one curious fact; the northerners who settled upon the Kansas prairie had remained largely
a leaderless mass. Intimidation and fraud had driven them into
a fatalistic resignation. However, if a prominent member of the
Democracy were to lead them to their just dominance—the
territorial government—then the National Democracy might
escape the full weight of the reaction. Events proved that the
true crime of Walker in the eyes of the radical southerner had
been his decision to provide the necessary leadership to encourage the free soilers to exercise their franchise against the
proslavery clique.[16]

The free soilers proved difficult to convince. Even as he found
himself subjected to a mounting crescendo of southern attacks, a
suspicion of his intentions prevailed among Kansas free soilers.

The Leavenworth *Times* charged sarcastically that the declaration by Walker stating he had accepted the Governorship in order to save the Union made them suspect that saving the Union was his favorite hobby. A suspicion lurked that behind the "flowery verbiage" he used on behalf of a free and fair election "something . . . of a venomous nature" lay concealed. Some believed the final explanation for his behavior was to be found in his deliberate efforts "to break up the free State and pro-slavery organizations and to establish the parties of Kansas upon the basis adopted throughout the States." [17]

Attempts at a peaceful solution came increasingly into conflict with the vested interests of Kansas. The bloody imbroglio had been allowed to drag along too long. The mass of Kansans might be heartily disgusted with the prospect of renewed warfare, but the leadership of both factions knew a final solution would undermine the basis of their long held power. This was especially true of the southern radicals who listened with growing disenchantment as their more moderate comrades conceded Kansas must inevitably be free. Nor did Walker misunderstand the general Kansan sentiment. With detachment, he advised Buchanan:

A very large majority of the *Squatters* who came to this territory from slave states are said to be for a free state, partly from conviction that their *claims* would bring a larger price, and partly because many . . . came . . . expressly to settle in a free state. The same is the case to a limited extent with pro-slavery men holding town lots & shares & interests in projected railroads. The rage for speculation here is universal & prices cannot be maintained.

He refused to believe that philanthropy had anything to do with emancipating slaves anywhere in the United States, and insisted most emphatically that it had little or no appeal in Kansas. When asked how he would handle the abolitionists of Kansas, he remarked, "they have never yet been understood. Touch their pockets—that is the way to reach them." [18]

Though his appeals received a generally unfavorable response among Kansas leaders, they had the opposite effect with the ordinary folk. The repeated assertion that he would tolerate nothing less than a free and fair election brought acts of public faith in his integrity. One nasty dispute between the free soilers and the "slavocracy" had raged over the question of whether to pay taxes levied by the proslavery legislature. Walker urged the free soilers to pay their taxes under protest. Early in June, the Anderson County taxpayers announced their "intention to ascertain the amount of their taxes with the view of paying them under protest." [19]

His determined effort to accord evenhanded justice involved him in a ludicrous dispute with a minority of Lawrence free soilers who had established a city council after Walker had declared it would be illegal. The Governor promptly issued a proclamation declaring the city in a state of insurrection. Walker, General Harney, and a force of federal troops then marched forth to reduce the recalcitrant town. Farce overtook the expedition, for upon its arrival at the town gates, Walker and his army found no hostile preparations. The free soilers found the proceedings galling. There existed a considerable suspicion that the abolitionist element in Lawrence had deliberately contrived the defiance in order to maneuver the Governor into embarrassing acts. Nonetheless, many felt that he had still to learn that harsh experience had taught Kansans to accept illegal government as the only sure way to get any government. The free soil propagandists set to work energetically ridiculing the whole expedition. One irreverent witness accused the Governor of being "tight" during the entire expedition. When it became obvious that Lawrence did not intend to resist the federal authority, Walker mulled over how best to extricate himself from this particularly hurtful situation. Fortunately for his dignity, the Comanche provided release. News that the dog warriors were marauding along the territorial frontier sent the prairie Don Quixote and his regiment in hot pursuit.[20]

Preoccupation with keeping the peace did not keep the Governor from mixing "political speculation" with "speculations in real estate." His attendance at the Paola land sales, though defended as the occasion for making a political speech, gave credence to accusations of extensive land speculations. It does appear that Walker and Stanton had become thoroughly acquainted with the promoters of the proposed Leavenworth, Pawnee, and Western Railroad, though no clear evidence exists to prove that a speculative understanding had been reached between Walker and Thomas Ewing, Jr., the leading speculator of the enterprise. One thing is certain: the meeting established a friendship which resulted in Walker and Stanton agreeing to lobby for a land grant and government loan to aid in the construction of the line westward. In return for their efforts, the railroad syndicate promised to give Stanton four sections of average quality land and an additional section of Pottawatomie lands to both Walker and Stanton. The entire transaction fell through in the continuing troubles that plagued Kansas, but again Walker had shown a marked proclivity for the easy chance.[21]

During his first weeks in Kansas, Washington had become aware that the Kansas Governor believed that most Kansans expected their territory to come into the Union as a free state. He frequently cited the extraordinary unanimity with which the Missouri Democrats applauded his actions. "If the free state party constitute a majority, and a constitution pro-slavery in its character should be adopted by the convention without submission to the people," proslavery Kansans reasoned "this party, driven by such a course into violent opposition to southern institutions, will elect an abolition state legislature, send two abolition senators to the senate of the United States, and a member to Congress entertaining similar sentiments." The avoidance of such a calamity preoccupied the gubernatorial attention. The Lecompton Convention, whose members had been elected to draw up a constitution, showed every intention that it would protect the slaves already in Kansas. It closed the territory to the further importation of slaves, and strictly enforced the fugitive slave

laws. He wondered uneasily whether such a constitution would
ever command the acceptance of any but a minority of Kansans.[22]

"The only practical way to maintain the peace of the territory,
and to inaugurate a party which would support the constitution
and the union," he warned, "is to unite the free-state democrats
here . . . with the pro-slavery party of Kansas." Any solution
which abandoned this course to placate the southern extremists
would force an "overwhelming . . . union of free-state democrats with the republicans." Such a union, he concluded, would
have the most serious consequences for "the harmony of the
union, if not the very existence of the government." Walker had
defined the categorical imperative without which the Democracy
could not hope to salvage its position in Kansas.[23]

Unfortunately, this imperative solution had fallen victim to a
distant party struggle which had transformed Kansas from an
issue of popular sovereignty to one of sectional supremacy.
While Walker sought to settle the future of a remote prairie, he
had become the symbol of a greater struggle—that of the southerner to establish a receivership for the entire Democratic party.
Slowly, almost painfully, he awakened to the realization that he
had become a marked man about whom whirled for a brief moment the national destiny. The futures of the Republic and of
Kansas had fused. Along the broad reaches of the Potomac
which he had left a short time before, the counterattack against
his policies had opened. Alone in a lonely outpost of the nation
he would soon taste the wormwood of betrayal.

13. He Will Not Presume

MR. BUCHANAN had a fine legal mind. It apprehended the nuance of the law and anticipated that the law once enunciated would command obedience. Above all, it thought of the law as fixed. Within the limits of the established definition, the President knew the bounds of legitimate action. He never understood that humans are capable of refusing to obey the law without a feeling of self-guilt. His was a mind obsessed with limits, a mind that had been trained to conserve rather than inaugurate. To the established order he gave reverence; to the written law he gave obedience. When confronted with a near-revolutionary situation, he was not the man to postulate a new solution; rather he drew the past more tightly about him. Forty years of politics had accentuated his natural caution. For him the Presidency came as a culmination of dutiful labor rather than as a challenge. A latter-day Jacksonian, he owned the rhetoric without the force. Obliged to lead, he attempted to reconcile. In his hands the Republic fell apart.[1]

Jeremiah Black, possessor of a glowering countenance and a fierce temper, dismissed his chief contemptuously when he wrote, "Mr. Buchanan has very little to do with a cabinet appointment and of course will not presume to have a will of his own." With equal forthrightness Black had pleaded with Cobb, when it seemed Frémont might be elected, "Do nothing rashly, and take no decisive step without first having a full and free consultation with your Northern friends." He reminded Cobb:

. . . that if the worse comes to the worse we will be sharers in a common calamity (disunion) and something more than sharers in the disgrace. I am very sure that our united efforts can accomplish more for the cause of justice and right than anything which you of the South can achieve alone and unaided. . . . If you will do this, even the election of Frémont may result in nothing worse than turning New England with her ignorance, bigotry and superstition out of the Union; and that is a consummation most devoutly to be wished.[2]

A unionist might well wonder to what kind of Union the Buchanan cabinet was pledged. Kansas made the answer painfully evident.

The decision of Buchanan to stand upon a full application of the theory of rotation led William Marcy to protest, "Pierce men are hunted down like wild beasts." Seething discontent flared in the South over the construction of the cabinet and the distribution of patronage. Stephen Douglas advised Walker when the southern attack against him was strongest that he had been made "the scapegoat" of southern dissatisfaction with the national administration. Henry A. Wise, the erratic governor of Virginia, had erupted, when certain Cabinet appointments were rumored, "I am not going to be exacting, but Cass, Cobb and Bright 'I ain't going to stand anyhow!' Now you may set that down— That is a Forney and Slidell move and they are bending their talons to devour me. . . . I mean to have a *fair* hearing about the formation of the cabinet or none at all." The appointment of Floyd to the War Department had placated Wise, but it had done little to reassure the Old Dominion's Senator R. M. T. Hunter of a just administration hearing.[3] Trouble aplenty threatened from the South; the obvious obligation upon Buchanan was to defend his appointees from such attack when they were pursuing his policies. But for a man who did not presume to have a will of his own, such an action proved beyond his scope.

That Buchanan and his cabinet had committed themselves to support Walker without qualification cannot be doubted. Nor can it be questioned that the administration, especially its southern members, was not fully aware of the extremes to which Kansas sentiment went within the South. They had all had occasion to read sentiments like,

Kansas must come in as a slave state or the cause of southern rights is dead. . . . We can't afford to lose the point. We must have it our way or we are ruined. To stop to cavil and dispute about this or that course being in accordance with the act of organization or not is a great folly as to open moot courts to argue constitutional questions when the citadel of our liberties and existence is surrounded and assaulted.

The intensity of this feeling led to the unveiled suggestion of one Georgian that "If Buchanan should secretly favor the free-state men of Kansas, as I see it charged he will, and succeed in bringing it in as a Free State, he will richly deserve death, and I hope some patriotic hand will inflict it." [4] The course marked out by the pledge Buchanan had given to support Walker demanded high courage. It would expect readiness from the President to challenge elements of the often fickle and whimsical Democracy. The critical question rapidly became whether the Buchanan administration proposed to lead or to be led.

Having assured Walker of its unwavering support, the first southern protests in response to the declaration by Walker that Kansas must inevitably come into the Union as a free state stirred serious uneasiness within the administration.[5] Buchanan, however, seemed determined to keep the ship of state on an even keel. He assured Walker, "The point on which your and our success depends is the submission of the constitution to the people of Kansas." Though he already knew members of the cabinet were uneasy over the effect of Walker's speeches, he carefully avoided mention of his own concern. The importance of a firm and unwavering course appeared to weigh uppermost in the presidential mind, but it did not take long for those who knew Buchanan best to realize that the spate of southern criticism weighed heavily upon his morbid sensitivity "to public reproach," and made him solicitous "beyond the wise sedateness of statesmanship, to please everybody." [6] The presidential wavering added to the confusion of the cabinet. An irate Thompson complained, "I get lost in following the path with the Administration and its true position on one side and Gov. Walker and his many givings out on the other. Walker evidently has one purpose and the Administration another; and it requires a tactician to do justice to the President and not wound the sensibilities of Walker." [7]

The ambiguous posture of the administration was accentuated as the tempo of southern protest increased. Buchanan chose to retreat rather than defy the justice of these complaints. Left to their own devices, the southern cabinet members succumbed to the wrath of home protests. In the cabinet, only the Pennsylvanian, Black, exhibited political nerve. Confronted with an inert President and a frightened group of southerners, he chose to defy regional sentiment. He deserted the North and committed himself to the fearful southerners.

The shift in administration policy on Kansas subsequent to July came only in response to the protests of a segment of southern opinion. As it worked to placate radical southerners, the administration only encouraged them to increase the tempo and heat of their attacks. The Walker inaugural which had for all practical purposes been given an official imprimatur brought a storm of protest from the radical southern editorial pen. The Charleston *Mercury* protested vehemently, "The cotton states will let Mr. Buchanan and Mr. Walker and all the national spoilsmen slide, even of Virginia. . . . In the broad road of abolition designs, all such may ere long slough off together from the South. . . . Defend us from such friends, and we will take care of our enemies." [8] The signs were most ominous for Walker since he was singled out to bear the brunt of the southern attack.

The Democratic State Convention meeting at Milledgeville, Georgia, castigated the territorial Governor. It left no doubt that it demanded nothing less than his removal when it asserted:

That the address of Governor Walker in prescribing the terms on which Congress should admit Kansas into the Union, and in attempting to dictate to the people as to the submission of their Constitution for ratification, and as to what class of persons votes constitutes a presumptious interference in matters over which he has no legitimate control, and that the same address, in expressing the official opinion that Kansas will become a Free State, and in presenting arguments to support that side of the question, is a gross departure from the principles of non-intervention and of neutrality which were established by the Kansas bill and that the Convention has full confidence that Mr. Buchanan will manifest fidelity to the principles which carried him into office, by recalling Governor Walker.[9]

Mississippi quickly joined Georgia in denouncing Walker, but withheld a similar denunciation of the administration "until officially informed how far his conduct meets with the approval of the President." The newly elected Governor of Florida used his inaugural address to castigate the course being pursued in Kansas. "If the northern wing of the Democratic party is not strong and faithful to the rights of the South," he warned, "there is an end of the Union and I shall be among those to advocate a dissolution of every National tie, and the taking of our destiny into our hands." [10]

Under the surging attack the administration, though seriously concerned, reassured its distant Governor that he need not lose confidence in its support.[11] Douglas, sensing that the southern protest, and the wavering course followed in response, prefaced a major political upheaval, came to the defense of Walker. He told the Governor that he was the victim of rivalries between southern politicians. Douglas reaffirmed his unqualified support for the Kansas policy enunciated in Walker's inaugural address. He might have added that within the divided cabinet there existed a strong suspicion that "Walker is playing a bold game for the succession." But out of the melee a fact pregnant with meaning for the future stood out; the first hesitant steps had been taken toward a Walker-Douglas axis as the storm gathered over the Southland.[12]

Yet, as Douglas had further indicated, the situation within the South had not deteriorated beyond hope. The southern defense of Walker was often as vociferous as was the attack. It revealed that a determined administration could draw upon ample support if it were to espouse a vigorous continuation of its proposed policy. Cobb spelled out for Lucius Lamar the southern strength that Buchanan possessed. "Mr. Buchanan," he argued, "is the first President, who recognized the right of the southern man to go into the common territories with his slave property, . . . thus putting himself upon the southern construction of the doctrine of popular sovereignty." Not only that, he appointed "a southern man Governor of Kansas . . . [a man] urgently recommended . . . by the extreme southern rights men for the first place in his cabinet." The territorial Secretary was not only a southern man, but one who had been "identified with the Southern Rights party." Nor could anyone deny that Buchanan had filled "all the offices in Kansas either with Southern men, or northern national democrats who were acceptable to our friends." In short, the South had a President who awaited its beck and call.[13]

Possessing an amplitude of strength, the administration needed only to mobilize its southern friends should the fire eaters insist upon a showdown. The Charleston *Mercury* centered as much of its vehemence against the Border State politicians as it did against Walker. It did so for good reason. The Richmond *Enquirer* calling for moderation editorialized, "Walker's course has been satisfactory to the pro-slavery men of Kansas and offensive to the anti-slavery men. . . . Walker is but carrying into practice, fearlessly and zealously the principles of the Kansas-Nebraska bill." As the radical attack increased, the same newspaper demanded, "Point us to a man in the ranks of the revilers of Walker to whom the South owes 1/10th the gratitude which is due Walker . . . he has left in the Treasury Department and the Senate monuments to his fidelity to the South which the voice of detraction cannot deface." [14]

The Virginia journals did not rest with a defense of Walker. They scathingly challenged the whole basis of the ultra critique of the Kansas program. The ultras had embraced a shortsighted policy which could only terminate in the South repudiating her own principle of popular sovereignty "upon no other pretext than the childish, petulant one that . . . in this case would benefit the North." If such were to be the southern position, could the North be expected to respect the same principle when the "tropical regions . . . shall present constitutions sanctioning negro slavery, and demand admission into the Union?" Repeatedly, Virginians read that the vast majority of Kansans were sickened unto death of turmoil and wished to settle down to the task of building a home and fortune. It was useless they were told to accuse Walker of unfaithfulness or traitorous intention for he had neither created nor could he change conditions in Kansas. The Virginia *Sentinel* defended Walker as "endeavoring to pacify Kansas; and to effect this, he is simply trying to hasten, not influence, the decision of the question on which peace depends. That decision," it concluded, "is already in the breast of the community—he is seeking to facilitate its utterance." [15]

Far to the South, an old friend of Mississippi days took up his pen in defense of Walker. Colonel Claiborne meant to question those who most fiercely protested Kansas developments and, more important, to diagnose the difficulties. He chose to direct his epistle to the New Orleans *Courier* which had never endeavored to conceal its fire-eating propensities. It reminded southerners that in the fight Walker had led to annex Texas "a powerful party, strong in wealth, talent and numbers . . . in Louisiana, Mississippi, and Georgia had opposed . . . the annexation." In New Orleans, he crisply reminded, strong opposition to the annexation developed "on the patriotic grounds that it would reduce the value of the sugar estates of Louisiana!" The impending crisis that threatened the South resulted from "a moral and pestiferous treason, deep in the vitals of the South," but its source was "not President Buchanan; not Governor Walker, gentlemen, but the South itself!" Instead of looking elsewhere to explain the loss of Kansas, Claiborne demanded to know what the South had done to warrant obtaining Kansas. For all the sound and fury, "not a dollar—not a man did Mississippi or Louisiana contribute to vindicate Southern rights in Kansas."

He ended with warning the South to take care lest it drive from its side the Northern democracy.[16]

But for the militant dissenters, these arguments missed the point. The desire of Northern Democratic politicians to bring in Kansas as a free state, they believed, granted that party ascendancy was "of more importance than the rights of the South." To designate Walker a friend of the South pricked them to recall that few "regarded him as a proslavery man." The administration scheme had the virtue of being ingenious, bold, and vigorous, but for the opposition it had brought to a test their fealty to the party or the South. They meant to establish the preeminence of their loyalty to section rather than to party.[17]

The moderate policy supported by Walker may have divided the South, but it received widespread approval throughout the North from both conservative politicians and the conservative press. Senator William Bigler of Pennsylvania expressed dismay at "the bad temper of some of our Southern friends" who "evidently do not understand the real state of parties in Kansas." The plodding Pennsylvanian, completing a tour of Kansas, thought Buchanan had better make it clear to the South that they had lost all chance of securing Kansas "when they agreed to let the majority decide." To continue the denunciations of Walker was to deny the facts.[18]

The northern press backed the Walker pacification plan with a varying response. Originally, the radical northern press had viewed Walker with profound suspicion, but as the tone of the southern attack became fiercer and the administration exposed signs of abandoning its support of the Governor, these journals, scenting political hay, threw their support to Walker.[19] The conservative journals agreed that his actions in Kansas had probably prevented civil war from exploding afresh. Some suggested that Walker added to the growing confusion on the prairie with "his restless officiousness." "He has no idea of the negative virtues of a judicious abstinence from acts and words," complained the Boston *Journal.* "He overdoes his part, and gets himself into trouble by talking, writing, and acting where there is not the slightest need for it." [20]

The rank and file of the Democracy professed bewilderment at the events which transformed Kansas from a local to a national issue. The editor of the New Hampshire *Patriot* complained to Pierce:

Kansas affairs seem to have come to another crisis and we are probably to see more trouble there. Walker's boasted "pacification" seems to have been deceptive; he was doubtless as much deceived as any of us. What the ultimate result is to be I have no doubt, but I fear it will come too late for our local benefit. The *end* which Walker is laboring to produce is desirable for us. . . . It is difficult to determine what it is proper and expedient to publish, . . . and I have therefore said but little on the subject. . . . And until I can see more clearly the right way of treating the subject, I do not intend to do more than give the current views from that region.[21]

As the New Englander retreated into a cautious attitude, the Pennsylvania democracy, rarely characterized by unified sentiment, displayed a surprising unity of opinion. Richard Vaux, the Mayor of Philadelphia and staunch friend of Buchanan, energetically pleaded:

If Governor Walker will *disregard* the monarchists, the enemies of free government, *in the South,* and the absurd nobodies of the North, Mr. Buchanan's administration will compare with that of Washington. Yes! Yes! . . . there are men in the South who hate *free* government and anything they can do will be done to destroy a Pennsylvania President or a republican form of government.[22]

Senator Bigler feared that "the open and covert enemies of Governor Walker's programme" concealed a purpose that had as its aim the complete rejection of any Kansas settlement, while Black reassured a Philadelphia audience the President wanted only "to restore peace." [23]

His original intention to support Walker gradually faded as Buchanan yielded to ultra-southern pressure. The crux of the administration policy had been to maintain a moderate posture which would keep the conservatives in control of the party.

Ultimately, there existed a dilemma for the northern democrat; he had to recognize the potency of the free soil appeal
among his constituents. Douglas had felt the power of that call
and had struggled to meet it while permitting the southern
politician a graceful withdrawal. Popular sovereignty had been
meant to emancipate the national politician from the difficulty
of resolving the fate of the territories. It appealed to the Jeffersonian dictum that the government closest to the people is
the best government. Similarly, the best decision is that which
springs from the people most directly concerned. It had the
virtue of combining an appeal to local decision and to majority
rule. It had one fatal drawback—it condemned the South to a
condition of decline which would be augmented with the admission of each new state.

So long as Buchanan seemed committed to the Walker settlement, Douglas could believe that the program with which he
had been most thoroughly identified was to be followed. The
moment the administration cut itself adrift from Walker, the
Senator from Illinois had no choice but to view it as an act that
renounced his guidance. Knowing that he must win re-election to
the Senate if he were to achieve the Presidency, he knew that he
faced disaster should he abandon popular sovereignty. His own
necessities dictated a fight. From this realization there emerged
an alliance between the troubled Governor of Kansas and himself that would undermine the Democracy.

Walker had watched the devious course of the administration with growing concern and suspicion. Jeremiah Black attempted to assure the Governor of his absolute authority.
"Everybody thinks, talks, and writes about Kansas and of
course everyone thinks his own views right," the Pennsylvanian
reported. He continued, "I venture to make a few suggestions
for which nobody but myself is responsible. . . . The great *official* duty which you have to perform and which you have shown
a determination to perform at all hazards is that of preserving
the peace and good order of the Territory." He concluded

emphatically, "This can be done only by making the law supreme." [24]

Since Black had chosen to write his letter to buttress Walker in his efforts to quell any extreme action taken by free soilers, it was only natural for Walker to assume that the law applied with equal force to overt proslavery action. Upon this, he proved sadly mistaken. When the territorial elections were held on October 5th and 6th, the frequent assurances by Walker of a free election brought out a heavy vote. The returns indicated not only the election of a Republican congressional delegate by a majority in excess of 4,000 but also of a proslavery legislature! Fraud could not be doubted. Angrily, Walker and Stanton set out to examine the returns. Their examination proved that outrageous fraud had been practiced in two sparsely settled localities, McGee County and the hamlet of Oxford. Walker quickly established that nearly fifteen hundred votes cast at Oxford had been copied from Williams *Cincinnati Directory*. Determined to make the law supreme, he threw out the illegal votes. If this action were sustained, the free soilers were certain to control the territorial legislature.[25]

Temporarily thwarted, the proslavery element consolidated their control of the constitutional convention meeting at Lecompton. Though the bulk of its membership opposed the submission of any constitution to the electorate, the Democratic managers were uncomfortably aware that nothing less would redeem administration pledges. The convention manager, Calhoun, seems originally to have intended submitting to the electorate a free soil and a slave constitution for their decision. A temporary lapse in the sitting of the convention resulted in Calhoun losing control of it. Only questionable tactics had enabled him to regain control of a thoroughly disreputable congregation of confused, and as some thought ossified, delegates. The constitution that was finally submitted permitted the Kansan to vote either for a continuance of slavery or for a halt to further slave importations but extended protection to slave property already in

Kansas. The complete termination of slavery was not allowed. To confuse the situation further, the convention voted to submit to the people only the "clause 'Constitution with slavery' or 'Constitution without slavery.' " The pledge to submit the entire constitution had been reneged upon. As if to prove McLean's assertion that they could undo any Governor, the convention voted to oust Walker and other federal officers and to replace them as of December 1, 1857, with a provisional government headed by Calhoun. To complete the debacle they declared that the power to adjudge the returns devolved upon the new government. The perpetrators of the McGee and Oxford frauds had voted to allow themselves to conduct another election. Small wonder that the free soilers of Kansas and of the nation expressed outrage. It was pure disaster for Buchanan when the free soilers were joined by numberless Democrats who refused to associate themselves with an obviously illicit action.[26]

The administration could hardly have been unaware of the divisions which resulted from the Lecompton actions. An administration supporter and friend of Walker who witnessed the proceedings informed Black:

The ultra pro-slavery men have enlisted the support of John Calhoun by promising to make him a U.S. Senator and he is using all his power and patronage to make Kansas a slave state. He has been the major cause of trouble from the start and has driven a wedge between the Democrats in Kansas. The Free State Democrats desire to form a solid Democratic party in Kansas without allowing the question of slavery to destroy the whole party; but the pro-slavery men led by Calhoun have their own objects. . . . The President's supporters in Kansas want an opportunity to vote for or against the constitution as a whole as well as for or against slavery.[27]

A confused, ill, and depressed Walker took stock of his position. Assured of constant support, encouraged to press a program of pacification, he found himself in mid-November officially abandoned. The *Union*, which served as an administration organ, carried an article written by Black committing the administration to support the Lecompton Constitution. Black's utter

indifference to the presidential opinion, one that seemed to prevail amongst other cabinet members, is startlingly shown in the
Attorney General's decision to alter the original article after
Buchanan had read and approved its contents. An unhappy
executive hastily wrote Black to complain:

In reading your article this morning (in the Washington *Union*) which
was excellent in the original form, I deeply regret that the notice of
Governor Walker has been stricken out, whilst the praises of the Convention remain. What is the reason for this? It will give just cause of
offense to Governor Walker's friends; and I confess I am much worried
myself at the omission.[28]

The man who had written "the President will not presume to
have an opinion of his own" understood Buchanan far too well
to concern himself with weak complaints.

As the President danced to the tune played by Black, Cobb,
and Thompson, an injured Walker left Kansas and indicated
upon his arrival at Washington that he had some definite ideas of
his own. Among them was his deepest conviction that an attempt to fasten the Lecompton Constitution upon the Kansas free
soiler would result in renewed warfare. A pleasant meeting with
Buchanan preceded a cabinet meeting at which Walker gave the
cabinet a description of his Kansas experience. All pleasantry
disintegrated when the Governor stated his unyielding determination to oppose the Lecompton Constitution at every opportunity.
The arrogant trio promptly informed him that they intended
to exterminate opposition in Kansas and, by implication, within
the Democratic party. The whip that meant to cow only enraged
Walker. He intended now to meet threats with action; action
which would entrap the authors of his discomfort. Mr. Walker
wrapped about him the garb of the martyr, stalked from the
meeting, and went forth upon a journey that would have a
sordid end.[29]

14. Principle Abandoned

AN ANGRY WALKER departed from the White House convinced that he had been betrayed. But he had prepared for this contingency. As he traveled eastward, he had joined Douglas to discuss the common cause. Both men agreed to resist administration support of Lecompton. In Kansas, Frederick Stanton now acting Governor, chose to press a strategy to which Walker had given an ambiguous assent prior to his departure. He convened a special session of the free soil legislature chosen the previous October. He proposed that it set a date for an election which would permit not only a vote for the constitution with or without slavery but one on the whole constitution. Though repudiated with alacrity by the administration, Stanton believed a "good deal of good" had been done "by providing the means of legally voting down the Lecompton fraud." Outmaneuvered, Buchanan now read a withering letter from Walker resigning his governorship. It bluntly accused the southern cabinet members of betraying the pledges they had originally made him. Shrewdly he spared Buchanan harsh criticism, implying that he had been misled about the scope of the Kansas frauds. The letter left the distinct impression that the President was not his own master.[1]

As the Democrats came to recognize the dimensions of the break affecting their party, frightened members pressed for a prompt reconciliation. The annual Presidential message was eagerly awaited. "We are holding our breath for the message," one concerned Democrat wrote. "I trust," he added, "it will commend itself to every man's conscience." The message contained the usual Democratic pledges to foster free trade, states rights, and democracy. On the Kansas issue alone it created controversy. Buchanan made it emphatic that he meant to force Lecompton upon his party, or as Black expressed it: "the test of membership in the Democracy is to be made on the Kansas question." [2]

Agitation and confusion seized the party. "The Kansas question," one Democrat wistfully complained, "seems to be more complicated than ever." Friends of the administration pressed for belligerent reprisals against the Lecompton rebels. "Everything appears to be going to the Devil because of Kansas," they complained. "The whole agitation is merely a ruse to make Douglas President in 1860," one asserted. "Can't you Democrats at Washington get ahead of those fellows," queried another, "and have those Kansas matters settled?" Some proposed a course of action that Douglas would dismiss contemptuously when it was attempted. "The President will have to take the animal that would gore him by the horns," came the belligerent word from one Pennsylvanian, "and Jackson-like cut off his head." But most often came the timid lament, "I regret the position of the Administration . . . [on] the Kansas Constitution, but hope that the question will be settled without seriously disturbing the peace of the Country, or impairing the unity of the Democratic Party." [3]

The administration proposed to take disciplinary action against those who dissented against Lecompton. It operated from the mistaken premise that the dissidents had provoked the party upheaval when the administration had left no alternative to opponents of Lecompton but an uncompromising opposition. In brief, the executive leadership ignored the dilemma of those northern Democrats who had to meet Republican opposition. There was left among these Democrats an untidy impression that Buchanan proposed to use discipline against men who had to contemplate the threat of proscription by the voter. The administration learned that humans, unlike the proverbial lamb, view unenthusiastically the sacrificial altar.

As Walker wrapped about him the martyr's mantle, there

seemed momentarily to be one opponent who had genuine reason to oppose the administration's course simply because it symbolized his betrayal. Yet, there existed an abiding difficulty; Walker's financial situation had been seriously affected by the depression of 1857. In his efforts to retrieve his position, he was destined to pursue a devious path.

Before his departure from Kansas he had consulted with the free soiler Lane and with his own temporary successor Stanton. Lane had proposed that a special session of the legislature be called to permit legislative authorization of a vote on the whole constitution. Stanton had immediately recognized the potent threat such a call would present to supporters of Lecompton. It would permit the Kansan to disavow any acceptance of the document. When Walker had been made aware of the proposal, he had replied to his subordinate's enthusiasm with the bland reminder that Stanton would assume full authority the moment Walker crossed over into Missouri. The obvious implication was that it would be up to Stanton to determine whether to take the risk. Once he had convened the legislature, Walker avoided indicating to Stanton whether he approved or disapproved. Almost diffidently, the acting Governor finally asked:

Of one thing I am still very desirous—that is to learn your opinion of my course in calling the Legislature. It would be a source of great regret to me if it has caused any embarrassment to you, or if it should even not meet your approval. I honestly believed, if you had been here, you would not have hesitated to do the same thing. . . . It seems palpable to me that your aim to defeat the Lecompton constitution, will be eminently promoted by a regular, legal vote of the people to the same effect.[4]

Walker continued to remain silent on the course set by Stanton.

Indeed, the former Governor had become thoroughly preoccupied with obtaining a favorable Supreme Court decision against a government effort to invalidate the Fossatt claim. At stake was the still unsettled New Almaden Mine claim. Jeremiah Black had launched a vigorous investigation of the claim, sending Edwin M. Stanton to examine in person the California

archives. That worthy quickly found considerable tampering
with archival deposits, but also concluded there existed formidable strength in the governmental challenge. Since Black
had once been a member of the Walker syndicate, he needed no
information about the mine's value.[5]

Simultaneously, Walker pressed a case in the Supreme Court
to invalidate the Fossatt claim in his own behalf. This stratagem
had been made necessary because of a falling out between himself and James Eldridge. Walker contended that the Quicksilver
Mining Company they had jointly formed in 1854 had been
dissolved with suitable compensation for Eldridge. It was to
Walker's interest to obtain a decision against the government
in the case of the *United States vs. Fossatt,* and then one which
supported his claim in *Walker vs. Fossatt.* Beset with severe
financial difficulties, Walker thought of the New Almaden Mine
as a release from these liabilities. Accentuating his problem was
the unrelenting pressure on him exerted by W. W. Corcoran,
the financial patron of the Democracy.[6]

It was against such a background that Senator Gwin began in
January of 1858, to press for a reconciliation between Walker
and Buchanan. Only a strenuous effort and beguiling promises
persuaded the recently deposed Governor to accede. When the
two men finally met, it was in a supercharged atmosphere of
emotion. Upon sighting one another, they gasped and fell into
one another's arms weeping and apologizing. Buchanan hastened
to supplement forgiveness with a positive sign of favor. He
directed the Attorney General to examine the brief which Walker
intended to submit to the Supreme Court in behalf of his own
claim. Jubilant, Walker apparently thought that he had been
assured a favorable judicial finding. Since he is reputed to have
received $500,000 when the case was finally settled in 1863, the
distinct impression remains that Walker's principle commanded
a high price.[7]

The first sign Walker gave that he no longer intended to press
with vigor his attack on the administration occurred on February

6, 1858, when he declined an invitation by Forney to address an anti-Lecompton meeting in Philadelphia. Though he did not intend to unfurl his own banners any further, he suggested to Forney,

All free Government is based upon *"The Consent of the Governed."* Let this truth be inscribed on your banners and written on your hearts. Let it be proclaimed by you, that this great principle shall neither be evaded by technical quibbles, nor subverted by frauds and forgeries.[8]

He had carefully avoided including bribery in his list of subversions. To compensate for his failure to attend the rally, he wrote to it reasserting the principle that every Kansan deserved the right to vote on his constitution. In defense of this principle, he pledged himself to march beside "the noble Democracy of Philadelphia . . . to the rescue of the liberties of our country." Within a few weeks, the Democracy of Philadelphia had been given to understand that Mr. Walker's march had deteriorated into a promenade down a path that led to reconciliation with and reward from the administration.[9]

Instead of attacking the administration, he now became preoccupied with justifying his stand to southerners. A blistering attack from the Texas legislature brought a quick rejoinder. The South would have possessed ample territory to expand its *peculiar institution* if all of Mexico had been annexed as he had originally advocated. The question of the fate that would have been meted out to the Mexican people he cavalierly defined. "It was not my intention," he announced, "to introduce the colored races of Mexico into any participation in the government of this country any more than the African race in our own confederacy." He invoked the name of Thomas Jefferson to justify the exclusion of Negroes everywhere from self-government. Should anyone question how he would have kept the 7,000,000 Mexicans subjugated, he stated simply "by military possession." Slavery could not expand into Kansas but its true hope for expansion lay southward. The man who had denounced the pernicious effects of slavery struggled to redeem his lost prestige by painting an image of a vast subtropical empire of slaves. Though not explicitly advocating the enslavement of the colored peoples of the Caribbean, he left the distinct impression that their color warranted such a result.[10]

As Walker sought to undo the worse consequences of his earlier course, the Lecompton dispute continued unabated. Whereas Douglas and Forney bore the brunt of administration invective, Walker received the gentle treatment. The contrast became increasingly apparent in the bitter attacks launched by Black against Forney when the latter persisted in filling the pages of his newspaper, the *Pennsylvanian*, with fiery attacks upon the administration and its Kansas policies. Black poured forth his vitriol after Forney had thoroughly castigated the administration in a speech given in Tarrytown, New York, in September, 1858. In an uncompromising editorial for the *Union*, he characterized Forney as a deserter to the "Black Republican Party"; waxing eloquent, Black described him further as "a miserable hypocrite, a liar, a fraud, a vulgar incompetent rascal." Particularly galling, according to the Attorney General, had been Forney's description of the cabinet meeting at which Walker had received his instructions prior to his departure for Kansas. This behavior had been heinous since "Forney attempts to create the impression that his story was told him by Walker." As for Mr. Walker, Black continued:

[He] has committed some grave political errors but he has been guilty of no behaviour towards the President which forfeits his character as a gentleman. Whilst he was in Kansas a question arose . . . concerning its admission into the Union as a State; which it was the sole duty of Congress and the President to decide. But on this question Gov. Walker saw proper to differ with the administration. He demanded the adoption of his own Kansas policy and his own views of Constitutional law, and *he made* this a test question with the administration. Of course Mr. Buchanan could not and would not surrender his convictions to anyone.[11]

Walker had earned more than the backhanded praise given him by Black. When the administration had retreated from its uncompromising Lecompton stand to support the English bill,

Walker officially abandoned his fight against the administration. This bill, proposed by William H. English, Indiana Congressman and member of Senator Jessie Bright's machine, gave the Kansan the right to reject the Lecompton constitution outright. If Kansas approved the constitution she would be given the same land grants as had been given other states plus five percent of all proceeds the government received in the sale of 2,000,000 additional acres. If the constitution were rejected, then Kansas could not reapply for admission as a state until the census established she had 90,000 residents. Walker had publicly supported the bill as one that met his original demand—total submission for popular approval of the Lecompton constitution. He announced that he expected Kansans would confirm his original objection by rejecting the constitution, an expectation that the polls confirmed. He almost convinced Douglas of the wisdom of allowing the bill to achieve its purpose. Only when Douglas realized the political danger of such a course did he renew the battle against the administration. But as Walker told Gwin, he had done what he could to restore the party.[12]

Once the English bill and the Kansans had settled the fate of Lecompton, an awkward fact revealed itself to the "puny Timon" of the Democracy. "He pleased nobody. . . . He was lost as a political factor of the nation and to the party forever." Mistrusted by all sides, he had a grim awakening. Far from the government relaxing prosecution of its case against the Fossatt claim, Black pressed it with such enthusiasm that Walker lapsed into an ever blacker mood against his protagonist. At one point, the disparaging arguments of Black before the High Court had provoked Walker to challenge the Attorney General to a duel. His anger had not been assuaged when Black refused to acknowledge receipt of the challenge. Walker spoke freely of his betrayal. His denunciations of Buchanan soon entered into the common gossip of Washington. The depth of his fury may have been measured by his outrage at realizing how cheaply his principles had been sold.[13]

The Republicans smelled a chance to reopen the Kansas wound. John Covode, a dour and fierce Republican Congressman from Pittsburgh, wanted above all the election of a new executive who would favor northern railroad interests. As often happens, he chose to exploit the congressional committee system as a means to ferret out the facts about Kansas. His success was to prove disastrously complete. As his first move he intended to extract from Walker certain letters, the mysterious contents of which were often privately discussed. The purpose of the Covode Committee, therefore, was explicitly political and, interestingly, one which northern Democrats opposed to Buchanan thought would advance their control of the party.[14]

A crowded committee room awaited Walker when he finally appeared to testify on April 17, 1860. He had hardly been sworn in when Mr. Olin, the committee's counsel, asked if he had received a letter from Buchanan "about July 12 or August 12 [1857] . . . in reference to the affairs of the Territory, and the policy to be pursued by you?" Walker said he had but declined to discuss the letter's contents or to turn it over to the committee. When pressed, he insisted that its "confidential and private" nature gave him the right to decide "the place, time and manner" of its revelation. Walker admitted under questioning that he had allowed several associates to read it. He added that a second copy existed in the hands of a relative as a safeguard against the loss of the original. When Walker had convinced the committee that he did not intend to comply with their request, it dismissed him. The committee then called various men the former Governor had allowed to read the letter to testify.[15]

The first witness, Ellis B. Schnabel, a long-time legal associate of Walker, quickly acknowledged reading the entire letter. He stated that as he read the letter, its "exceedingly indignant and angry" recipient had expressed forcefully his fear "that the President would not only destroy the Democratic Party, but the country with it." The testimony of Schnabel took an unexpected

twist when he related that during a meeting earlier in the week
with Attorney General Black, the cabinet official had denied the
letter existed while Schnabel reiterated that he had seen it.
Black, obviously ignorant of the letter's existence, insisted to
Schnabel that if the letter were in existence, it was the duty of
Walker to produce it. When Schnabel reasserted that he had
seen it, Black, never a man to contain his anger, shouted:

> . . . that the President never wrote such a document, it was a mere
> pretense to cover up a perpetrated or intended treason to the Demo-
> cratic party, or a mere pretext for deserting to the Black Republican
> ranks . . . that if anyone attacked the administration on this ground,
> *"we will put a shirt upon him from which he will never escape."*

The succession of witnesses after Schnabel merely confirmed
that the letter did exist. But Walker decided to reveal the letter
once he became aware of Black's denunciation. Too much abuse
had come from that quarter for him to ignore the chance to settle
a bitter score.

When Walker returned to the stand, he poured forth his
grievances. The letter, which he now proposed to reveal, he had
hoped to keep secret for he "was very much alarmed about the
condition of the country" and he feared its publication would
precipitate further controversy and division. He ascribed his
reluctant acceptance of the Governorship to extreme pressure
from both Buchanan and Douglas. He admitted that he had intended to bring Kansas into the Union as a Democratic state by
uniting "the Free State democrats with the proslavery party and
all those whom I regard as conservative men against the more
violent portion of the Republicans." He made no effort to conceal his belief that the administration had betrayed him in his
effort.

A gasp of astonishment went up from the audience as he detailed his interview with John Calhoun on the details of the
Lecompton constitution. When Walker protested that this was
contrary to administration policy and produced the letter from
Buchanan to support his claim, Calhoun promptly informed

him that the administration had altered its policy without informing him of the change. He revealed that Calhoun had been the especial friend of Douglas in Kansas and had been appointed surveyor general on Douglas's recommendation. The Illinoisan had acted in the expectation that Calhoun would support a submission of the constitution to the people. However, Walker noted, loyalty ceased when Cobb and Thompson dangled the senatorship before the surveyor general. Astonishment gave way to amazement when the former governor insisted that the President had denied at their private November interview that he had consented to the policy change. The letter when finally produced was an anticlimax; it bore out Walker's testimony. The incontrovertible fact that Mr. Buchanan had been a servant in his own house was revealed to the nation. Another investigating committee had achieved success: it had discovered a damaging issue, the incompetence of Buchanan and the perfidy of his administration.[16]

Public vindication had exacted a high price from Walker. All efforts to deceive himself about the nation's future ended. Gloomily he forecast a period of long and bloody strife. He returned to the practice of the law and continued to pursue the wealth of New Almaden. The last poor hope to keep the Union intact, he believed, would be the nomination of Stephen A. Douglas for President. His limited influence was at the disposal of that presidential candidate. But he knew that the Union of old was beyond salvage. Like himself, it lived in the shadow of fading hopes.[17]

15. A Sixty-Year-Old Public Man

THE AMERICAN PUBLIC MAN of 1861 had ample reason to doubt the future. The United States, a republic scarcely seventy-five years old, seemed on the verge of collapse. The labored compromises of the previous decades had exhausted their promise. Pathetic efforts at renewed compromise crumbled as determined Republicans insisted upon making the new territories free while militant southerners determined to force the supremacy of states' rights. For Robert Walker, however, the war brought release. Secession gave him a purpose for being: he must labor to restore the Union—without slavery.

Walker, in Washington at this time, was grimly certain that only a total effort would insure northern victory. He did not hesitate to predict "a long war," one that would "last till one section or the other is completely exhausted." His past knowledge of Jefferson Davis convinced him that the Confederate President's obstinacy, as well as his absolute conviction of the justice of his cause, made certain a fight to the finish. "There will be a holocaust of lives, rivers of blood, millions of wasted property"; he insisted, "but we shall emerge from the conflict with the stain of slavery wiped from the country." Through the long years of the War, Walker remained convinced that only a "terrible struggle of rule or ruin" would settle the conflict.[1]

He described slavery as the cause of the War and anticipated that it would end only with the destruction of this pernicious institution. But the northern public had not yet recognized this necessity and still remained unprepared for immediate emancipation. "The Abolitionists, after thirty years of agitation, are merely a corporal's guard, and not a party," he observed coldly. "They have appealed to the moral sentiment of the people," he mourned, "and the people, absorbed in money getting, have given the old answer: 'Am I my brother's keeper?'" The North might refuse for a time to admit that "the cause of causes, lying back of the whole wide gulf of difference in Northern and Southern politics is . . . slavery," but the southern attack had forced it to "fight to sustain our nationality when it would not to destroy slavery." [2]

Walker, always the passionate exponent of manifest destiny, managed to discern some hope even in the prospect of a temporary disruption since, with the extermination of slavery, "Canada . . . would soon seek admission to the Union." Never once did he entertain a permanent rupture "for disunion is opposed to the physical laws of this continent." Actually, as the war lengthened, Walker accepted it as a necessary step in the universal fulfillment of the democratic mission. There had come into existence in America "a race," he declared, "that should build up a free, enlightened, all powerful country, to lead the van in the great march of the nations." But to merit that holy task the North had to pledge the destruction of slavery. Once it had recognized the stakes, the North would "insist on continuing the war until slavery is utterly exterminated." [3] It was the abstract identity of the slave that had to perish, for Walker did not think of the Negro as either innately or potentially the equal of the white man.

Dedication to the Union demanded a tangible demonstration of his loyalty. Now a war Democrat, Walker plunged with gusto into the self-appointed task of propagandist for the Union. He entered into partnership with James R. Gilmore, militantly antislavery, to publish the *Continental Monthly*, a magazine designed to educate the public on the meaning of the War. As he rushed its preparation, Walker hurried about New York City, then in turmoil over war preparations. When he arose to speak at a patriotic rally sponsored by John Dix and Hamilton Fish on

April 20, his introduction as a "loyal Southerner" brought a roar of approval. He responded with deprecations at efforts to conciliate the wayward sisters. "Secession was political suicide," he argued, "and if not stopped at the threshold, we should fall into universal anarchy, and become the scoff and scorn of the civilized world." The issue transcended party, and though a loyal Democrat, he would subordinate his party affiliation to his first loyalty—America. The senatorial predecessor of Jefferson Davis paused a moment, looked about him, and as the multitude subsided into silence, softly uttered the most belligerent words of the gathering: "We must fight it out, until our glorious flag floats over every fort, and every vessel, and every acre of soil recognizes it as our national symbol." A thunderous reply shook Union Square as the slight figure bowed and retired, content at having made known publicly the profundity of his national loyalty.[4]

Walker then settled down to the publication of the *Continental Monthly*. It struck out to encompass a wide and varied number of interests, "avoiding all petty jealousies and exclusiveness," and was meant to attract the interest of influential persons. Both editors fostered the idea that the magazine had a semiofficial character, enabling it to obtain advance information of administration policy. Within a short time, it had a substantial and growing circulation.[5]

The editorials of the magazine were dedicated to establishing the need for the obliteration of slavery. Both men thought it an uphill task. "I have not talked with a single individual who would not, for the sake of peace," reported Walker glumly to a friend in the spring of 1861, "take the South back with slavery, and all our disagreements unsettled." Appalled, he insisted, "that we can have no permanent peace without the destruction of slavery." When Lincoln proposed gradual emancipation, Walker seized upon the proposal with approval, contending "that the immediate action theory has been delaying the cause for thirty years." It also served as a pledge for further and

fuller action.[6] The prospect of gradual total emancipation moved
the editors to describe its consequences in glowing terms. "The
press would glow with enthusiasm," according to these worthies,
"and the procession of nations march in the grand ovation, not
to national airs, or under the national banners, but under the
world's new flag, and to the music of the world's new anthem
of universal freedom and regenerated man." Walker was moved
to pronounce the Civil War as a demonstration of human progress.[7]

Any threat to the cause of the Union provoked a belligerent
reaction from the *Continental*. It regularly condemned the British
for their unfriendly attitude toward the cause of freedom. "We
all know, and so does every Englishman," it reminded, "that
the emancipation of the slave, to a greater or less degree, must
inevitably follow our success. When it comes to the pinch,"
Walker mocked, "the British will endure nothing for . . . abolition, but slide off at once towards aiding the inception of the
foulest, blackest, vilest slaveocracy ever instituted on earth!" [8]
At one point he publicly discussed renunciation of his free trade
commitments. Great Britain received the further warning that it
stop displaying in "a thousand ill-disguised ways an itching
impatience to aid the South," else the North decide to "manu-
facture for herself." Such an action would wreck all prospects
for a free trade alliance between the British workshop and the
American treasure trove of raw materials. "Drive us to manufacturing for ourselves," he promised, "and we shall manu-
facture for everyone." [9]

A belligerent nationalism increasingly agitated Walker's
writings. Provincialism, the foundation of a divisive sectionalism
could no longer be tolerated. Differences between the sections,
whether social, political, or economic, had to give way to the
democratic imperative of equality. Once achieved, a unity of
spirit would obliterate divisive sectionalism. The indictment
against slavery struck increasingly at its disruptive effects. The
institution had precipitated the war; its destruction would pref-

ace the emergence of a true nation. Upon the rock of black bondage a unique rebellion had been forged. "Other revolts," the
Continental contended, "have been against tyranny, but this is a
rebellion of slavery against freedom, of the few against the
many, of the bayonet against the ballot, of capital invested . . .
as a chattel against free labor and free men." The slightest in-
timation from Lincoln that he would accept reunion with slavery
brought a dismayed warning against an uneasy peace with the
peculiar institution again looming "up like a black mountain,
dividing us." Once again every political issue would be overshadowed by the exacerbating question; "will any measure, or
any construction of the constitution . . . weaken or strengthen
slavery?" [10]

Walker accepted the need for emancipation, but it did not
alter his view of the Negro. "The negro, altho to be regarded as
a man, and treated with humanity, belongs to an inferior race,
communion or association with whom is not desired by the
whites;" a view shared by most northerners. He clung to the
hope that a permanent separation of the races might still be
achieved. Massive deportation or deliberate segregation seemed
the only possible solution. With chilling precision, he challenged:

Those who regard the slavery question as the only, or the principal
difficulty, are greatly mistaken. The negro question is far deeper. It is
not slavery, as a mere political institution, that is sustained in the
South, but the greater question of the intermingling and equality of
races. . . . Abolition alone, touches then merely the surface of the
question. . . . In this respect there is a union of sentiment between
the masses, North and South, both opposing the introduction of free
blacks.[11]

One detects in the grim description Walker gave to the racial
question the fundamental difficulty contained in efforts to trace
a sense of moral urgency to the Civil War. Slavery as an abstract
thing had to end for it endangered the tranquillity of the white
man's world. Free soil, though directed against slavery, drew
its strength not from the abhorrence of the moral degradation

that bondage inflicted upon its victims, but from the selfish belief of free white yeomen that the new western territories belonged to them alone. Slavery was presented as an impediment to white fulfillment; few thought of it as the democratic dilemma in which Americans were obliged to erect a society founded on a color-blind equality. Walker, incapable of transcending his environment, accurately predicted the emancipated slave would exist as a black alien in a white world.[12]

The Emancipation Proclamation marked for Gilmore the fulfillment of the *Continental's* purpose. He proposed to end his participation in the magazine. Walker vigorously dissented for he felt that the growing fiscal difficulties of the Republic now superceded the slavery problem. "It is not the Rebel armies that can ever overthrow the Union," he contended, "it is the alarming increase of the public debt and expenditures, and the still more appalling depreciation of the national currency, that most imperil the great Republic." [13] Walker finally agreed to assume full responsibility for the magazine and use it to agitate for fiscal reforms. He had hardly started on his new course when Salmon P. Chase offered him a delicate fiscal mission to England and Western Europe. The prospect of being able to serve the Union in a field where he possessed an international reputation brought an immediate assent. Martha Cooke accepted with delight her brother's invitation to edit the magazine in his absence. The only stipulation was his injunction that she publish all articles he sent to her on the condition of America's finances.[14]

The mission gave Walker an opportunity to achieve a dual purpose. He meant first to discredit Confederate credit and, subsequently, to tap new sources of European capital with which to finance the war effort. Chase viewed the appointment as a chance to secure the services of a prominent war Democrat, further emphasizing the national dimensions of the conflict. Walker's eminence among conservative financiers who knew him as a staunch defender of hard money would help secure their support for Chase's greenback issuance.[15]

When Walker announced his decision to continue the *Continental,* devoting it to discussions of northern financial problems, he elicited a favorable response from both Chase and Greeley. The *Tribune* characterized as able and lucid a long letter in which the former Treasury chief set forth the basic fiscal situation. Greeley had also energetically agreed "that the restoration of the Union is more imperiled this day by our financial condition and prospects than by all the forces of Jeff. Davis, and that whoever shall assure the return of the Government to solvency will do more for the National cause than the General who shall win for it a decisive victory." [16]

As the inflation worsened during the winter of 1863, Walker strongly urged the use of paper currency as a temporary war measure. To secure the greenbacks and make them a hard currency, he would have them redeemable in bullion after the war ended. In a vigorous defense of Chase's Financial Report of 1862, he contended, "I would differ from him on such a question only on the clearest convictions, and then only upon the condition that I had a better plan as a substitute." The War, he believed, provided an obvious opportunity for the federal government to assert its supremacy over all money issuances. Such an assertion would complete the subordination of states' rights to federal authority.[17]

Chase had seen in the former Treasury chief's vigorous defense of his policies final evidence of Walker's absolute reliability. War Democrats did not frown upon the appointment of a fellow who unwaveringly insisted, "Let no man talk of a separation of the Union . . . let none speak now of peace or compromise with armed Treason." Walker provided those Democrats who feared the Republicans would emerge from the war as the saviours of the Union with an opportunity to remind the nation that Democrats too loved the Union. And he had wide influence in official Washington. All these made his appointment to the delicate mission of undermining Confederate credit abroad expedient.[18]

Not overlooked in the final choice was the wide circle of friends Walker possessed in Parliament, the Cabinet, and among British intellectuals. Though he had been outspokenly critical of British policy toward the North, privately he urged a cautious foreign policy toward Great Britain. He shrewdly recognized the political potency of twisting the lion's tail when rallying Anglophobic northerners to the Union cause. He also realized that the North would risk total disaster to invite a war with Britain while attempting to subdue the South.[19] Furthermore, his strongly voiced sentiments on the British position had not been wholly overlooked in London. Numerous rising politicians of the Bright school openly argued the northern case. With such prospects, Walker, after a suitable delay, "concluded that it is my duty to go, & to receive nothing but my actual expenses." His willingness to donate his services may well have resulted from the Supreme Court's favorable decision in the New Almaden Mine case. The decision paved the way for Walker to sell his claim for a reputed $500,000.[20]

No sooner had he accepted the mission than he pressured Chase into helping prepare the groundwork for his forthcoming campaign against southern credit by persuading Lincoln to issue a proclamation declaring that all Confederate bonds were "*null & void*, the acts of *rebels & traitors*, and that they will *never* be recognized or paid by the U[nited] States." Walker had given the first evidence that he would do anything to undermine Rebel finances. Once abroad, in full command, he would treat London to a campaign that would titillate the staid old city.[21]

Benjamin Moran, first Secretary to the American legation in London, recorded on April 20, 1863, "The Hon. Robert J. Walker has been here this morning. He is a very small person, not being more than five feet, three inches high; but he has a good head and a well cultivated mind. He is one of the best talkers I ever knew." But he neatly balanced his compliments with a few less favorable observations. "He is an odd-looking fellow about 60 years of age," Moran noted, "is most slovenly in his dress, has thin hair which has been dyed almost black, and is evidently very proud of himself." The first Secretary, who scarcely needed instruction about European attitudes, listened impatiently as the new agent insisted, "there was a good feeling towards us in Ireland," although "the French and English were [for] secession." [22] Charles Francis Adams, the Northern Minister, courteously arranged a large breakfast party for the following morning in order to reunite Walker and several of his British friends, among them Cobden and Bright. The breakfast left Adams musing, "this mission is growing more and more difficult." The vivid energy of the wayward southerner annoyed the dour New Englander. Privately, Adams confessed his amusement at finding Walker "changed into a thorough anti-slavery man, determined upon emancipation as the only condition of pacification." [23] Within a short time, he had ample reason to wonder whether the government had not sent him human proof of perpetual motion.

In the ensuing days Walker busily renewed his friendships with numerous English politicians he had known during his earlier trip to England. Late in April he attended the House of Commons and heard with gratification Cobden attacking "the pretended neutrality of England in the war . . . the shameless violations of the law, both municipal and international, in building pirate ships here and arming them for the rebels." The forceful language of Cobden exhilarated Walker. The insulting speech of a Mr. Horsman which followed, pointedly contrasting Confederate gentility and Yankee coarseness, left Walker puzzling how a gentleman could lie so deliberately. Moran who had "witnessed too many of such painful exhibitions in the British Parliament . . . to be vexed by them" explained sardonically, "it was a part of an English gentleman's business to lie when it suited him." [24]

Cobden confirmed Walker's expectation that the North could do substantial damage to southern propaganda by defining with exactitude the position "in which creditors would be placed in case of war." So long as the hint of war between Britain and the North remained, "the partisans of the South in this country in raising the cry of war have a cunning eye," the British liberal observed, "on the effect which they know it will have on the value of U.S. Securities." Walker promptly conveyed this intelligence to his Washington chief. Concurrently, the Aspinwall and Forbes mission to raise loans in the London money market actively pursued its mission. Chase had been careful to avoid any conflict of purpose between the two missions. Aspinwall and Forbes understood that the Walker mission had as its primary purpose the task of acquainting "European capitalists with the actual circumstances and resources of our country." Though Aspinwall and Forbes had full information about the purposes of the Walker mission, the reverse was not true. He remained ignorant of the temporary loan being negotiated with Baring Brothers, and for the time restricted his activities to those of a propagandist.[25]

To achieve his purpose Walker conducted a careful examination of British public opinion. The working classes he estimated correctly "are all for us & most enthusiastically, mainly on slavery, & a just appreciation of their identification with us on the great question of popular rights." On this stand the workers were joined by the middle class. Opposition to the northern cause existed only in the governing classes and in Parliament where Walker asserted a majority "are against us." All signs of bellicosity toward England disappeared when the propagandist admitted that no more eloquent reason for avoiding war with Britain existed than in his slogan, "Peace and survival; war and destruction." One war, already gigantic in its scope, had tempered Yankee aggressiveness. Another would be disastrous.[26]

The near universal rejection of slavery among all segments of the British population convinced Walker that the North ought to avoid raising doubts about its intention to emancipate the Negro. Once doubts about northern sincerity had been overcome, "England," he asserted, "cannot go to war with us—it would produce a revolution." As proof of northern honesty, he urged a multiplication of black regiments and black sailors. The induction of the Negro into the armed forces, added to large scale emancipation, promised "next to victories to help us most." [27]

Throughout the month of May, Walker remained preoccupied with the preparation of pamphlets intended to lower southern credit prospects while increasing those of the North. Emancipation, together with southern repudiation of past state debts, gave the Union an unbeatable propaganda. "Slavery takes the philanthropic, the sentimental, & the religious classes, & the *people*," he observed, "but repudiation touches the pocket nerve, & sweeps away the lenders of money." [28] Two separate themes emerged in the pamphlets. One emphasized the retarding influence of slavery upon the development of American wealth. The other concentrated upon the poor credit reputation of the South. It developed, in particular, the role Jefferson Davis had played as a defender of Mississippi's bond repudiation. It slyly permitted the words of the Confederate President to convey the message intended. The sceptre of defaulted Union and Planters' Bank bonds rose to plague a beleaguered South.[29]

As he composed his pamphlets, Walker consulted with Cobden and Bright who convinced him that a northern triumph would hasten the British along the path to democracy. "So soon as England is *thoroughly convinced* that the triumph of the Union cause will extinguish slavery in our country," he prophesied, "the popular feeling will become so strong here, that the British government must studiously avoid a war with us." Then he continued, "The success of Bright & Cobden's party would be immediate—then would follow in quick succession, the abolition of church rates, of the remaining rotten boroughs, of the law of primogeniture, a great extension of the suffrage, accompanied by free schools, & the vote by ballot." [30] These dramatic events hinged upon "victories in the Field." Repeatedly Walker returned to the idea that a battle for British democracy would be won on the riptide of Union victory.[31]

As friendship with Britain buoyed his hopes, open enmity came to permeate his view of France. He was convinced Louis Napoleon understood only the deterent of cold steel, and waited vulturelike to swoop down upon a Union which flagged in its determination. Once reunion had been successfully imposed, the North could not avoid a war with the French in Mexico. Walker feared that a bellicose Napoleon, seeking to avoid this consequence, might precipitate overt action on behalf of the Confederacy. Such a development might encourage the prosoutherners in Great Britain to attempt a forced peace. To forestall this grim result, only a constant emphasis upon the victories and vast war potential of the North would deter the Gallic Hotspurs.[32] In the midst of these efforts came the grim news of Lee's invasion of Pennsylvania. Though Walker regretted "any suffering by the people of my native state," he was convinced that "this invasion will silence the voice of treason, & unite the people in maintaining the Union." No matter what was the result in the East, however, he believed the true triumph of the Union had been insured by the rapid advance of the northern armies through the Mississippi Valley. The western farm boys not only emancipated millions of slaves but also freed millions of depressed southern white yeomen. The war often left him deeply uneasy for the safety of his son, Duncan, a Union captain serving in the infantry outside Port Hudson, Louisiana. Upon this village he fastened his most intimate concern, for not only his country but his flesh was involved.[33]

As the summer turned to autumn, Chase voiced increasing disappointment at the delay in issuing the first pamphlet. Beset with a rocketing inflation, the dismayed Treasury chief communicated his conviction that "a steady demand in the New York market for the foreign account of even $20,000 a day will be worth a million to us in the course of the year, in the enhance-

ment of the value of our bonds, in the cheapness of exchange &
in the facilitation of loans at home, which will enable us to pay
promptly for munitions, supplies, & troops." [34] But Chase also
insisted upon keeping foreign credits at a minimum. Fully con-
scious of increasing northern dependence upon foreign bullion,
he nevertheless feared lest too heavy a reliance upon foreign
credit undermine federal finances should foreign investors suddenly contract their purchases. The Secretary of the Treasury had
repeatedly stressed the psychological boon a ready access to
foreign capital had as an inducement for home investors to ab-
sorb federal bonds. Walker who had conservatively administered
the Mexican bond issuances proudly pronounced the Chase policies a confirmation of his earlier wisdom. [35]

Publication of the first pamphlet revealed a stinging indictment of Jefferson Davis. It questioned whether a man who had
publicly defended a state's repudiation of bonds could resist
repeating his performance if the postwar fiscal condition of a
victorious Confederacy were to encourage repudiation. Walker
indicted the southern chief executive as the living symbol of
those "who insist upon forced labor, and repudiate all compensation to the toiling millions of slaves—who repudiate, among
slaves, the marital and parental relation . . . who forbid emancipation—who make it a crime to teach slaves to read or write—
[and] who keep open the interstate slave trade more horrible
than the African, making Virginia a human stock farm." The
free wheeling attack united appeals both to moral sensibility and
to the pocketbook. Throughout, Walker carefully avoided reference to his own defense of repudiation when he had courted the
favor of the Mississippi electorate. [36] The repudiation pamphlet
preceded a series of "Letters on the Finances and Resources of
the United States" published in the autumn. These glowingly
described the material wealth, both real and potential, of the
young republic. With bland self-assurance, he associated the national bounty with an Almighty whose sole preoccupation was his
American children. His insistence upon the geometric progres-

sion of American wealth led him to conclude that by the beginning of the twentieth century America would revel in a national wealth that approached four hundred and twenty-five billion dollars. The letters ached with expectations.[37]

The publication of the pamphlets left speechless the large "corps of Confederate writers in London & Paris." At least so reported the ebullient author, who assured Chase their failure to give a suitable answer resulted from his incontrovertible facts. Angry denunciations and friendly approvals flooded his mail. Confederate sympathizers deluged Walker "with abusive & menacing letters" similar to those he had received during the Kansas imbroglio. The upper echelons of the British government, however, expressed considerable interest in the arguments of the pamphlets. Gladstone, then Chancellor of the Exchequer, sent a special invitation requesting an interview with the pamphleteer. The meeting impressed Walker with the Britisher's conversational powers. These he described as "surpassing those of anyone I ever met except the great Historian [Macaulay]." Superlatives had always come easily to the American. A rushing enthusiasm assigned to Gladstone "more varied information, & greater intellect, than any man now living except perhaps, that miracle of acknowledged genius, Lord Brougham." [38]

News that Lee's invasion of Pennsylvania had been repulsed sent soaring the flagging spirits of the northern community residing in England. Walker sputtered his joy when further news reached him of the fall of Vicksburg and Port Hudson, doubly so, since his beloved Duncan had been removed from immediate danger. Victory simplified the task of wrecking southern credit. Confederate bonds declined some twenty percent once news reached London of the crushing defeats of July 3 and 4, 1863. Rumors circulated in London that several prosouthern bankers had sustained heavy losses. The insignificance of his own contributions reduced Chase's agent to unusual humility. "I think my 2nd letter will accelerate its [Southern credit] descent," he wrote, "but it is our military & financial success, that has mainly caused the decline." When he received information about efforts among some conservative members of Congress to revoke the Emancipation Proclamation in the hope that this act, added to the defeats at Gettysburg and Vicksburg, would persuade the Confederates to end the War and rejoin the Union, he warned that such a course "would ruin the cause here." Furthermore, "the proclamation was legal," so far as anyone could determine. "As such it did emancipate the slaves & they are *now free.*" "How," he asked, "can Mr. Lincoln reinslave them? The past is irrevocable, even by the Almighty Power. Besides," he added almost as an afterthought, "it would be a breach of faith to the slaves." [39]

Prominence attracts to it not only the highly placed personage but also those of questionable repute. As Walker cemented his relations with prominent politicians, he also made the acquaintance of a free lance journalist of vague background named Pliny Miles. The two men soon became fast friends. The incongruity of the relationship moved Moran to observe, "This connection is astonishing to me, for Miles is as complete a Yahoo as ever lived, and totally unfit for companionship with Mr. Walker." [40] Astonishment gave way to total confusion when he realized that Miles had appealed to the bizarre in Walker's nature. The tiny man, who remembered with pride that during his term as Treasury chief he made an experimental descent into Chesapeake Bay in a primitive submarine, readily acceded to a suggestion that he make a balloon ascent as a propaganda stunt. [41]

Miles had introduced Walker to Henry Coxwell whom the fiscal agent subsequently characterized as "the celebrated British aeronaut." Coxwell had experimented extensively with balloons and needed only to *suggest* an ascent to interest Walker. The bewildered American embassy marvelled at a "daring" which "surpasses . . . common sense." His decision to take along Miles did not help lessen the embassy's suspicion that Walker had lost his mind. But the enterprise's unfavorable reception hardly deterred the thoroughly converted air-enthusiast from his heavenly explorations. If anything, it increased his contempt for that conservative timidity which feared the unknown. Though the presence of Miles had raised eyebrows, none could object to Walker's personal guest, "Mr. Glasher, the eminent Meteorologist of the Greenwich Observatory."

Chase read the startling account of his agent's triumphal "celestial journey." Unsuppressed delight suffused Walker's description of the forty mile journey over London at heights which varied "from a few hundred feet to more than two miles." From his skyborne perch Walker had beheld with ever increasing awe "The scenery of the Earth & of the Heavens, the views of the works of God & Man, of the clouds sweeping below us, especially of the Sunset." All "were beyond description grand & sublime." He had descended from the heavens certain of the "omnipresence & omnipotence of God." [42] Lest his Chief dismiss the trip as useless, he sought to justify it in practical terms. Despite his conviction "that an aerial trip with Mr. Coxwell is safer than a voyage by steam across the Atlantic," he realized that "the world, & many friends, & my family think otherwise." Therefore, he had made the trip only "for a good purpose." Nowhere is his penchant for the novel more explicitly expressed than in his concluding proposal to Chase; and few writers of science fiction have ever exceeded Walker in his appalling insight into the future of war as he wrote:

It occurred to me that besides the use of the balloon for military reconnaissance, it might be made a most potent engine in war, for the destruction of *ships, cities, forts, & armies* . . . I beg you . . . to call the attention of the President & of the Secretary of War & Navy to this subject . . . Small pilot balloons without an aeronaut could ascertain the current of air, & how . . . balloons sent up *at night in rapid succession* . . . could be made to carry shells . . . , also Greek fire or other more terrible chemical compounds to burst in & destroy any place.[43]

Though partially invalided as the result of a severe attack of lung hemorrhages,[44] Walker did not neglect propaganda; how-

ever he shifted its approach during the fall of 1863. The War had
passed from one of mobilization for victory to one of steady
attrition that appalled the world. On a thousand scattered fields,
in gloomy forests, in soggy swamps and marshes, upon the
treacherous slopes of mountains, tens of thousands died. The
gentleman and his code of chivalry passed; the citizen soldier
and grim revenge arrived. Walker who had once thought of the
abolition of slavery as the sacrifice to be exacted from a defeated
South now demanded a conspicuous display of loyalty from the
wayward southerner in order to justify his restoration to full
citizenship. But he protested against vindictiveness once loyalty
had been demonstrated.[45]

As inflation at home worsened during the winter of 1864,
Chase called upon Walker to locate new supplies of foreign
bullion with which to replenish depleted northern coffers.
Walker sprang at the new chance to do service and prepared to
scour the continent. As he sent out preliminary feelers to European bankers, he painted for them a vivid portrait of an America
bursting with abundance—once victory for the Union had been
assured. He also predicted final resolution of the long struggle
between proponents of states rights and federal supremacy. No
matter what else resulted, he now believed, the future of America
would always be "determined by the will of Federal authorities."
Secure in that conviction he worked to meet the fiscal needs of
the struggling republic.[46]

16. The Search

PROPAGANDA HAS RARELY had a more proficient agent than Walker. He used distortion of fact, avoidance of precise truth, indeed, made an art of the half truth, and never scorned novel ways to attract maximum attention. As he floated above London in his balloon, marvelling at the beauties made by man and God, he had also occupied himself with the prosaic task of dumping upon startled Londoners large quantities of leaflets denouncing Jefferson Davis and the Confederacy. The result had been to focus attention upon both pamphlets and author. One hardly knew which pleased him more. Just as the sensation of his air flight began to fade, he launched into a dispute with the aggressively prosouthern ambassador from Vienna. The controversy culminated when Walker rode through the streets of London "behind six milk-white horses in an equipage more glorious than that of the Austrian Ambassador to show the British and the contemptuous Austrian that the 'rail-splitter' had money." [1] Charles Francis Adams, presiding at the American Legation, suffered from the publicity, but Walker refused to desist. Everyone conceded he had made an obvious if unseemly impression.

The reserved New Englander, acutely mistrusting the behavior of his bumptious agent, agonized as Walker persisted in intruding upon diplomatic negotiations. After considering the festering issue of the ironclads being constructed at British yards for the Confederacy, Walker reached the obvious conclusion that further aggravation of the issue blocked friendly relations between the North and Great Britain. Several efforts by Adams to obtain an injunction against continued construction brought adverse decisions in the British courts. When one court found there could be no legal bar to construction, so long as the ironclads remained unarmed, several friendly British officials proposed that the North station war ships off the "marine league" to capture the unarmed ironclads as they left the safety of the harbor. Walker promptly pressed the administration to employ the solution offered.[2]

At every opportunity he warned of the threat that Louis Napoleon posed to both the United States and Great Britain. Blood ties united the two great Anglo-Saxon powers; together they must prevent French intervention in Mexico. "Juarez is fighting our battles" became his theme. Napoleon III would "expunge the Reformation & carry us back to the dark ages." Neither of the English speaking powers could permit "Catholic Monarchies" to dominate the hemisphere "South of the United States." Once the United States had been dismembered, Britain would learn that nothing could halt the rapacious appetites of the French tyrant. Though claiming he abhorred "a church war" and detested "religious intolerance," Walker declared "I must resist the overthrow of liberty & my country." The stake, he argued, was no less for England.[3]

Cassius Clay, writing to Walker from his ministry at St. Petersburg, concurred fully with his friend's suspicions of Napoleon. At the behest of the fiscal agent, Clay had distributed Walker's pamphlet on repudiation among influential Russians and members of the diplomatic colony. He had, however, neglected to supply any to the French mission, "who," he concluded, "may now be considered our avowed enemy." With a familiar belligerence, Clay insisted, "we ought to swear and wage against him [Napoleon III] an eternal war." Though Britain had not fully understood, as yet, her own best interest, she ultimately would have to join the United States "to 'move the boots' of a certain gentleman—whose stride is by no means Jacksonian!" Both Clay and Walker agreed that Britain ought not help the

French "set up a *Catholic reactionary* Poland." Instead, they gave common subscription to Clay's conclusion:

The Russians are our friends—tolerant in religion, and progressive in civil administration: We know what Catholicism is, and that we have nothing in common with it. You see they have crowded out the *democratic* party from any control in the revolution (then racking Poland.) So I say once more what folly our press is guilty of in denouncing our liberal friend, the Emperor [Alexander II], for the sake of our *conservative enemy*, the New Poland.[4]

The warmth of the friendship between Clay and Walker had grown since they first met crossing the Atlantic in the spring of 1863. Between the two, there buzzed the idea that a friendly Russia might wish to part with Alaska. Already Walker had decided to visit the Slavic Empire sometime in the coming year.

When Lincoln designated November 26, 1863, as Thanksgiving Day, Walker promptly arranged a dinner for the Americans in residence at St. James Hall. Some of those present thought it unusual to have a former Senator from Mississippi stand in silent prayer as a former slave delivered benediction. In a militant speech, the "loyal Southerner," as he had chosen to have himself introduced, announced "Our cause is that of humanity, of civilization, of Christianity." America remained "the best, the brightest, the last experiment of self-government." And, in a moment of extraordinary foresight, he declared the capture of "Chattanooga, the climax that preceded northern victory. From Chattanooga, which may be regarded as the great geographical central point of the rebellion, the armies of the Republic will march through the heart of Georgia, and join our troops upon the sea-board of that State, and thus terminate the rebellion." Hardly anyone who heartily applauded Walker's optimism realized that they had heard a soon-to-be fulfilled prophecy.[5]

In response to an appeal by Chase, and much to Adams's relief, Walker hurried to the Continent in a bid to unloosen con-

tinental purse strings. His success exceeded his wildest expectations. The stolid German and Swiss burgers, captivated by the
vision of abundance painted in his statistical pamphlets, poured
more than one hundred and fifty millions in bullion into federal
securities. Since continental investors relied upon their bankers
for advice, the energetic agent cultivated the "favorable opinion
. . . of Bankers," who were able to direct a flood of gold into
the northern war effort. The subsequent outpouring of assistance
provoked tears from the peripatetic patriot. Tenderly he would
reminisce that in the darkest moments of 1864, the Dutch, German, and Swiss investor had retained a buoyant optimism, even
as he had approached despair over the Union.[6]

One defect of the loans floated among the Rhinelanders ultimately led to unfortunate repercussions. The "5–20 bonds"
lacked a specific guarantee for their redemption in gold. When
suggestions were made that these bonds be subjected to a "paper
redemption," Walker protested on behalf of the continental
investor, who had gambled on a northern victory, and had "not
understood that we reserved the right to extinguish bonds on
which six percent interest in gold was distinctly promised and
regularly paid, by giving dollar for dollar in our own naked
promises, drawing no interest, redeemable never, and only made
to be broken." Appalled, Walker was unable to believe his country would deliberately repudiate an implied obligation to redeem bonds in the same medium in which they were purchased.
He pleaded lest the nation should forget when, despite opposition
to the North by the French and English moneyed and governing
classes, "the people of the continent and especially of Germany,
Holland and Switzerland came to our rescue." "That their faith
in us and in republican institutions, in the darkest hour, now
rebounds in their favor," the confirmed bullionist protested, "in
no way detracts from the value of their services."[7]

Specie redemption for specie debt became his watchword.
Since the European believed the whole of American currency
had a bond backing, Walker feared "to repudiate [a bullion

redemption] would destroy the currency." Nor could the United
States, a debtor nation, ignore the importance of foreign capital
investment in the exploitation of its national resources. "Strange
that we, a country with a large debt," he commented, "have not
fully realized the immense importance of our national credit."
To those who thought there existed a short cut to national solvency, he delivered the pungent reminder, "National credit is a
part of the national wealth, especially with a nation in debt, or
engaged in war, and, in maintaining the credit of the nation, we
not only sustain its honor, but we diminish the interest upon its
public debt, with a corresponding decrease of taxation." The
conservative financier showed cautiousness when he wrote,
"Whilst contraction . . . is death by a slow and lingering process, expansion of a depreciated paper is . . . financial suicide." [8]

Caution permeated his thinking about national finances. One
drew upon foreign loans only when compelled by dire necessity.
The creation of an unbacked paper currency "deranges all business by constant fluctuations in prices, renders all calculations
unreliable, and all pursuits uncertain." Although a large portion of the Democracy contemplated explorations in paper currency, the old Jacksonian preached anew, "each nation is but a
part of the great community of States, united by ties of commerce, business and interchange." If this be understood, "how
can we," he asked, "who are dealing with depreciated paper,
expect to compete successfully with those countries whose money
is gold?" The Democracy already moved toward the great battle
of the currency which would fragment it in 1896. There is no
doubt that had Walker been alive as Bryan flung down the gaunt-
let, he would have joined the "goldbugs." [9]

As the first echoes of the currency fight reverberated, other
battles loomed on the horizon. As the War exacted its savage
conclusion, a sick and worn Walker returned home after a hectic
tour of Europe. Briefly, he emerged as the prospective negotiator
of a peaceful conclusion to the War. When he appeared in Mon-

treal, some feared he had entered into secret talks with Confederate agents; others thought he sought to purchase Canada for one hundred million dollars. Actually, he had conducted fruitless conversations with the Confederate adventurer, George N. Sanders. At no point did he obtain official support. Seward specifically disavowed all knowledge of his activities. Unkind observers described him as a cantankerous old man bent upon reminding the indifferent world of his continued capacity for mischief.[10]

The old man wearily protested no other intention than to spare his land further bloodshed. Would America not remember how he had ruined "the second confederate loan of $75,000,000," thereby sparing the North "an immense destruction of property, the burning of many of our cities, . . . probably terminating in a war with France and England?" Could they not appreciate that "this was in part my humble contribution in aid of our Country?" Amidst the indifference of a people whose suffering had drained them of gratitude, no one listened to his apology: "It was all I could do, but it cannot be compared with the arduous labors of the President and Cabinet, nor with the services of those who risked their lives or shed their blood upon the battlefields of their country." America had become to him a strange and hostile place. She no longer recalled with reverence the men who had led her blindly into a Walpurgis Night. Walker had become a living artifact of a dead time. Four years more of life remained to him; they gave him not peace but trial, not hope but the humiliation of despair.[11]

Debt, endless irredeemable debt, had always plagued his family. Jonathan had died encumbered and now his sole surviving son faced the same prospect. For a brief time during the war, the successful liquidation of the New Almaden claim had given him an unusual affluence. But abroad his patriotism had permitted him to receive compensation only for the direct expenses of his mission; he had met his personal needs from his own resources. For almost two years he had drawn upon capital to support his family and the *Continental Monthly*. Now the ceaseless toil exacted its toll; a rapidly deteriorating health had already sent him on a wild pursuit of the illusive fountain of youth. The long journey home had taken him through the Riviera, Italy, Greece, Egypt, Syria, Turkey, Russia, Germany, and France. When puzzled requests for his whereabouts reached the London Embassy, Charles Francis Adams confessed that he knew only that "Mr. Walker is somewhere on the Continent." Sickness and debt seemed permanently attached to the old man.[12]

With the restoration of peace came a final reckoning. W. W. Corcoran whose prosouthern sympathies had sent him into temporary exile in France returned to settle accounts. Due him from Walker was more than $12,000. But there existed judgments against the property of the aging Democrat that increased the accumulated debt to more than $35,000. Against these debts, Walker held some $175,000 in real estate and stocks. Superficially, the books balanced in his favor, but so much of the property had been tied up in litigation, that only $75,000 possessed a clear title. The bulk of this free property consisted of his beloved home *Woodley* and its furnishings. On April 27th, 1867, all Washington read that a public sale of his property had been scheduled to meet a judgment of $15,000. An anguished Walker pleaded with Corcoran to spare him this ultimate humiliation. The old banker, moved by friendship, agreed to consolidate the indebtedness of his old crony and allow Walker to retire it in the most convenient manner possible. As security, the once proud Democrat surrendered to Corcoran two hundred shares of Illinois and Wisconsin Land stock, nominally valued at $20,000; and sixteen shares of Memphis and Charleston Railroad stock valued at $400. The remainder of the security consisted of five insurance policies valued at $23,500. But consolidation of a debt is not repayment; Walker had now to earn enough money to meet his obligations.[13]

His renown as a lawyer settled him upon a resumption of

his law practice. Though he had denounced the folly of secession, he treated the radical Republican program of reconstruction as even more abhorrent. President Johnson received his unreserved support. As a delegate at large to the 1866 National Union Convention in Philadelphia, he made a conspicuous effort to revive his old southern friendships. His name and that of his son Duncan appeared on a petition to Johnson for the release of Jefferson Davis. It was hardly surprising, therefore, that Mississippi should turn to him to argue its case against the Reconstruction Act of 1867. Before the Supreme Court he applied "for leave to file an injunction against Andrew Johnson, preventing him from enforcing the Reconstruction Acts of 1867." In conjunction with two other lawyers, he argued that the President, "the creature of the Constitution," is not exempt from the "process of the court whose duty it is to guard it [the Constitution] against abuses, because he is the chief executive . . . of the government." Toward the congressional concept of reconstruction, he directed withering scorn. The congressional radicals by depriving the southerners "of their rights and privileges as American citizens," had violated the Constitution they had been pledged to uphold. Unless this deprivation ceased, he argued, "So far as constitutional liberty is concerned, they might as well be living under a Czar or a Sultan upon the banks of the Bosporus or the Neva, as in this free country." The fundamental guarantees of life, liberty, and property, he charged, had the air of a vast mockery. Eloquence was exerted in full, but the Court chose to avoid an open dispute with a belligerent Congress by denying the brief.[14]

Next he joined with Jeremiah Black to argue the case of Georgia against the Reconstruction Acts. With exact logic, he challenged the ambiguity of a position which asserted that secession had been originally impossible, but which now enacted laws as if secession had in fact occurred. Walker insisted the court needed to clarify a confused issue. Again the Justices retreated, asserting that they possessed no jurisdiction. Now convinced that Congress could not be halted, he advised the South to accept the congressional program as the inescapable price of defeat.[15]

A long political career had taught him to estimate accurately political currents. The Johnson administration could scarcely hope to divert the uncompromising determination of its congressional opponents. The Whig suspicion of a strong executive and the Jacksonian concept of a powerful national executive lay at the base of the emerging dispute. The Republicans had borne with Lincoln; the War had left them little alternative. They did not expect to endure Johnson whom they suspected of working to restore a Democratic congressional majority. Appeals to war bitterness and the desire of fellow Republicans to preserve their party had helped the radicals box an inept Johnson into utter helplessness. Walker understood the Republican necessity which Horace Greeley had expressed with such painful accuracy when he wrote:

The truth is, there *is* but one question of moment remaining to be settled; and that is, Manhood Suffrage. Enfranchise the Blacks, and further rebellions at the South are impossible; and we can have a great National party, which can hopefully contest nearly every State in the Union; while if we reconstruct on the basis of the . . . Blacks remain [ing] underfoot, the Vallandigham Democracy will have nearly every one of the 15 ex-Slave States as fixed capital to begin with.[16]

The South and the Democracy had no alternative but to endure until the ballot box rendered an adverse decision to their antagonists.

Once again family and indebtedness preoccupied Walker's attention. An unsettling fear gripped him as his health rapidly deteriorated: what would happen to his widow and family if he were to die before the debt had been retired? When he received news that his eldest daughter Mary had been afflicted with tuberculosis, and that death claimed the most precious of his grandchildren, he wondered if God had chosen to submit him to the tests of Job. Undaunted, he did not protest, but trusted that reward would follow resignation. Hardly able to appear before court, he increasingly settled for rendering advice privately. It was in this capacity that he entered into his last moment of notoriety.[17]

The Russian and Danish governments had both indicated an eagerness to dispense with their New World real estate. They had first to persuade Congress to appropriate the necessary funds for any purchase that might be negotiated. Walker, who had been characterized as "territory mad," seemed to Baron de Stoeckl, the Russian ambassador to the United States, the perfect lobbyist to persuade Congress to purchase Alaska. He could hardly have chosen better. Walker had envisioned such a purchase ever since he had labored to convince Polk to add the northern territory to the American domain. Disciplining his waning energies, the incorrigible expansionist set to work button-holing numberless congressmen. Vicious rumors circulated in Washington of his efforts to convince uncertain members with large bribes, and after his death, outright accusations charging extensive corruption were made against him.[18]

Walker admitted before a congressional committee that de Stoeckl had paid him $26,000, of which $5,000 had gone to his associate counsel, Frederick P. Stanton. This sum had been paid, he claimed, in return for legal services. He mentioned that John Forney, editor of the Washington *Chronicle*, had refused $3,000 in gold as a reward for services, which had consisted of using his journal to propagandize the purchase. Walker was enthralled by such dispassionate honesty, or so he led the committee to understand. He never admitted that he knew Forney had received a payment of $30,000 in gold from de Stoeckl to help push the appropriation bill paying for the purchase of Alaska through the House of Representatives. In addition, N. P. Banks, the Chairman of the Committee on Foreign Affairs, received $8,000, while Thaddeus Stevens had been compensated with $10,000. All payments had come directly from de Stoeckl.[19]

Yet, despite the large payments that were supposedly made

to Walker, a strange fact remains: his financial condition showed no evident improvement; in fact, it worsened. Obviously, a payment of $21,000 ought to have provided some relief. The only reasonable explanation is that Walker had used his payment to reward other interested participants. This becomes even more evident if the payment to Stanton is considered. As associate counsel and Walker's law partner, it is implausible that he should have received a substantially smaller sum. A more likely explanation is that both had received equal payments of $5,000 and had used most of the remaining $16,000 to persuade certain congressmen of the measure's import. There is the added factor that Walker hardly needed to be bribed to support expansion. His whole life had been dedicated to the extension of American dominion over the Western Hemisphere. Cassius Clay remembered vividly in later years the enthusiasm with which Walker had discussed the prospect of the purchase of Russian America in 1863. It is not unlikely that the real reward for the old expansionist had been a further step toward fulfillment of America's destiny.[20]

Once launched upon agitation for further expansion, Walker's appetite seemed without end. He reasoned that if the Danes were willing to dispense with their West Indian real estate, they would be willing to sell their northern possessions of Greenland and Iceland. He wrote a pamphlet arguing for the purchase of both Alaska and the Virgin Islands as "adhering to my life-long principles." Since the pamphlet appeared in its original form only in the Washington *Chronicle,* the suspicion arose that the firm of Walker and Forney was exploring the money-making possibilities of Danish diplomacy. Again it is uncertain whether continental expansion or personal profit dominated his thoughts. Seward received assurances from Walker that he intended to print an "immense issue" of his pamphlet advocating the purchase of the Virgin Islands "at my own expense." There is something irrational about a man with Walker's straitened finances expending money on such an agitation. Since nothing exists to contradict his assertion, one can only assume that Mr. Walker could not control himself when an opportunity for territorial expansion existed.[21]

Though his expansionist proclivity predisposed him to support territorial purchases, there also existed a compelling political reason behind Walker's energetic pursuit of new territory. The Democratic party desperately needed to find an issue independent of the late war. He suggested, therefore, that the Democracy meet the Radical Republican cry for vengeance against the South with the lure of manifest destiny. Intent upon rallying the Democrats in Congress behind expansion, he wrote Seward:

I have done all I can here for Alaska—Now I go to New York. The *Tribune* will come out for Alaska. I think & I wish the democracy to put it on their banner—this would rally the Democratic members—& alarm the Rads. Now, excuse me for saying that in a matter so *vital*, of such *transcendent* importance to the country, should not you & the *President* exert yourself with every Democratic member by fair argument to support the appropriation. . . . Immortal as will be the vetos of the President, sublime as was his conduct during the impeachment— Yet, the great *act* of his administration, will be the acquisition of Alaska. The theatre of our greatest triumph is to be the Pacific where we will soon have no formidable European rivals—The consequences are *ultimately*, the political and commercial control of the world.[22]

The future of the Democratic party, he thought, depended upon its ability to identify itself with the glorious future rather than with the painful past. Therefore, pressure for the purchase of Alaska, the Virgin Islands, Nova Scotia, Greenland, Iceland, and British America aimed to avert the destruction of a party irretrievably identified with the unsettled South as much as it intended to fulfill manifest destiny.

While seeking an issue to reverse the trend toward Radical Republican ascendancy, Walker dispensed shrewd political advice to President Johnson. Nothing disturbed supporters of the President more than his inept use of patronage. The elder statesman pleaded with Johnson to balance his appointments between Democrats and "Johnson Republicans." As for an adequate political issue, he pressed upon the President "a review of the great issue—*Union or no Union—constitution or no constitution.*" [23] Nor did he hesitate to advance suggestions on how best to challenge radical Reconstruction legislation. If the Supreme Court would not meet the challenge, then a strong executive must provide the necessary leadership. Even as he had sought to force the Supreme Court to act, Walker urged the struggling President to pursue a course which would place him in unwavering opposition to the congressional Reconstruction legislation but, which would, at the same time, commit him to a strict enforcement of the legislation should it pass over his veto. To avoid further complicating the plight of the South and to prevent further congressional excesses, he urged Johnson "to advise the South to submit, 1st, Because *delay* will certainly make their case worse. 2nd, Because such delay may ruin the country, and imperil the cause of civil liberty throughout the world—." This latter threat led Walker to fear that "the country is in far greater danger than it ever was during the war—." [24]

Even as the Civil War raged, the old Jacksonian had foreseen that a major political reorientation must inevitably follow the War. His instinctive commitment to moderation led him to advocate a new Democracy, constructed upon a coalition of conservative Republicans and Democrats. The fracturing issue of free soil, now resolved, could no longer prevent this natural union. When the Union ticket of Lincoln and Johnson had been nominated in 1864, he had advocated support of it by fellow Democrats. It would transform the War's effort from one of a single party to one of a united nation. Time and again he claimed that the Democrats had supported the Union as loyally as any Republican. Only when Lincoln suspended civil liberties did he vigorously dissent. After the War he had joined other prominent Democrats in an effort to sponsor a meeting of Union soldiers and sailors "who are opposed to radicalism." Throughout his arguments, there appeared an appeal to an old fashioned Jacksonian sentimental nationalism.[25]

Failure to check radical excesses in Congress convinced Walker that only a successful appeal to the ballot box would assure a reversal of the radical trend. As the 1868 Democratic convention met, an invalid Walker, unable to participate, insisted upon making his sentiment known. "If Hancock cannot be nominated, I go next for Johnson," he wrote. "I go for Hancock, 1st, because our volunteer soldiers during the war numbered 2,700,000 or more than one half the vote of the North at present." Sagaciously, he added, "We must divide this vote or we are lost." Since Hancock alone could hope to divide the veterans, the ailing politician concluded, "I therefore go for him." However, if the General could not carry the Convention, then Walker would "go for Johnson, because his anti-rebel views are clear, and all the other candidates named are more or less implicated with the Peace Party." [26]

The Peace party carried the day. Neither Hancock nor Johnson was chosen. Horatio Seymour, whose suspect loyalties had aggravated Walker during the War years, picked up the Democratic banner and, as Walker predicted, carried it to defeat. But his commitment to the Democracy prevented him from deserting Seymour. The distortion of Reconstruction by Congress justified for him the opposition to Grant. However, once the electorate had rendered its verdict, the invalid felt "at perfect liberty" to reassess his position. To Ulysses S. Grant he sent the advice that the new President act upon "the Annexation to the United States of all British America" and "the settlement of the Alabama claims." Again his eyes turned southward as he urged the victor of Appomattox to redeem Cuba from its Spanish oppressors. From his pen came a rambling letter advocating the annexation of Nova Scotia and British America.[27] As his illness deepened, the future and fulfillment of America's continental destiny obsessed him. His mind rushed back to the years of glorious struggle when his generation had swept up Texas, California, and Oregon. A feverish imagination stirred within him a vision of the seat of the empire moving westward until the new capital of the world rested not in London but in New York. Even in the clutches of death, his belief in the future prevailed.

Humiliation overtook him: Corcoran pressed upon him the urgency of settling his debts. No longer able to argue cases, his income had been reduced to the occasional sums of charity which came disguised as requests for legal advice. To secure his wife from want, he agreed finally to sell the *Woodley* estate and its furnishings. The sum he received retired his debts and there remained enough to insure his remaining wants. But he reached a debt free existence only as life ebbed away. Then he made a touching discovery. Devoid of all but a few possessions, with only a tattered fragment of his once great power, he learned how deeply his family loved him. They struggled to prolong his life. A summer at Long Branch, New Jersey, spared him the rigors of a final Washington summer. Late in October, 1869, he begged Duncan to take him back to Washington. He returned to the one place where nothing needed to be explained to him. In Washington he had made his mark. There he would escape life.

Frequent lapses into unconsciousness left him uncertain as to time and mercifully spared him added physical torment. His family kept vigil as early November marked the ending hours. He hovered in a coma. Then early in the morning of November 11th he awakened and looked about at his gathered family, and the ever loyal Negress who had tended him through his countless illnesses, and gasped, "What have I done to deserve such love?" Torn with pain, he beseeched: "Look! Look! I see God! Let me go to God! I will not! I don't want to live a little more! Give me up! Give me up!" And so death came.[28]

Notes

1. THE YOUNG AMERICAN

1. Claiborne, *Mississippi*, p. 417; Rowland, *Encyclopaedia of Mississippi History*, Vol. II, p. 891; Aptheker, *American Negro Slave Revolts*, pp. 325–27; *Niles' Register*, Vol. XLVIII, pp. 403–04.

2. Catterall, *Judicial Cases Concerning American Slavery and the Negro*, Vol. III, p. 299; Walker to Runnels, July 6, 1835, *Governor Papers, Series "E," 29;* Thompson, "Reforms in the Penal System of Mississippi, 1820–1850," *Journal of Mississippi History*, Vol. 7, p. 57.

3. Gwin to Claiborne, Vicksburg, May 8, 1841, *Gwin Papers;* Walker to Samuel Gwin, December 20, 1836, *Walker Papers;* Butler to Walker, May 31, 1836, *Robert J. Walker Papers;* 40 Peters, Appendix, *Brightly's Notes*, p. 652; Gilmore, *Personal Recollections of Abraham Lincoln*, pp. 37–41.

4. "Memoir of Robert John Walker," *Walker Papers; Dallas Diary*, p. 86.

5. *The Blenheim Roll*, p. 42; "Indian Incursions," *Hurja Papers; Patent Book "A,"* Vol. 12; *Genealogy of the Dallas Family; Cumberland County Assessments*, East Pennsboro Twnshp., 1750–53, 1767–68–69, 1770–71–72–73–74–76–78–79, 1780–81–82–85–86–87–88–89, 1795; *Records of Deeds in Cumberland County*, Book V, p. 76; Book "O," p. 83; Book "F," p. 273; *D.A.R. Lineage Book* LVI, p. 133; *Pennsylvania Archives*, 5th Series, Vol. VI, p. 604; "Memoir of Robert John Walker," *Walker Papers;* "Memory of Jonathan Hoge Walker," *Walker Papers; Scranton Republican*, July 23, 1932; *Speech of Robert J. Walker at the Banquet to Lewis Kossuth at Southampton;* Rapps, *History of Cumberland County*, p. 128.

6. Jonathan Walker to Wylie, September 26, 1817, *Autograph Collection;* although Robert and Mary Walker were to have five children, he named none after his father. He did not neglect his mother naming his youngest daughter Charlotte Lucy after his sister and mother; and named his youngest son after himself.

7. Godcharles, *Freemasonry in Northumberland and Snyder Counties, Pennsylvania,* p. 564; Bell (ed.), *History of Northumberland County, Pennsylvania,* p. 180, 241, 244; Meginness, *Biographical Annals of the West Branch Valley,* p. 261; *Census of 1790 for Pennsylvania,* p. 84; *Northumberland County Deed Book "F" and "I" Sunbury,* pp. 347–350.

8. Author unknown, *History of the Susquehanna and Juniata Valleys,* p. 463; Egle, *History of Pennsylvania,* p. 512; "Memoir of Robert John Walker," *Walker Papers;* Jonathan Walker to the People of the 4th District of Pennsylvania, July 24, 1818, *ibid.;* Beccaria's *Essay on Crimes and Punishments,* profoundly influenced the judge. Phillipson, *Three Criminal Law Reformers: Beccaria, Bentham, Romilly,* pp. 3–106.

9. "Memoir of Robert John Walker"; Jonathan Walker to the People of the 4th District of Pennsylvania, July 24, 1818; Jonathan Walker to Poyntelle, Bedford, Pa., September 14, 1815, *Walker Papers.*

10. "Memoir of Robert John Walker," *Walker Papers;* Walker to Bache, July 5, 1843; Walker to Bache, August 4, 1843, *Hurja Papers;* Zeamer, "The Early Patriots of the Silver Spring," *One Hundred and Seventy-fifth Anniversary of the Silver Spring Presbyterian Church,* passim.

11. Walker to Wylie, Bedford, Pa., September 26, 1817, *Autograph Collection;* Sprague, *Annals of the American Pulpit,* Vol. IX, Pt. 5, pp. 36–37.

12. Walker to Wylie, September 26, 1817, *Autograph Collection;* Walker to Poyntelle, Bedford, Pa., September 14, 1815; "Memoir of Robert John Walker"; Walker to Poyntelle, Bellefonte, Pa., December 21, 1816; Walker to the People of the 4th Judicial District, Pa., July 24, 1818, *Walker Papers;* Nevin, *Men of Mark of Cumberland Valley, Pa.,* p. 211.

13. "Memoir of Robert John Walker"; Walker to Wylie, September 26, 1817, *Walker Papers; Alumni Records,* University of Pennsylvania; *The University of Pennsylvania Illustrated,* Vol. II, pp. 30–31; Brown, *Reminiscences of Governor R. J. Walker,* p. 24.

14. Walker to Wylie, Pittsburgh, February 24, 1821; Walker to Wylie, Pittsburgh, December 25, 1821, *Dreer Papers;* "Memoir of Robert John Walker," *Walker Papers.*

15. "Memoir of Robert John Walker," *Walker Papers; Pittsburgh Gazette,* July 24, 1820; *Biographical Directory of the American Congress 1774–1924,* p. 1701; *Genealogy of the Dallas Family.*

16. "Memoir of Robert John Walker," *Walker Papers; Pittsburgh*

Statesman, undated, 1824; *Pennsylvanian,* Harrisburg, March 6, 1824; Occasional Records of the United States District Court for the Western District of Pennsylvania, 1822–23, *Hurja Paper;* Pittsburgh *Gazette,* September 28, 1821; November 16, 1821; Pittsburgh *Statesman,* January 7, 1823, indicates that Walker was active in the law; James A. Kehl, *Ill Feeling in the Era of Good Feeling,* p. 146, 214–16, 221, 231.

17. Walker to Wylie, Pittsburgh, February 24, 1821; Walker to Wylie, Pittsburgh, December 25, 1821; Walker to Wylie, Pittsburgh, November 19, 1823, *Dreer Collection;* Walker to William Tilghman, Pittsburgh, October 31, 1823, *Hurja Papers;* "Memory of Jonathan Hoge Walker, "Memoir of Robert John Walker," *Walker Papers,* Natchez *Gazette,* March 27, 1824; Pittsburgh *Statesman,* March 13, 1824.

18. William Tilghman, Chief Justice of Pennsylvania's Supreme Court was a close friend. His uncle Thomas Duncan was a member of the same court. See Walker to Tilghman, October 31, 1823, *Hurja Papers; 16 Sergeant & Rawle's Reports,* p. 440; *17 Sergeant & Rawle's Reports,* p. 457; *Records of Christ Church,* Philadelphia, Vol. VIII, p. 4807; *ibid.,* Vol. III, Baptisms, 1795–1818, p. 1804 which records Mary's baptism; Pittsburgh *Statesman,* April 16, 1825; *American Daily Advertiser,* April 5, 1825; *Aurora & Franklin Gazette,* April 5, 1825; "Memoir of Robert John Walker," *Walker Papers;* J. N. Moffitt to *Southwestern Advocate,* 1837; a typical example of that poetry is "To Charlotte" by Walker's sister Marianne Walker McElroy.

19. *Dallas Genealogy; Bache Genealogy; Dictionary of American Biography,* Vol. V, p. 36–39; E. Digby Blatzell, *Philadelphia Gentlemen,* pp. 136–38; Raymond Walters, Jr., *Alexander James Dallas, passim.*

20. "Memoir of Robert John Walker," *Walker Papers;* Meginess, *ibid.,* p. 262; *Sunbury Daily,* April 18, 1931.

2. THE CONFIDENCE MAN

1. Charles Sydnor, *Benjamin L. C. Wailes,* pp. 68–70; George J. Leftwich, "Robert J. Walker," *Mississippi Historical Society Publications,* Vol. VI, pp. 360–61; Joseph G. Baldwin, *The Flush Times of Alabama and Mississippi,* vividly demonstrates the turbulence of the region.

2. Baldwin, *Flush Times,* pp. 59, 174.

3. Notebook 1, 1828 citation, *Hurja Papers;* The Walker Collection of Autographs, *ibid.,* notes Walker's appointment to a lieutenancy in the Natchez Fencibles, April 7, 1828; Leftwich, *Robert J. Walker,* pp. 360–61.

4. H. Donaldson Jordan, "A Politician of Expansion: Robert J. Walker," *Mississippi Valley Historical Review*, Vol. XIX, 1932, p. 363; Claiborne, *Mississippi*, pp. 415–16, 422.

5. "Memoir of Robert John Walker," *Walker Papers*; Jordan, *A Politician of Expansion*, pp. 363–65; Leftwich, *Robert J. Walker*, pp. 361–64; William E. Dodd, "Robert J. Walker, Imperialist," *Randolph-Macon Bulletin*, Vol. I, 2, 1915, pp. 3–6.

6. "Memoir of Robert John Walker," *Walker Papers*; J. F. H. Claiborne, *Life and Correspondence of John A. Quitman*, Vol. I, pp. 96–98; Dunbar Rowland, *Mississippi the Heart of the South*, Vol. II, p. 423.

7. Rowland, *Mississippi*, Vol. II, pp. 432 and 615.

8. *American State Papers, Public Lands*, Vol. VII, pp. 272–84, 414–507, 732–72; Vol. VIII, pp. 711–88; Jordan, *A Politician of Expansion*, pp. 363–65; Hallie Mae McPherson, *William McKendree Gwin, Expansionist*, pp. 59–60; Magdalen Eichert, "Some Implications Arising from Robert J. Walker's Participation in Land Ventures," *Journal of Mississippi History*, Vol. XIII, pp. 41–46.

9. *American State Papers, Public Lands*, Vol. VII, pp. 494–506; Deed Book "Z"; Barnard to Walker, April 6, 1835; Walker to Clifton, Washington, March 13, 1850, *Walker Papers*; Quitman to Walker, June 22, 1846; Archer to Walker, Port Gibson, Miss., August 28, 1846, *Hurja Papers*.

10. Claiborne, *Mississippi*, pp. 415–16; Edwin A. Miles, "Franklin E. Plummer, Piney Woods Spokesman of the Jackson Era," *Journal of Mississippi History*, Vol. 14, pp. 18–22.

11. *American State Papers, Public Lands*, Vol. VII, pp. 492–93; Rowland, *Mississippi*, Vol. I, pp. 558–62; Dallas C. Dickey, *Seargent S. Prentiss Whig Orator of the Old South*, p. 204.

12. Rowland, Mississippi, pp. 599–600, 621–24, 636–37, 699–700; Dickey, *Seargent S. Prentiss*, pp. 198–228.

13. Walker to Black, March, 1834, quoted in *Niles Weekly Register*, Vol. XLIX (1835), p. 93; Turner to Quitman, November 5, 1834, *Claiborne Papers*, Mississippi Department of Archives and History; Gwin to Claiborne, May 6, 1879, *J. F. H. Claiborne Papers*, Columbia University Microfilm; Edwin A. Miles, *Robert J. Walker—His Mississippi Years*, p. 24, note 78.

14. Leonard D. White, *The Jacksonians*, pp. 107–08.

15. *American State Papers, Public Lands*, Vol. VII, pp. 377–447; Vol. VIII, pp. 740–42; Miles, *Robert J. Walker*, p. 23.

16. Gwin to Claiborne, May 6, 1879, *J. F. H. Claiborne Papers*; Miles, *Robert J. Walker*, pp. 19–20; William B. Hamilton and Ruth K.

Nuremberger, "An Appraisal of J. F. H. Claiborne with his Annotated 'Memoranda' (1829–1840)," *Journal of Mississippi History*, Vol. VII, p. 155.

17. Claiborne, *Mississippi*, p. 416; Henry Stuart Foote, *Casket of Reminiscences*, pp. 218–19; Turner to Quitman, November 5, 1834, *Claiborne Papers*; *Niles Weekly Register*, Vol. XLVII, p. 200.

18. *Niles Register*, Vol. XLVII, pp. 453–54; *United States Telegraph Extra*, January 10, 26, 1835.

19. Washington *Globe*, January 22, February 11, 14, 16, 1835; Columbus *Democrat*, February 13, 1835; Miles, *Robert J. Walker*, pp. 36–37; Claiborne, *Mississippi*, pp. 402–07.

20. *American State Papers, Public Lands*, Vol. VIII, pp. 733, 743, 755.

21. Miles, "Franklin E. Plummer: Piney Woods Spokesman of the Jackson Era," *Journal of Mississippi History*, Vol. XIV, pp. 1–34; Gwin to Claiborne, May 6, 1879, *J. F. H. Claiborne Papers*; Series "M," 5 and 6, *Miscellaneous Archives*, Mississippi Dept. of Archives and History; Claiborne, *Mississippi*, pp. 416, 427.

22. Jackson to Campbell, July 29, 1835; Jackson to Donelson, July 30, 1835, *Donelson Papers*; *Niles Register*, Vol. XLIX, p. 92; *Mississippian*, September 4, October 2, 1835; Clinton *Gazette*, January 2, 1836; McPherson, *William McKendree Gwin*, p. 18.

23. Claiborne, *Mississippi*, p. 417, 430; *Mississippi Free Trader*, September 29, October 20, 1835; Clinton *Gazette*, October 10, 1835; Miles, *Robert J. Walker*, pp. 44–47.

24. Black to Quitman, December 15, 1835, *Claiborne Papers*; "Gwin-Caldwell Duel," *J. F. H. Claiborne Papers*; White, *The Jacksonians*, pp. 108, note 10.

25. Miles, *Robert J. Walker*, pp. 50–52; Quitman to Quitman, January 10, 1835 (misdate should be 1836), *Quitman Papers*; Clinton *Gazette*, January 12, 1836.

3. TEXAS

1. *Congressional Globe*, Twenty-seventh Congress, first session, p. 793; *National Intelligencer*, February 27, 1836; *Congressional Globe*, Twenty-seventh Congress, first session, Appendix Vol. III, p. 138.

2. "Memoir of Robert John Walker," *Walker Papers*; Deed transferring seven leagues of land from Duncan to Robert J. Walker, *ibid.*; James C. N. Paul, *Rift in the Democracy*, p. 26.

3. "Memoir of Robert John Walker," *Walker Papers*.

4. *Congressional Globe,* April 26, 1836, p. 401; *ibid.,* May 9, 1836, p. 436.

5. *Congressional Globe,* p. 394; *ibid.,* pp. 436–37; J. S. Bassett, *Correspondence of Andrew Jackson,* Vol. V, pp. 381–82; *Congressional Globe,* p. 83; *ibid.,* p. 214.

6. Claiborne, *Mississippi,* pp. 417–18; George P. Garrison, *Diplomatic Correspondence of the Republic of Texas,* Vol. I (American Historical Association, 1907–08), p. 186; *Democratic Review,* Vol. XVI, p. 161; *Mississippi Free Trader,* July 7, 1837; *Journal of the House of Representatives of the Republic of Texas,* First Congress, second session (Houston, 1838), pp. 77–79.

7. *Mississippi Free Trader,* March 21, 1839; Jordan, *A Politician of Expansion,* p. 368; *Congressional Globe* Appendix, February 26, 1839, p. 213; *ibid.,* February 27, 1839, p. 259; *ibid.,* March 1, 1839, p. 312; *Congressional Globe,* March 2, 1839, p. 225.

8. Dallas to Gilpin, Washington, March 12, 1837, *Gilpin Papers; Congressional Globe* Appendix, January 28, 1837, pp. 216–21; *National Intelligencer,* April 21, 1837, deals with a recurrent rumor that Walker had been killed in a duel with Benton.

9. *Congressional Globe,* May 5, 1836, p. 419 in which Walker insisted "that the land bill, by taking 20 to 30 millions from the Treasury of the Union, leaves not enough money to defend the country without increasing the Tariff"; *ibid.,* April 21, 1836, p. 381; *ibid.,* April 25, 1836, p. 397; *ibid.,* April 14, 1836, in which the "lecture" incident is discussed; Roy Marvin Robbins, *Our Landed Heritage, The Public Domain, 1776–1936,* pp. 67, 74–76, 88; St. George L. Sioussat, "Andrew Johnson and the Early Phases of the Homestead Bill," *Mississippi Valley Historical Review,* Vol. V, p. 258, describes Walker as the originator of Homestead Legislation.

10. *Congressional Globe,* March 31, 1836, p. 309; *ibid.,* March 16, 1836, p. 259.

11. *Ibid.,* June 15, 1836, p. 556.

12. *Congressional Globe,* December 12, 1836, p. 18; *ibid.,* January 3, 1837, p. 68; *ibid.,* December 12, 1837, p. 91; *Speech of Mr. Walker of Mississippi on the Bill Presented by Himself, limiting The Sale of the Public Lands to Actual Settlers* (Washington, 1837), p. 1, hereafter referred to as *Mr. Walker on Public Lands.*

13. *Mr. Walker on Public Lands,* pp. 4, 15.

14. Miles, *Robert J. Walker,* p. 71.

15. *Congressional Globe,* February 9, 1837, p. 172; *ibid.,* December 7,

1837, p. 15; January 26, 1838, p. 139; *ibid.*, Appendix, pp. 129–42; *ibid.*, January 30, 1838, p. 149.

16. *Congressional Globe*, April 6, 1836; Gwin to Claiborne, Natchez, Miss., June 3, 1837, *Hurja Papers*.

17. *Congressional Globe*, September 15, 1837, p. 32; *ibid.*, September 18, 1837, p. 37; *ibid.*, September 27, 1837, p. 80; *ibid.*, Appendix, September 27, 1837, p. 77; Washington *Globe*, September 26, 1837.

18. Washington *Globe*, June 14, 1838.

19. Columbus *Democrat*, May 25, 1839; *Niles Register*, Vol. LVI, pp. 412–15; Dickey, *Prentiss*, pp. 164–65.

20. *Niles Register*, Vol. LVI, pp. 412–15; George Prentiss, *Memoir of S. S. Prentiss*, Vol. II, pp. 142–43; pp. 147–48, in which Prentiss wrote his brother: "I shall feel no chagrin at defeat, for success will disturb my entire plans of life."

21. Prentiss, *Memoir*, p. 147; Hamilton and Nuremberger, "An Appraisal of J. F. H. Claiborne" p. 155; Vicksburg *Weekly Whig*, September 24, 1839, cited in Miles, *Robert J. Walker*, p. 80, note 78.

22. Natchez *Mississippi Free Trader Extra*, October 10, 1839; Columbus *Democrat*, October 19, 1839; Prentiss, *Memoir*, Vol. II, p. 144; *ibid.*, Vol. I, p. 94; Dickey, *Prentiss*, pp. 44–45.

23. *Journal of the State of Mississippi* (Jackson, 1840), pp. 68–69; *Congressional Globe*, December 2, 1839, p. 1.

24. *Congressional Globe* Appendix, January 20, 1840, p. 726.

25. *Congressional Globe* Appendix, pp. 137–38; Washington *Globe*, January 25, 1840; Allan Nevins (ed.) *The Diary of Philip Hone, 1828–1851*, Vol. I, p. 455; John Barbour to Mrs. Barbour, Baltimore, January 23, 1840, *Robert J. Walker Papers*, New-York Historical Society, hereafter referred to as *Miscellaneous Papers*.

26. Buchanan to Walker, Bedford Springs, Pa., August 1, 1839, *Miscellaneous Papers; Congressional Globe* Appendix, January 16, 1840, pp. 123–24; *ibid.*, January 21, 1840, p. 137, noted that Walker has not completed "recovery from severe illness."; *ibid.*, February 12, 1840, p. 185; *ibid.*, January 10, 1840, p. 112; Walker to McNutt, January 10, 1840, quoted in *Nine Years of Democratic Rule in Mississippi 1838–1847*, pp. 150–51 observed "At the request of the delegate from Florida, I conceived it to be my duty to bring forward the proposition of the people of East Florida, to make two states out of Florida. It has produced much feeling, and seems to portend another Missouri question."

27. Hancock to Walker, Daleville, September 18, 1841, *Walker Papers;* Claiborne, *Mississippi*, p. 420.

28. Walker to Walker, Philadelphia, May 18, 1841, *Tyler Papers*; *Congressional Globe*, June 1, 1841, p. 5.

29. *Congressional Globe*, July 12, 1841, p. 185; *ibid.*, July 20, 1841, p. 231; *ibid.*, July 12, 1841, p. 187; *ibid.*, July 21, 1841, p. 234.

30. Lyon G. Tyler, *The Letters and the Times of the Tylers*, Vol. II, p. 72; *Congressional Globe*, August 16, 1841, p. 339.

31. Buchanan to Clay, July 21, 1843, *Dreer Collection*; F. T. Claiborne to Walker, October 13, 1841, *Claiborne Papers*; Nevins (ed.) *Philip Hone Diary*, p. 621; White, *The Jacksonians*, p. 311.

32. Claiborne, *Mississippi*, p. 420; Walker to Gwin, June 2, 1843, *Claiborne Papers*; *Congressional Globe*, September 11, 1841, in which Walker announced he favored the restoration of the Independent Treasury "if the President was (not) against that."

33. Walker to Claiborne, Natchez, October 7, 1839, *Claiborne Papers*; Gwin Memoir, *J. F. H. Claiborne Papers*; Walker to Frazier, Havana, December 15, 1841; Walker to Bates, July 19, 1841; Walker to Lapice, July 1, 1841, *Walker Letterbook*; *Congressional Globe*, December 14, 1841, p. 15; December 16, 1841, p. 22.

34. Walker to Duncan, June 9, 1843; Walker to Duncan, Washington, February 7, 1840, *Walker Letterbook*, indicates Walker indifference to his cousin's view of his trustworthiness.

35. Walker to Gwin, December 9, 1840; Walker to unknown, March 4, 1842; Walker to Bainbridge, April 1, 1845; Walker to Gwin, November 30, 1840, *Walker Letterbook*, are but a few of the numerous letters dealing with paper transferrals.

36. Gwin Memoir, *J. F. H. Claiborne Papers*.

37. McPherson, *William McKendree Gwin*, pp. 59–66.

38. Walker to unknown, March 24, 1843, *Walker Letterbook* expressed a lively interest in the disposition of the Chickasaw lands; *Congressional Globe*, April 5, 1842, p. 385; *ibid.*, April 25, 1842, p. 441; *ibid.*, July 23, 1842, p. 781; *ibid.*, July 25, 1842, p. 786; *ibid.*, July 26, 1842, p. 790; *ibid.*, January 29, 1845, p. 212.

39. Gwin to Claiborne, New York, August 15, 1840, *Claiborne Papers*.

40. Walker to the editor of the Washington *Evening Express*, April 8, 1844, *Walker Letterbook*.

41. Holman Hamilton, "Texas Bonds and Northern Profits: A Study in Compromise, Investment, and Lobby Influence," *The Mississippi Valley Historical Review*, Vol. XLIII, pp. 579–94; confirmed in Holman Hamilton letter to author, September 26, 1958; Walker to Corcoran, September 21, 1850, *W. W. Corcoran Papers*.

42. James E. Winston, "Robert J. Walker, Annexationist," *The Texas Review*, Vol. II, 4, p. 300. Winston notes that Mississippi's interest flagged "for a period (1838–42) of several years" p. 298.

43. Charles G. Sellers, Jr., *James K. Polk: Jacksonian, 1795–1843*, pp. 464, 490.

44. Walker to Van Buren, February 8, 1841; August 31, 1842; August 4, 1843, *Van Buren Papers;* Calhoun to Clemson, Washington, D.C., April 3, 1842, *Annual Report of the American Historical Association,* 1899, Vol. II, hereafter referred to as *Calhoun Papers;* Walker to Claiborne, May 23, 1842; Walker to Quitman, September 15, 1842, *J. F. H. Claiborne Papers.*

45. William M. Meigs, *The Life of Charles Jared Ingersoll*, p. 261.

46. Johnson to Walker, White Sulphur, Ky., April 29, 1842, *Hurja Papers.*

47. Tyler to Walker, July 9, 1842, *Hurja Papers;* Walker to Tyler, August 15, 1842, *Hurja Notebook 4.*

48. Walker to Blair, April 13, 1844, *Walker Letterbook;* E. Blair Lee to Walker, April 13, 1844, *Walker Papers.*

49. Tod to Walker, Washington, Texas, December 18, 1844, *Walker Papers.*

50. Walker to Jackson, January 10, 1844, *Andrew Jackson Papers;* also in *Walker Letterbook;* Marquis James, *The Raven: A Biography of Sam Houston,* pp. 345–47.

51. Meigs, *Charles Jared Ingersoll*, p. 263.

52. Tod to Walker, December 18, 1844, *Walker Papers.*

53. Tod to Walker, December 31, 1844; Tod to Walker, December 18, 1844; for ample evidence of Walker's fear of the growing British influence in Texas, see Atkins to Walker, November 13, 1843; Allen to Walker, November 27, 1844, *Walker Papers.*

54. Wright to Van Buren, February 27, 1843, *Van Buren Papers;* Wright to Van Buren, February 19, 1843, *ibid.;* Paul, *Rift in the Democracy,* pp. 64, 65; E. I. McCormac, *James K. Polk*, p. 226; Garraty, *Silas Wright*, p. 241.

55. Hays to Polk, January 8, 1844; Howry to Polk, Oxford, Miss., January 17, 1844, *Hurja Notebook 4.*

56. *Richmond Examiner,* undated, clipping in *Walker Papers;* Jackson to Houston, March 15, 1844, in Amelia W. Williams and Eugene Campbell Baker (eds.), *The Writings of Sam Houston 1813–63*, Vol. IV, p. 267.

57. On Jackson's fiscal situation see Marquis James, *Andrew Jackson Portrait of a President,* pp. 472–73; Walker to Jackson, February 13,

1844, *Jackson Papers;* Walker to Jackson, Washington, February 14, 1844, *ibid.; Congressional Globe,* February 13, 1844, p. 273; on background of fine see Marquis James, *Andrew Jackson the Border Captain,* pp. 282–87.

58. Walker to Jackson, Washington, D.C., February 14, 1844, *Jackson Papers;* Butler to Walker, Carrolton, Ky., February 24, 1844, *Hurja Papers.*

59. Robert J. Walker, *Letter on the Annexation of Texas,* February 5, 1844, hereafter *Texas Letter; The Globe,* February 5, 1844; Walker to Blair and Rives, undated, *Walker Letterbook;* Sanders to Walker, Carroll County, March 4, 1844, *Walker Papers;* Dallas to Walker, February 5, 1844, *ibid.*

60. Rush to Walker, February 15, 1844, *Hurja Papers;* Johnson to Walker, White Sulphur, February 24, 1844, *ibid.;* Tappan to Walker, March 6, 1844, *Miscellaneous Papers;* Bancroft to Walker, Boston, May 25, 1844, *ibid.;* Pillow to Horn and Kane, Columbia, Tenn., July 2, 1844, *Bancroft Papers,* described impact of letter in Tennessee; Baron Howden to Walker, London, May 25, 1844, *Miscellaneous Papers,* describes favorable British reaction; New Orleans *Bulletin,* March 27, 1844, although Whig, emphatically endorsed the letter; Paul, *Rift in the Democracy,* pp. 114–18.

61. Philip A. Hoyne to Van Buren, Galena, Ill., February 4, 1844, demanded that the former President make his opinion known on Texas and the Oregon Territory; William H. Miller to Van Buren, New Orleans, March 2, 1844; Thomas Ritchie to Van Buren, Richmond, March 20, 1844, reported the receipt of a letter from a member of Congress that pronounced General Jackson "the originator of this movement and *will see it through.*" The Congressman warned: "Unless there is great imprudence or folly, Van Buren will be re-elected— but if he goes against Texas (which I deem impossible) *all is gone.*"; W. L. Marcy to Van Buren, Southbridge, March 20, 1844, who was composing the candidate's campaign biography, noted: "You will be required to speak out on the subject in some way or another." Silas Wright to Van Buren, Washington, March 22, 1844 suggested as much; Jefferson Davis to Van Buren, Warren County, March 25, 1844, demanded to know where the candidate stood on "the annexation of 'Texas' to the Territory of the United States . . ."; William H. Hammet to Van Buren, March 27, 1844, found this Mississippi congressman, a collaborator in Walker's subsequent actions to capture control of the Baltimore convention, demanding to know Van Buren's "opinions as to the Constitutionality & expediency of immediately annex-

ing Texas to the United States." An unusually large number of letters signed by several people, representing themselves as spokesmen for larger groups, are in the *Van Buren Papers*. One of which represents itself as a request from "citizens of Cincinatti," March 30, 1844, has as its first signature that of S. P. Chase. Perhaps the most interesting letter is that of Congressman T. M. Tucker of Mississippi to Van Buren, Washington, April 12, 1844, warning: "I have strong reasons to conjecture, that political *moves* are about being taken (sic), by persons claiming to be of the Democratic party . . . to weaken your strength. . . . The reasons, as I understand them, for this conjectural *move*, is based on your silence on the all-engrossing subject of the re-annexation of the Republic of Texas to the United States. . . ." One detects the fine Italian hand of the senior Senator from Mississippi in the large number of letters Van Buren received from that state.

62. Jackson to Blair, September 19, 1844, *Jackson Papers;* Hunt to Walker, April 8, 1845; Hunt to Walker, March 24, 1845, *Walker Papers.*

4. THE SUBSTANCE OF POWER

1. Charles Varle, *Complete View of Baltimore, passim.*

2. New York *Evening Post*, May 27, 1844.

3. John O'Sullivan to Martin Van Buren, May 27, 1844, *Van Buren Papers.* On the first ballot Van Buren was assured of 146 votes out of a total of 266.

4. Paul, *Rift in the Democracy*, p. 182.

5. Mississippi Delegation to the *Globe*, Washington, May 4, 1844, *Walker Letterbook;* James E. Winston, "The Lost Commission: A Study in Mississippi History," *The Mississippi Valley Historical Review*, Vol. V, 2, September, 1918, p. 164.

6. Proceedings of the Mississippi Delegation, May 26, 1844, *Walker Letterbook.*

7. "Kremer" to John Van Buren, May 21, 1846, *Van Buren Papers.*

8. Walker to J. F. H. Claiborne, May 23, 1842, *Claiborne Papers*, Misc. Book "C."

9. Walker to Quitman, September 15, 1842, *Claiborne Papers*, Misc. Book "C"; W. A. Butler, *A Retrospect of Forty Years, 1825–1865*, p. 146.

10. Pickens to Calhoun, May 28, 1844, *Calhoun Collection.*

11. New York *Evening Post*, May 28, 1844. The *Post* gave the most comprehensive treatment of the convention. Its commitment to Van

Buren provides a vivid insight into the bewilderment of the Van Burenites as the convention quit their candidate. N. B. Wright to Walker, Philadelphia, March 15, 1845, *Hurja Papers.*

12. John R. Dickinson (ed.), *Speeches, Correspondence, Etc., of the Late Daniel S. Dickinson,* Vol. II, pp. 369.

13. O'Sullivan to Van Buren, May 27, 1844, *Van Buren Papers;* Ritchie to Cobb, May 6, 1844, describes the party factions; Ritchie to Cobb, May 23, 1844, *Toombs, Cobb, Stephens Correspondence,* threatened a third party nomination of Tyler should Van Buren win the Democratic nomination.

14. Simpson to Van Buren, May 31, 1844; June 10, 1844, *Van Buren Papers.*

15. O'Sullivan to Van Buren, May 27, 1844; Butler to Van Buren, May 27, 1844; Bancroft to Van Buren, June 14, 1844, *Van Buren Papers;* Pickens to Calhoun, May 28, 1844, *Calhoun Collection;* New York *Evening Post,* May 27, 1844; Paul, *Rift in the Democracy,* pp. 149–56.

16. J. G. Harris to Bancroft, September 13, 1887, *Bancroft Papers.*

17. New York *Evening Post,* May 31, 1844; Arthur M. Schlesinger, Jr., *Age of Jackson,* pp. 436–37.

18. Bancroft to Harris, August 30, 1887, *Bancroft Papers;* New York *Evening Post,* May 31, 1844; Schlesinger, Jr., *Age of Jackson,* p. 437; "Letters of James K. Polk to Cave Johnson, 1833–1848," *Tennessee Historical Magazine,* Vol. I, pp. 239–40; Eugene H. Roseboom, *A History of Presidential Elections,* p. 128.

19. New York *Evening Post,* May 31, 1844; Butler to Van Buren, May 30, 1844, *Van Buren Papers.*

20. Proceedings of the Mississippi Delegation, May 26, 1844, *Walker Letterbook;* Walker Memoir in Answer to Southern Attacks, p. 18, *Walker Papers;* Laughlin to Polk, May 31, 1844, *Polk Papers;* Paul, *Rift in the Democracy,* pp. 159–65; Garraty, *Silas Wright,* pp. 274–77.

21. Paccidey to Van Buren, May 31, 1844, *Van Buren Papers.*

22. Harris to Bancroft, September 13, 1887, *Bancroft Papers;* Paul, *Rift in the Democracy,* p. 166; Garraty, *Silas Wright,* pp. 281–83; New York *Evening Post,* May 31, 1844.

23. Paul, *Rift in the Democracy,* pp. 166–67; Walker to Polk, Philadelphia, May 31, 1844; Walker to Polk, May 30, 1844, *Polk Papers.*

24. Henry Simpson to Van Buren, Philadelphia, May 31, 1844; Butler to Van Buren, May 30, 1844; *Van Buren Papers;* Walker Memoir in Answer to Southern Attacks, p. 18, *Walker Papers.*

25. Polk to Walker, Columbia, Tenn., June 8, 1844, *Miscellaneous Papers.*

26. Walker to Polk, July 10, 1844, *Polk Papers.*

27. Lyon Gardiner Tyler, *The Letters and Times of the Tylers*, Vol. III, p. 139.

28. Walker to Polk, July 10, 1844, *Polk Papers;* Tyler, *The Letters and Times of the Tylers*, Vol. III, p. 141.

29. Polk to Jackson, July 23, 1844, *Polk Papers;* Jackson to Polk, August 3, 1844, *Jackson Papers.*

30. Walker to Polk, Washington, D.C., July 11, 1844, *Polk Papers.*

31. Jackson to Blair, July 26, 1844, *Jackson Papers.*

32. Jackson to Polk, July 26, 1844, *Polk Papers.*

33. Tyler to Jackson, August 18, 1844, *Jackson Papers;* Tyler, *The Letters and Times of the Tylers*, Vol. II, p. 338 and 342; Vol. III, p. 144.

34. Jackson to Polk, July 26, 1844; see also Anderson to Polk, Washington, D.C., July 11, 1844, *Polk Papers.*

35. Walker to Quitman, September 15, 1842, *Claiborne Collection,* Misc. Book "C."

36. Walker to Polk, Baltimore, May 30, 1844; Walker to Polk, Washington, D.C., June 18, 1844, *Polk Papers;* Walker to Polk, Washington, D.C., June 18, 1844, *Walker Letterbook.*

37. Walker to Polk, Washington, D.C., June 18, 1844; Walker to Polk, Baltimore, May 30, 1844, *Polk Papers;* see also Simon Cameron to Walker, Middletown, June 7, 1844, *Walker Papers,* which expressed certainty that Polk would carry Pennsylvania "unless the Whigs can get an impression that Polk is hostile to the tariff"; Lewis Eaton to Walker, New York, June 25, 1844, *ibid.,* expresses similar views for New York State. S. H. Laughlin to Polk, June 11, 1844, *Polk Papers,* also presses for "incidental protection."

38. Polk to Kane, June 19, 1844, *ibid.;* on Kane see Henry Simpson, *The Lives of Eminent Philadelphians*, pp. 614–17; *Appleton's National Cyclopaedia of American Biography*, Vol. III, p. 492.

39. Milo Quaife (ed.), *Polk Diary*, Vol. I, p. 43; see also Gideon J. Pillow to Henry Horn and J. K. Kane, Columbia, Tenn., July 2, 1844, *Polk Papers.*

40. Alex Anderson to Polk, August 22, 1844, *Polk Papers;* Wilmington *Gazette* quoted in the *Southern Reformer*, April 12, 1845; Daniel to Van Buren, Richmond, June 11, 1844, *Van Buren Papers;* Dunbar Rowland, *Jefferson Davis*, Vol. I, p. 7, suggests that some Southern politicians were reluctant to settle the Texas issue because of their conviction that it made votes.

41. Catron to Walker, July 27, 1844, *Hurja Notebook 4.*

42. Walker to Robertson and others, Washington, D.C., July 30, 1844, *Madisonian,* August 24, 1844; *Madisonian,* September 26, 1844; Walker to Whitfield and others, August 28, 1844, *Hurja Papers,* in declining an invitation to a Mississippi barbecue, noted "The duties assigned to me at this place are most arduous, requiring great labor and constant attention and they cannot be neglected, even for a day, without serious injury to the democratic cause."

43. Bancroft to Walker, Boston, June 19, 1844, *Miscellaneous Papers.*

44. *Journal of Commerce,* March 21, 1846.

45. Wright to Van Buren, January 17, 1845, *Van Buren Papers.*

46. Van Buren to New York Committee to Protest the Baltimore Convention, June 3, 1844, *Van Buren Papers;* Garraty, *Silas Wright,* p. 308; *Appleton's National Cyclopaedia of American Biography,* Vol. V, p. 298.

5. INTO THE VINEYARD

1. Calvin Colton, Frelinghuysen to Clay, November 9, 1844, *The Private Correspondence of Henry Clay.*

2. Colton, Fillmore to Clay, November 11, 1844, *ibid.*

3. Colton, Hone to Clay, November 28, 1844, *ibid.*

4. "The South in Danger," *Hurja Papers.*

5. Washington *Globe,* September 30, 1844, warned: "We believe it to be our duty to put the democracy on their guard against this forgery"; Walker to Washington *Globe,* October 3, 1844; Adams, *Memoirs,* XII, p. 87; Columbus *Democrat,* October 26, 1844, approved Walker's efforts to make "known to the people of the South the assaults made upon them by Whig presses and statesmen of the North."

6. Daniel to Van Buren, November 19, 1844, *Van Buren Papers.*

7. Gilpin to Van Buren, December 13, 1844, *Van Buren Papers.*

8. Polk to Van Buren, January 4, 1845, *ibid.*

9. Polk to Wright, Columbia, Tenn., December 7, 1844, *Polk Papers;* Polk to Van Buren, January 4, 1845, *Van Buren Papers;* Garraty, *Silas Wright,* pp. 340–41.

10. Jackson to Blair, November 29, 1844, *Jackson Papers;* Mason to Polk, Washington, D.C., November 16, 1844, *Polk Papers,* in which Mason, an old friend of Polk, pleaded for retention as Secretary of Navy since the salary was almost the sole support of his family.

11. Van Buren to Polk, Lindenwold, N.Y., February 15, 1845, *Bancroft Papers,* in which Van Buren indicated he still expected ample recognition despite Wright's refusal.

12. Dallas to Polk, December 15, 1844, *Bancroft Papers*.

13. Dallas to Polk, January 10, 1845, *Polk Papers*.

14. Johnson to Polk, January 11, 1845, *Polk Papers*.

15. Group of Democratic Supporters to Polk, Pittsburgh, November 21, 1844, *ibid.*; Dallas to Polk, December 15, 1844, *Bancroft Papers*, feared antagonism toward his family would adversely affect Polk's judgment.

16. Polk to Buchanan, February 17, 1845, *Buchanan Papers*; Polk to Walker, Washington, February 19, 1845, *Polk Papers*.

17. Jackson to Polk, Hermitage, December 15, 1844, *Bancroft Papers*.

18. Harris to Bancroft, September 13, 1887, *Bancroft Papers*.

19. Simpson to Dallas, February 25, 1845, *Dallas Papers*.

20. Dallas to Walker, November 6, 1844; Dallas to Walker, February 7, 1845; Dallas to Walker, February 11, 1845, *Dallas Papers*.

21. Gwin to Claiborne, undated, *Claiborne Papers*; Cameron to Walker, Middletown, January 20, 1845, *Hurja Papers*; Dallas to Sophy Dallas, February 22, 1845; Dallas to Sophy Dallas, February 23, 1845, *Dallas Papers*; Polk to Walker, February 19, 1845, *Polk Papers*; Dawson to Walker, February 20, 1845, *Miscellaneous Papers*; New York *Tribune*, February 21, 1845; New York *Evening Post*, February 22, 1845; New York *Herald*, February 22, 1845; *National Intelligencer*, February 21, 1845.

22. Polk to Van Buren, February 22, 1845, *Van Buren Papers*.

23. Bancroft to Van Buren, January 22, 1845, *Van Buren Papers*; Van Buren to Polk, February 15, 1845, *Bancroft Papers*; Van Buren to Polk, January 18, 1845, *ibid.*

24. Butler to Van Buren, February 27, 1845, *Van Buren Papers*; Butler to Polk, February 27, 1845, *ibid.*; Garraty, *Silas Wright*, p. 345.

25. "Democratic Congressional Delegation from Indiana" to Polk, February 12, 1845, *Polk Papers*.

26. Disney to Walker, Columbus, Ohio, January 24, 1845, *Hurja Papers*; Wood to Gwin, February 2, 1845, *ibid.*

27. Walker Memoir in Answer to Southern Attacks, *Walker Papers*; Baldwin to Hammett, February 19, 1844; *Democratic Review*, February, 1845; Irwin to Polk, February 6, 1845, *Polk Papers*.

28. Walker to Dallas, January 24, 1845, *Dallas Papers*.

29. Johnson to Polk, Washington, D.C., January 2, 1845, *Polk Papers*; Brown to Polk, December 29, 1844, *ibid.*; Howvy to Johnson, Oxford, February 5, 1845, *ibid.*; Johnson to Polk, Washington, D.C., January 11, 1845, *ibid.*; Cass to Walker, May 12, 1844, *Hurja Papers*; Mississippi Congressional Delegation to Polk, Washington, D.C., January

12, 1845, *ibid.*; Sturgeon to Polk, January 17, 1845, added the support of Pennsylvania's junior Senator for Walker, *ibid.*; Tallmadge to Polk, New York, January 15, 1845, *ibid.*; Brown to Polk, January 5, 1845, *ibid.*

30. Walker to Claiborne, Nashville, December 13, 1844, *Claiborne Papers; Congressional Globe,* December 2, 1844; December 5, 1844.

31. Smith Van Buren to Martin Van Buren, March 3, 1845, *Van Buren Papers;* Garraty, *Silas Wright,* pp. 345–46.

32. Polk to Van Buren, March 3, 1845, *Polk Papers.*

33. Smith Van Buren to Martin Van Buren, March 3, 1845, *Van Buren Papers.*

34. *Washington Globe,* March 5, 1845; New York *Herald,* March 5, 1845; New York *Tribune,* March 5, 1845; *National Intelligencer,* March 5, 1845.

35. Adams to Mrs. A. B. Adams, Washington, D.C., April 2, 1845, *Adams Papers;* Jackson to Polk, March 2, 1845, *Polk Papers.*

36. Stevenson to Marcy, March 2, 1845, *Marcy Papers.*

37. Worth to Marcy, March 8, 1845, *ibid.*

38. Jackson to Polk, March 2, 1845, *Polk Papers;* Spencer to Walker, March 15, 1845, *Hurja Papers; Southern Reformer,* March 29, 1845; New York *True Sun,* March 8, 1845.

39. Cambreling to Van Buren, March 14, 1845, *Van Buren Papers.*

40. Winston, *The Lost Commission: A Study in Mississippi History,* p. 165; *Proceedings,* May 26, 1844, *Walker Letterbook.*

41. Walker to Brown, February 11, 1845, published in the *Sentinel and Expositor,* January 31, 1846, February 3, 1846; also Columbus *Democrat,* February 7, 1846; *Speeches and Messages and Other Writings of Albert Gallatin Brown,* pp. 87–88.

42. Brown to Walker, February 21, 1845, *Brown Papers.*

43. *Free Trader,* April 29, 1845.

44. *Free Trader,* July 31, 1845; Vicksburg *Sentinel,* July 21, 1845, quoted Walker's letter to Brown which contained the damaging assertion, "Dr. Gwin, we all think, who have conversed together, might surely be relied on, and so think some of the special friends of the President." Brown to Walker, Jackson, Miss., September 28, 1845, *Miscellaneous Papers.*

45. Winston, *The Lost Commission,* p. 177; *Mississippi House Journal* (1846), p. 348 and pp. 390–94.

46. Winston, *The Lost Commission,* p. 176; *Niles Register,* Vol. LXVIII (1845), pp. 330–31; Thompson's contention is supported by

his subsequent refusal to accept appointment for the Senate from Governor Brown. See *Free Trader*, April 29, 1845.

47. Thompson to Claiborne, June 3, 1878, in Percy L. Rainwater (ed.) "Letters to and from Jacob Thompson," *Journal of Southern History*, Vol. VI, pp. 103–04; Claiborne, *Mississippi*, p. 439.

48. Winston, *The Lost Commission*, pp. 185–86.

49. Winston, *The Lost Commission*, p. 188; Miles, *Robert J. Walker*, pp. 168–69; *Mississippi House Journal* (1846), pp. 399–400.

50. Brown to Claiborne, May 29, 1879, *Claiborne Papers*, cited in Miles, *Robert J. Walker*, p. 171.

51. Quaife (ed.) *Polk Diary*, Vol. I, p. 239; Washington *Daily Union*, May 23, 1845, reported that Thompson had claimed that "Had the commission reached me while in Washington, I should have accepted the Honor and entered upon the discharge of its duties."

52. Quaife, *Polk's Diary*, Vol. I, p. 175.

53. Quaife, *Polk's Diary*, Vol. I, p. 176.

54. Quaife, *Polk's Diary*, Vol. I, p. 239.

55. The *Mississippian*, January 7, 1846, quotes the Vicksburg *Sentinel; Free Trader*, July 31, 1845.

56. Rowland, *Jefferson Davis*, Vol. I, pp. 26–28.

57. "Kremer" to Van Buren, May 21, 1846, *Van Buren Papers*.

6. TALLEYRAND OF THE TREASURY

1. Jackson to Polk, Hermitage, June 6, 1845, *Jackson Papers;* Jackson to Polk, March 2, 1845, *ibid.;* James, *Portrait of a President*, pp. 496–99; Tyler, *The Letters and Times of the Tylers*, Vol. III, Jackson to Polk, May 2, 1845; Bassett, *Correspondence of Andrew Jackson*, Vol. VI, p. 405.

2. Polk, *Diary*, Vol. III, p. 241–42; White, *The Jacksonians*, p. 76.

3. Polk, *Diary*, Vol. II, pp. 126–28; Vol. III, p. 229; *Congressional Globe*, March 3, 1845, p. 389, in which Walker had earlier announced his opposition to federal redemption of Indian script. One suspects his opposition shrewdly attempted to avert the possibility that his reputation as speculator might be revived to attack his appointment.

4. Sellers, *James K. Polk*, pp. 249, 280, 491; William Ernest Smith, *The Francis Preston Blair Family in Politics*, Vol. I, pp. 144–81.

5. Polk to Donelson, March 28, 1845, St. George L. Sioussat, "Letters of James K. Polk to Andrew J. Donelson, 1843–48," *Tennessee Historical Magazine*, Vol. III, March, 1917; Polk to Cave Johnson, Decem-

ber 21, 1844, in St. George L. Sioussat, "Polk-Johnson Letters," *ibid.*, Vol. I, September, 1915; Schlesinger, Jr., *The Age of Jackson*, pp. 444–45.

6. Harris to Calhoun, July 11, 1845, *Calhoun Papers;* Cameron to Heiss, May 27, 1847; Coryell to Heiss, December 12, 1847, St. George L. Sioussat, "Heiss Papers," *Tennessee Historical Magazine*, Vol. II, September, 1916; Lewis to Coryell, September 16, 1845, *Coryell Papers.*

7. Walker to O'Sullivan, Washington, D.C., June 30, 1845, *Dreer Collection;* Walker to Cameron, November 16, 1847, *Treasury Records, Executive Documents*, Doc. 4, Thirtieth Congress, first session; Cameron to Walker, August 25, 1845, *Hurja Papers;* Cameron to Walker, June 21, 1845, *ibid.;* Wright to Walker, April 18, 1845, *ibid.; Tennessee Historical Magazine*, Vol. III, pp. 62–63; Cameron to Coryell, March 31, 1845, *Coryell Papers.*

8. Marcy to Walker, June 15, 1845, *Miscellaneous Papers;* Law to Van Buren, March 25, 1845, *Van Buren Papers;* see also Walker to Polk, June 12, 1845, *Polk Papers.*

9. Duval to Walker, St. Augustine, Fla., April 9, 1845, *Miscellaneous Papers;* Lumpkin to Walker, April 23, 1845; Polk to Jackson, May 12, 1845, *Polk Papers;* Foote to Walker, Jackson, Miss., May 24, 1845, *Hurja Papers.*

10. Haywood to Walker, March 24, 1845; Higgins to Polk, April 25, 1845, *Polk Papers;* Medary to Van Buren, May 22, 1845, *Van Buren Papers;* Miles to Walker, Hartford, Conn., April 17, 1845; Hamlin to Walker, Hampden, Me., May 26, 1845, in which the future Vice President protested patronage distribution at Belfast, Me., *Hurja Papers.*

11. Walker to the senior editor of *The Mississippian*, June 5, 1845, published in *The Mississippian*, June 18, 1845.

12. Sheldon to Van Buren, October 30, 1845, *Van Buren Papers;* Quaife, *Polk Diary*, Vol. I, p. 94.

13. Quaife, *Polk Diary*, Vol. III, p. 229; White, *The Jacksonians*, p. 76.

14. George M. to Sophy Dallas, December 2, 1845, *Dallas Papers.*

15. Walker, *1845 Treasury Report*, pp. 4–14; the arguments used by Walker often recurred during much of the subsequent tariff debate of the 19th century. Carl Schurz, for example, in a tariff address delivered on October 20, 1890, before the Massachusetts Reform Club, cited the 1845 tariff proposals and the Tariff of 1846 as evidence that a revenue tariff would work. Carl Schurz, *Speeches, Correspondence, Political Papers*, Vol. V, pp. 47–49 and 67.

16. Walker, *1845 Treasury Report,* pp. 14–18.

17. New York *Tribune,* August 3, 1846 and December 4, 5, 1845; New York *Herald,* December 4, 1845; *National Intelligencer,* December 4, 1845; New York *Evening Post,* August 4, 1846, noted the compliment paid Walked had a precedent. Twenty years earlier, Representative Francis Baylies of Massachusetts had his report on Oregon so honored.

18. *Niles National Register,* December 21, 1844.

19. *Niles National Register,* October 5, 1844.

20. *Niles National Register,* October 5, 1844, quotes the Richmond *Enquirer.*

21. *Niles National Register,* September 21, 1844, quotes *The* [London] *Times.*

22. *Niles National Register,* December 28, 1844, quotes *Wilmer and Smith's European Times; Journal of Commerce,* March 26, 1845.

23. *Niles National Register,* November 1, 1845, quotes the *London Economist;* see also Graebner, *Empire on the Pacific,* pp. 137–41.

24. *Niles National Register,* February 14, 1846, quotes the Baltimore *American; National Intelligencer,* November 1, 2, 5, 1845; Quaife, *Polk Diary,* Vol. I, pp. 268, 275, 453.

25. *Niles National Register,* March 7, 1846, quotes the *Union;* ibid., July 12, 1845, quotes the *Mississippian;* Davy to Walker, January 28, 1846, *Hurja Papers;* Persinger, "The Bargain of 1844 as the Origin of the Wilmot Proviso," *Annual Report of the American Historical Association,* Vol. I, 1911, pp. 189–95, which states that an agreement between the South and West had pledged Dixie to support western territorial gains in return for support of tariff reform. This assertion overlooks that the West, already burdened with huge staple crop surpluses, had much to gain with a reform of British tariff practices.

26. Graebner, *Empire on the Pacific,* pp. 141–45; McGrane, *William Allen,* pp. 103–20; Coleman, *Life of John J. Crittenden,* Vol. I, pp. 234–36.

27. Quaife, *Polk Diary,* Vol. I, p. 452; Coleman, *John J. Crittenden,* Vol. I, p. 235.

28. *Phillips* (ed.) *Toombs, Stephens, and Cobb Correspondence,* p. 73; Heilman and Levin, *Calendar of Joel R. Poinsett Papers,* p. 202, notes on April 28, 1846 that "war with England *or* Mexico is still a possibility." (Italics mine, J.S.).

29. Gardiner to Tyler, New York, February 22, 1846, *Tyler Papers; Journal of Commerce,* July 2, 1846; Tansill, *The Canadian Reciprocity Treaty of 1854,* pp. 18–19.

30. *Daily National Intelligencer,* May 10, 1845, quotes the *Union; ibid.,* August 22 and 29, 1845.

31. *Daily National Intelligencer,* September 15, 1845, quotes the New York *Tribune;* Isely, *Horace Greeley and the Republican Party,* p. 214.

32. *Daily National Intelligencer,* August 29, 1845, quotes the *Union.*

33. *Daily National Intelligencer,* September 3, 1845, quotes New York *Evening News.*

34. Walker to Van Buren, August 31, 1842, *Van Buren Papers;* Walker, *1845 Treasury Report,* pp. 8–9.

35. *Daily National Intelligencer,* July 11, 1845, quotes letter of Walker to the editor of the *Mississippian.*

36. *Daily National Intelligencer,* November 6, 1845; *Journal of Commerce,* May 12, 1845.

37. Rhett to Calhoun, September 18, 1845, *Calhoun Collection;* Poinsett to Van Buren, August 8, 1845, *Van Buren Papers; Correspondence of Toombs, Cobb and Stephens,* pp. 81–82.

38. *Daily National Intelligencer,* February 18, 1846.

39. Haskin to Cleveland, February 7, 1885, *Polk Papers;* Bancroft to Walker, September 10, 1845, *George Bancroft Papers,* Harvard University, reports of W. H. Prescott's desire to aid tariff work.

40. *Journal of Commerce,* January 17, 1846.

41. *Daily National Intelligencer,* July 16, 1846; Dixon Hall Lewis to Walker, July 7, 1846, *Walker Papers.*

42. Walker, *1845 Treasury Report,* p. 12; Tansill, *The Canadian Reciprocity Treaty of 1854,* p. 20; Thirty-first Congress, first session, *H. Ex. Doc. 64,* pp. 12–13; "Memoir of Robert John Walker," *Walker Papers.*

43. *Congressional Globe,* June 15, 1846, p. 976; see *ibid.,* June 18, 1846, p. 991 for a typical Pennsylvanian Democratic argument that "war" was not "the time to repeal it"; *ibid.,* p. 994, for Pennsylvanian Whig argument that Pennsylvania "never would have voted for James E. Polk" if they had known he was not an "advocate of protection." Lee F. Crippen, *Simon Cameron,* pp. 63–68; C. B. Going, *David Wilmot, Free-Soiler,* pp. 86, 145–50; New York *Tribune,* July 10, 1846. Of the 114 favorable votes 88 were cast by Southern and Western delegations. Of the 95 unfavorable votes 64 were cast by Middle Atlantic and New England delegations.

44. George M. to Sophy Dallas, July 15, 1846, *Dallas Papers; Congressional Globe,* July 27, 1846, p. 1141.

45. *Daily National Intelligencer,* July 25, 1846, quotes New York *Evening Post; ibid.,* quotes New York *Telegraph;* George M. to Sophy Dallas, July 15, 1846, *Dallas Papers.* Senatorial defections were small.

Only Cameron and Sturgeon of Pennsylvania and Cilley of New Hampshire deserted the Democrats. The latter suffered prompt retribution, being denied re-election by his democratically controlled legislature. Only Atchison of Missouri deserted the Whigs.

46. *Congressional Globe*, July 14, 1846 to July 28, 1846, pp. 1089–1151.

47. *Ibid.*, July 27 and 28, 1846, pp. 1143–1152; Malcolm Rogers Eiselin, *The Rise of Pennsylvania Protectionism*, p. 195; *Dallas Diary*, p. 94; *Daily National Intelligencer*, July 29, 1846.

48. George M. to Sophy Dallas, July 30, 1846, *Dallas Papers*; John B. Moore, *Works of James Buchanan*, Vol. VII, pp. 46–47; Albert D. Ramsey to Buchanan, July 25, 1846, *Buchanan Papers*.

49. Welles to Van Buren, July 28, 1846, *Van Buren Papers*; "Kremer" to Van Buren, May 21, 1846, *ibid.*; the author was making an obvious allusion to Congressman George Kremer, who had exposed the supposed Quincy Adams–Clay deal to Jackson. This "Kremer," also a Pennsylvanian, made a similar effort to expose Walker's 1844 role.

50. F. Randolph Hulbert to Walker, New York, July 29, 1846, *Walker Papers*; William Mullin to Walker, Natchez, Miss., August 21, 1846, *ibid.*

51. James G. Blaine, *Twenty Years of Congress*, Vol. 1, p. 194.

52. New York *Tribune*, September 23, 1846.

7. BULL OF THE WOODS

1. Walker to O'Sullivan, Washington, D.C., June 30, 1845, *Dreer Collection*; "Treasurer's Account," Ex. Doc. 5, *Ex. Doc.*, Twenty-ninth Congress, first session, shows that a general decline in deposits occurred between the third quarter of 1844 and the fourth quarter of 1845. A deposit of $653,680 at the Bank of Baltimore had been withdrawn before the third quarter of 1845; one of $3,671,587 at the (Boston) Merchant's Bank had been reduced to $877,891; that of $932,035 at the Philadelphia Bank had declined to $165,464. New York was unaffected.

2. *Congressional Globe*, Twenty-ninth Congress, first session, p. 10.

3. *Ibid.*, pp. 594–95.

4. *Daily National Intelligencer*, April 13, 1846, quotes the *Journal of Commerce*; *ibid.*, quotes *The Morning Telegraph*, "At the present moment there is a general fear pervading the business portions of this community, lest the line of measures about to be adopted with regard to the public moneys will carry widespread ruin with it. . . . [The] very doubt, caused by the constant introduction of new measures, is almost as fatal as the catastrophe anticipated."

5. *Daily National Intelligencer*, April 20, 1846.

6. New York *Tribune*, August 2, 1846; Glyndon G. Van Deusen, *The Jacksonian Era*, pp. 204–06; Coleman, *Crittenden*, Vol. I, pp. 248–49.

7. *Congressional Globe*, Twenty-ninth Congress, first session, Appendix, pp. 583–85, 592–94, 820–21, 1176; Lucien B. Chase, *A History of the Polk Administration*, p. 367.

8. *Ex. Doc.* Twenty-ninth Congress, first session, deposits at the Bank of America increased from $228,377 in the last quarter of 1845 to $1,310,284 in the first quarter of 1846; the Bank of the State of New York had no deposits in the first quarter of 1845 but had $808,394 in the first quarter of 1846.

9. Walker to Worthington, August 10, 1846, *Hurja Papers;* Swain to Walker, Philadelphia, August 11, 1846, *ibid.*

10. Pittsburgh *Morning Chronicle*, August 14, 1846, denounced Walker as an "Apostate." It recalled his earlier pungent defenses of protectionism. The impression it had was that Walker adjusted his politics to suit the latest basis of his political support.

11. Sanders to Crittenden, Natchez, Miss., September 20, 1846, *Crittenden Papers.*

12. Davis to Walker, August 24, 1846, *Miscellaneous Papers;* Varina Davis to Mary Walker, September 4, 1846, *Hurja Papers,* suggests the closeness of the relationship between the two families.

13. Allan Nevins (ed.), *Polk Diary*, p. 118; Chase, *Polk Administration*, p. 134.

14. *Daily National Intelligencer*, October 21, 1846, quotes the *Journal of Commerce.*

15. *Ibid.*, October 21, 1846; Board of Assistant Aldermen to Walker, New York, October 7, 1846, *Hurja Papers.*

16. *Journal of Commerce*, October 12, 1846.

17. Quaife, *Polk Diary*, Vol. II, p. 200; *Daily National Intelligencer*, October 24, 1846, quotes the *Union;* Young to Walker, October 7, 1846, *Hurja Papers,* urged the Secretary to obtain one and a half million "to transfer to N. Orleans *at once*. We have requisitions since you left for near ⅔ of this sum to meet expenses of the War—most of which are requested to be paid at N. Orleans in specie."

18. Margaret G. Meyers, *The New York Money Market*, Vol. I, pp. 184–85.

19. *Daily National Intelligencer*, November 16, 1846, quotes the *Journal of Commerce.*

20. Walker, *1846 Treasury Report*, p. 121; *Daily National Intelligencer*, January 2, 1847; New York *Tribune*, January 3, 1847, charged

the Secretary with abandoning his democratic pretensions since he chose to tax a basic commodity.

21. Walker, *1846 Treasury Report*, p. 121.

22. *Daily National Intelligencer*, April 5, 1847, quotes the New York *Herald*; New York *Herald*, April 2, 1847; New York *Tribune*, April 6, 1847; Walker to Polk, June 10, 1847, *Walker Letterbook*; Justin Smith, *The War with Mexico*, p. 263.

23. New York *Tribune*, January 30, 1847; February 9, 1847; New York *Evening Post*, February 9 and 10, 1847; *Congressional Globe*, Twenty-ninth Congress, second session, p. 203, contains a typical Whig comment. Congressman Vinton noted approvingly the amendment's intention "To strengthen the public credit and induce capitalists to lend their money to the Government." The bill was carried by 166 to 22 in the House and 43 to 2 in the Senate as a result of mixed support and opposition. See *ibid.*, pp. 230 and 267. On Walker's active intervention, see Quaife, *Polk Diary*, Vol. III, pp. 241–42, which Polk described as necessary "to prevent mischevious amendments."

24. New York *Tribune*, February 13 and 18, 1847.

25. George M. to Sophy Dallas, April 13, 1847, *Dallas Papers*.

26. New York *Tribune*, April 16, 1847.

27. *Corcoran Papers, passim* for late 1846 and 1847.

28. *Ibid.*, April 24, 1847.

29. *Ibid.*, April 26, 1847, quotes the Philadelphia *Bulletin*.

30. *1847 Treasury Report*, Appendix gives a detailed breakdown of distribution; *Daily National Intelligencer*, June 4, 1847, quotes the *Union*.

31. Winthrop to Corcoran, March 24, 1847, *Corcoran Papers*.

32. New York *Tribune*, May 5, 1847; Coryell to Dallas, December, 1845, *Dallas Papers*; Belmont to Walker, July 2, 1847; Belmont to Walker, August 3, 1847, *General Records of the Treasury Department*, Record Group 56.

8. THE PRICE OF SUCCESS

1. N. P. Trist to Walker, April 10, 1847, *Trist Papers*; James Thompson to Walker, Erie, March 30, 1847, *Hurja Papers*; George Evans to Walker, New York, March 8, 1847, *ibid.*; A. G. Brown to Walker, Jackson, March 1, 1847, *ibid.*; Daniel Webster to Walker, February 13, 1847, *ibid.*, pressing for help for "Mr. Fletcher Webster to get his compensation owing him as acting secretary of state." S. F. B. Morse to Walker, January 28, 1847, *Miscellaneous Papers*, are but a

few of numerous examples of the continuing demand for patronage.

2. Quaife (ed.), *Polk Diary, passim* for frequent references to the presidential suspicion that cabinet members were vying for the presidential nomination. See especially Nevins (ed.), *Polk Diary,* pp. 285–86.

3. Nevins (ed.), *Polk Diary,* p. 247.

4. Wright to Polk, October 18, 1846, *Polk Papers;* Walker to Wright, October 26, 1846, *Walker Letterbook;* Walker to Rogers, October 23, 1846, *ibid.*

5. Walker to Gould, October 23, 1846, *Walker Letterbook;* Walker to Wright, October 26, 1846, *ibid.;* Quaife (ed.), *Polk Diary,* Vol. II, pp. 176–77; Nevins (ed.), *Polk Diary,* pp. 160–61, establishes that Polk also suspected Wright was being undermined by Marcy; Garraty, *Silas Wright,* pp. 371–76.

6. Dallas to Walker, November 2, 1846, *Hurja Papers;* Observer to New York *Ledger,* Washington, D.C., October 31, 1846, *ibid.*

7. Broderick to Walker, New York, November 16, 1846, *Miscellaneous Papers;* Bancroft to Polk, December 3, 1846, *Bancroft Papers.*

8. *Toombs, Cobb, Stephens Correspondence,* pp. 86–87.

9. Quaife (ed.), *Polk Diary,* Vol. II, p. 218; Callaghan to Gilpin, January 1, 1846, *Gilpin Papers.*

10. New York *Tribune,* July 16, 1846; Quaife (ed.), *Polk Diary,* Vol. I, p. 495.

11. Walker to Polk, July 1, 1846, *Polk Papers;* Davis to Walker, July 22, 1846, *Hurja Notebook 5;* Davis to Walker, August 24, 1846, *Miscellaneous Papers;* Davis to Walker, Monterey, October 12, 1846, *Hurja Notebook 5;* Quitman to Walker, November 18, 1846, *ibid.;* Gaines to Walker, undated, *Miscellaneous Papers;* Stevens to Walker, February 5, 1847, *Hurja Papers.*

12. Quaife (ed.), *Polk Diary,* Vol. I, p. 495; Vol. II, p. 473.

13. Bancroft to Marcy, London, October 27, 1847, *Hurja Papers;* Landa to Trist, December, 1847, *Trist Papers.*

14. "Memoir of Robert John Walker," *Walker Papers;* Walker to Davis, New Orleans, November 30, 1846, *ibid.;* Walker to Polk, May 11, 1847, *Walker Letterbook.*

15. Rhett to Calhoun, June 21, 1847, *Calhoun Papers;* Niles to Van Buren, January 20, 1848, *Van Buren Papers;* Quaife (ed.), *Polk Diary,* Vol. III, pp. 402–04.

16. Welles to Van Buren, Washington, June 30, 1848, *Welles Papers.*

17. *Toombs, Cobb, Stephens Correspondence,* p. 88, letter that of South Carolinian Congressman Isaac E. Holmes.

18. Walker to Davis, New Orleans, November 30, 1846, *Walker Papers;* Kellogg to Walker, New York, January 13, 1848, *Hurja Papers,* describes Tammany enthusiasm for the "doctrine of free trade," while suggesting doubt about further expansion.

19. Hayden to Walker, New Orleans, May 16, 1846, *Walker Papers; Toombs, Cobb, Stephens Correspondence,* pp. 76–77; Coleman, *Crittenden,* Vol. I, p. 334.

20. Hayden to Walker, New Orleans, May 15, 1846; Hayden to Walker, New Orleans, April 29, 1846; Hayden to Walker, May 4, 1846, *Walker Papers;* Walker to Bache, July 5, 1843, *Hurja Papers.*

21. W. Dean Burnham, *Presidential Ballots 1836–1892,* pp. 34–35; Going, *David Wilmot, Free Soiler,* pp. 117–41.

22. Daniel to Van Buren, November 19, 1847, *Van Buren Papers, Toombs, Cobb, Stephens Correspondence,* pp. 113–14.

23. Tyler to Portsmouth *Pilot;* Tyler to Gardiner, Charles City, Va., March 2, 1847, quoted in Tyler, *Life and Times,* Vol. II, pp. 477–79.

24. Robert Selph Henry, *The Story of the Mexican War,* p. 104; New York *Tribune,* February 20, 1849 which published an account of an interview between Wilmot and Polk; Dallas to Van Buren, November 2, 1847, *Van Buren Papers;* Cooke to Walker, December 14, 1847, *Walker Papers;* Dallas to Walker, October 16, 1846, *ibid.;* Dallas to Phillips, December 11, 1848, *Dreer Papers.*

25. *Toombs, Cobb, Stephens Correspondence,* pp. 138–39.

26. Walker to Leach and others, Washington, D.C., December 15, 1847, *Walker Letterbook,* reports his dependence upon "an amanuensis" to do his writing. Quaife (ed.), *Polk Diary, passim* for frequent references to long illnesses of Walker.

27. *The Mississippian,* March 24, 1848, quotes the *Whig Courier and Enquirer; ibid.,* March 10, 1848, quotes the Philadelphia *Ledger;* Vicksburg *Weekly Sentinel,* February 16, 1848, quotes the Philadelphia *Ledger; Alton Union,* November 24, 1845; Tallmadge to Walker, Cincinnati, June, 1846, *Walker Papers.*

28. Vicksburg *Weekly Sentinel,* February 16, 1848, quotes the Philadelphia *Ledger; Courier and Inquirer,* January 3, 1848.

29. Niles to Van Buren, April 18, 1848, *Van Buren Papers;* Martin to John Van Buren, May 3, 1848, *ibid.*

30. Frank B. Woodford, *Lewis Cass,* pp. 254–57; "Memoir of Robert John Walker," *Walker Papers.*

31. Woodford, *Lewis Cass,* pp. 260–61; Nevins (ed.), *Polk Diary,* pp. 337–38; Avery Craven, *The Growth of Southern Nationalism,* pp.

48–49; John L. Hayes, *A Reminiscence of the Free Soil Movement in New Hampshire 1845*, pp. 10–17.

32. *The Mississippian*, May 26, 1848; Crittenden to Foote, New Orleans, December 21, 1848, *Walker Papers;* Abert to Coryell, Washington, D.C., March 12, 1848, *Coryell Papers;* Burnham, *Presidential Ballots*, pp. 36–39.

33. "Memoir of Robert John Walker," *Walker Papers.*

34. *Dallas Diary*, p. 46; Cobb to Walker, Athens, Ga., June 2, 1849, *Miscellaneous Papers;* Walker to Gaines, June 26, 1847, *Walker Letterbook;* Blair to Van Buren, June 10, 1849, *Van Buren Papers.*

9. THE BUSINESS CONSTITUENCY

1. Walker to Ward, February 28, 1849, *Record Group 56, General Records of the Treasury Department.*

2. Walker to unknown, September 18, 1847, *Walker Letterbook.*

3. Bancroft to Walker, May 26, 1848, *Miscellaneous Papers;* Bancroft to Walker, May 26, 1848, *Bancroft Collection;* Corcoran to Walker, August 4, 1848, *Corcoran Papers.*

4. Walker to Bancroft, August 9, 1848, *Corcoran Papers;* Walker to Bancroft, August 9, 1848, *Bancroft Collection.*

5. Corcoran and Riggs to Baring Bros., November 7, 1848, *Corcoran Papers;* Corcoran to Ward, February 4, 1849, *ibid.;* Corcoran to Walker, December 15, 1848, *ibid.;* Corcoran to Walker, December 22, 1848, *ibid.;* Walker to Bancroft, April 17, 1848, *Walker Letterbook.*

6. *Journal of Commerce*, January 15, 1849; Lawrence to Walker, November 17, 1848, *Letters Received; 1843–1849, Secretary of the Treasury*, hereafter *Treasury File;* Lawrence to Walker, November 18, 1848, *ibid.;* Walker to Lawrence, November 22, 1848, *ibid.;* Walker to Lawrence, November 26, 1848, *ibid.;* Walker to Lawrence, December 2, 1848, *ibid.*

7. Joly Freres and others to Walker, New York, April 13, 1847, *Hurja Papers;* Walker to Lawrence, April 5, 1847, *Hurja Notebook 5;* Walker to Lawrence, May 21, 1847, *ibid.;* Walker to Lawrence, September 26, 1846, *ibid.;* Walker to Richard Smith, *Autograph Letters*, Vol. V.

8. Walker to Forney, June 27, 1847, *Walker Letterbook.*

9. Walker to Dow, April 12, 1848, *Walker Letterbook;* for further examples of Walker's belief in Manifest Destiny see Walker to Messrs. I. L. Scott and others, June 28, 1847; Walker to Green, July 2, 1847; Walker to Young Men's Democratic Association of Philadelphia, July 2,

1847; Walker to Forney, July 1, 1847; Walker to Jacksonian Democratic Association, January 12, 1848, *ibid.*; New York *Tribune*, July 16, 1846.

10. *The Dictionary of National Biography*, Vol. X and XII, pp. 230–31 and 540–41; Walker to Bancroft, Washington, March 27, 1847, *George E. Bancroft Papers*.

11. Bancroft to Walker, May 3, 1847, *ibid.*; also in *Miscellaneous Papers*; Bancroft to Walker, London, October 2, 1847, *George E. Bancroft Papers*; Bancroft to Walker, London, August 17, 1847, *ibid.*; Walker to Pakenham, Washington, D.C., May 19, 1847, *Miscellaneous Papers*.

12. Bancroft to Walker, London, March 24, 1848, *George E. Bancroft Papers*; Bancroft to Walker, April 1, 1848, *ibid.*; Washington *Union*, April 3, 1848.

13. Walker to Warden and Barhydt, July 29, 1847, *Walker Letterbook*; *Journal of Commerce*, February 27, 1849; Herbert Wender, *Southern Commercial Conventions*, pp. 50 and 61; the report is to be found appended to the 1848 Treasury Report. It is more than 200 pages long and is the definitive work on the development of the British Warehousing System to 1848.

14. H. B. Learned, "The Establishment of the Secretaryship of the Interior," *The American Historical Review*, Vol. X, p. 765.

15. *Ibid.*, pp. 765–66; see also "Memoir of Robert John Walker," *Walker Papers*, describing Walker's pride at establishing the Interior Department; New York *Tribune*, February 14, 1849.

16. George M. to Sophy Dallas, April 2, 1847, *Dallas Papers*; George M. to Sophy Dallas, March 28, 1847, *ibid.*; George M. to Sophy Dallas, April 21, 1847, *ibid.*; Walker to Sibbald, August 7, 1848, *Hurja Papers*.

17. Polk to Walker, September 30, 1848, *Hurja Papers*; Polk to Walker, Nashville, May 9, 1849, *Miscellaneous Papers*.

18. A. T. Steward, Theodore Sedgwick, Prosper M. Wetmore, F. B. Cutting, William H. Aspinwall, and fifty other prominent New York businessmen to Walker, September 8, 1848, invite him to a testimonial dinner in gratitude for his labors on their behalf, *Hurja Papers*.

10. PRIVATE INTERLUDE

1. Walker to Claiborne, May 8, 1849, *J. F. H. Claiborne Papers*; see also New York *Tribune*, late February and March, 1849, *passim*, setting forth reports of Walker's plans.

2. Walker to Douglas, New York, September 21, 1850, *Douglas Papers;* *50 U.S. (9 Howard)*, p. 647; *54 U.S. (13 Howard)*, p. 518; Marshall to Walker, April 26, 1850; Forney to Walker, May 13, 1850, *Walker Papers;* Campbell to Walker, March 6, 1850; E. M. Stanton to Walker, Pittsburgh, March 28, 1850, *Hurja Papers,* Stanton assisted Walker in the preparation of his case. Walker to Walworth, January 7, 1851, *Walworth Papers; Mississippian,* April 26, 1850. At an earlier time, while serving as Senator from Mississippi, Walker had argued strongly in defense of the reserved powers, see Charles Grove Haines and Foster H. Sherwood, *The Role of the Supreme Court in American Government and Politics 1835–1864,* pp. 214–15.

3. Quitman to Walker, Jackson, February 13, 1850; Cobb to Walker, June 2, 1849, *Miscellaneous Papers;* Cobb to Buchanan, Athens, June 2, 1849, *Toombs, Cobb, Stephens Correspondence,* p. 159; Blair to Van Buren, June 10, 1849, *Van Buren Papers;* L. M. Sears, *John Slidell,* p. 86, indicates that the still potent political influence of Walker checked open attacks upon him.

4. Sanders to Walker, New York, April 20, 1850, *Walker Papers.*

5. Davis to Walker, New York, May 2, 1849, *Walker Papers;* Walker to Douglas, Lancaster, Pa., May 4, 1850, *Douglas Papers;* Washington *Chronicle,* April 23, 1869.

6. Quitman to Walker, Jackson, February 13, 1850, *Walker Papers.*

7. Walker to Forney and others, New York, November 21, 1850, *Hurja Papers;* Henry to Walker, New York, April 20, 1850; Henry to Walker, New York, March 12, 1850; Tammany Memorial to Walker, New York, May 7, 1850; Latham to Walker, Washington, D.C., May 21, 1850, *Walker Papers;* Washington *Union,* May 18, 1850.

8. Buchanan to Gwin, Wheatland, May 22, 1850, *Gwin Papers.*

9. Leonard William Ascher, "The Economic History of the New Almaden Mine, 1845–1863," *Unpublished dissertation, University of Southern California,* p. 102; Dix to Van Buren, June 9, 1849, *Van Buren Papers.*

10. Ascher, *New Almaden Mine, passim;* Janin to Walker, San Francisco, July 31, 1855; Walker to Janin, March 6, 1855; Janin to Walker, San Francisco, July 19, 1855; Janin to Walker, Baltimore, September 18, 1855; Rose to Middleton, New York, May 28, 1853, *Walker Papers.*

11. Frank H. Tick, "Political and Economic Policies of R. J. Walker," *Unpublished dissertation, University of California, Los Angeles,* p. 239; Green to Walker, New York, November 25, 1850, *California Assembly Journal* (Second session, 1851); Walker to Green, November 26, 1850, *California Historical Document VII, 2,* which urges the con-

struction of a University in California which "if properly organized and conducted would contribute, even more than your gold, to the glory and happiness of advancing generations in your great state." Corcoran to Walker, July 18, 1851, recording quicksilver investment; Corcoran to Walker, July 23, 1851, *Corcoran Papers,* acknowledges receipt for $3,277 investment.

12. Janin to Walker, San Francisco, July 19, 1855; Janin to Walker, July 31, 1855, *Walker Papers,* describes the difficulties besetting the Almaden mine's status. Janin complained, "The fees which lawyers here charge for ordinary court business, are fabulous. 10% upon large amounts for an ordinary procedure or mortgage. Notwithstanding they complain for there is not much business doing. All the property is mortgaged, all credit paralyzed. No office is open, nobody works here after four o'clock. The lawyers are flitting about, from one town to another so that I have to make many calls, before meeting anybody." Walker's neglect of his legal practice is graphically illustrated by his declining appearances before the Supreme Court. During 1850, he argued fourteen cases; in 1851–52, he appeared seven times; between 1853–58, he argued no cases.

13. Robert E. Russel, *Improvement of Communication with the Pacific Coast as an Issue in American Politics, 1783–1864,* pp. 96–97; *American Railroad Journal,* Vol. XXVI, p. 728 and Vol. XXVII, pp. 394–96.

14. Russel, *Improvement of Communication with the Pacific Coast,* pp. 128–29; *Am. R.R. Jour.,* Vol. XXVII, p. 541; *Congressional Globe,* Thirty-third Congress, first session, Appendix, pp. 1031–36; Roy Franklin Nichols, *Franklin Pierce,* pp. 268, 280, 309.

15. Russel, *Improvement of Communications with the Pacific Coast,* pp. 128–29; *Am. R.R. Jour.,* Vol. XXVII, pp. 394–96; *Circular to the Stockholders of the Atlantic and Pacific R.R. Co.,* (New York, 1855), *passim;* see also the New York *Herald* for the months of December, 1854, January and February, 1855, *passim.*

16. Russel, *Improvement of Communications with the Pacific Coast,* pp. 128–29; Walker to Wigfall, March 19, 1855; Janin to Walker, New Orleans, June 9, 1855, *Walker Papers;* Walker to Buchanan, April 28, 1856, *Buchanan Papers.*

17. Russel, *Improvement of Communications with the Pacific Coast,* pp. 148–49, 177, 193; Allan Nevins, *Ordeal of the Union,* Vol. II, pp. 48, 62, 122; *Congressional Globe,* Thirty-third Congress, first session, Appendix, pp. 1031–36.

18. Janin to Walker, New Orleans, June 9, 1855; Janin to Walker,

Thibodamville, May 22, 1855; Janin to Walker, New Orleans, June 6, 1855; Janin to Walker, off Acapulco, June 23, 1855, *Walker Papers*.

19. Agreement between Walker and Peter Cooper confirming purchase by Walker from Cooper of 1,000 shares of The Trenton Iron Company, May 23, 1853; Watterson to Walker, November 2, 1853, *Hurja Papers;* Corcoran to Whitehouse, Washington, D.C., November 16, 1853, on sale of 2700 shares of Illinois and Wisconsin Rail stock belonging to Walker, *Corcoran Papers;* Whitehouse to Walker, November 16, 1853, on sale of Janesville City bonds, *Hurja Papers;* Corcoran to Walker, December 13, 1853; list of Walker collateral guaranteeing his obligations which Corcoran ordered sold at auction, December 14, 1853, consisted of Janesville City Script, Sussex Iron Company, Rock River Valley R.R., and Marysville & Lexington R.R. stock worth $21,000; Corcoran to Camman & Co., December 16, 1853, complains "Mr. Walker has given me a great deal of trouble in the business"; Corcoran to Walker, January 9, 1854; Corcoran to Walker, Washington, November 17, 1854, *Corcoran Papers;* Walker to Coryell, February 24, 1854, *Coryell Papers,* asks aid in influencing congressional vote on Wisconsin railroad grant. Jordan, *A Politician of Expansion,* pp. 366–67.

20. Walker to Corcoran, New York, July 30, 1851, *Corcoran Papers;* Walker to Douglas, New York, September 21, 1850, *Douglas Papers.*

21. Walker to Corcoran, New York, July 30, 1851; Corcoran to Walker, August 1, 1851, describes the offer as of "too great moment to decide hastily." Corcoran to Walker, August 2, 1851, gives Corcoran decision, *Corcoran Papers;* Howard G. Bronson, *History of the Illinois Central Railroad to 1870,* pp. 11–21; the *Illinois Central Railroad Papers* at the Newberry Library has no identifiable references to Walker.

22. Walker to Corcoran, August 16, 1857, *Corcoran Papers;* Dallas to Aspinwall, August 22, 1851, *Hurja Papers.*

23. *An Account of the Proceedings at the Dinner Given by Mr. George Peabody,* pp. 34–36 and *passim.*

24. *The League,* January 24, 1846; March 14, 1846; April 18, 1846; this official British free trade publication invariably called him "able and enlightened"; Peabody to Corcoran, October 3, 1851, *Corcoran Papers;* Monckton-Milne to Walker, Devon, December 23, 1851; MacGregor to Walker, Hyde Park, October 21, 1851, *Walker Papers;* London *Daily News,* December 9, 1851 and December 11, 1851; *Speech of Hon. Robert J. Walker at Liverpool, England,* November 24, 1851, *Hurja Papers;* "William Peter: Her Majesty's Consul at Philadelphia 1840–1853," *Pennsylvania Magazine of History and Biography,* Vol. 80 (1956), p. 440.

25. Arthur Davies, *An Outline of Empire of the West as Foreshadowed in the Correspondence of Robert J. Walker and Arthur Davies, MP*, pp. 3–7, 16–18, 22.

26. Billing to Brayman, January 8, 1852, Schuyler to Brayman, February 10, 1852; Billing to Brayman, New York, February 20, 1852, *Brayman Collection*; Markham to unknown, 1851, *Hurja Papers*.

27. Walker to Woodbury, Washington, D.C., February 16, 1853, *Hurja Papers*; Walker to Cushing, Washington, D.C., February 7, 1853, notes that Walker had been in ill-health "for fourteen months." Walker to Pierce, Washington, D.C., March 8, 1853, *Cushing Papers*; Power of Attorney to E. George Squier, January 13, 1853; Edwards to Squier, March 5, 1853; Walker to the President of San Salvador, January 13, 1853; Edwards to Squier, September 19, 1853, *Squier Papers*; Nichols, *Franklin Pierce*, p. 228.

28. Walker to Marcy, New York, February 2, 1854; Walker to Marcy, New York, November 6, 1853, *Marcy Papers*; Walker to Buchanan, Washington, D.C., April 28, 1856, *Buchanan Papers*; New York *Tribune*, July 2, 1853; July 15, 1853; July 27, 1853.

29. Kendall to Walker, October 16, 1853, *Miscellaneous Papers*; Corcoran to Walker, June 26, 1855; Walker to Corcoran, Baltimore, July 7, 1855; Hyde to Walker, December 3, 1855; Hyde to Corcoran, Washington, D.C., July 3, 1856; Walker to Corcoran, New York, September 27, 1856, *Corcoran Papers*.

11. WITHIN A BUDDING TRAGEDY

1. Davis to Walker, New York, May 2, 1849, *Walker Papers*; Buchanan to Corcoran, July 15, 1850, *Corcoran Papers*.

2. Buchanan to Walker, Wheatland, Pa., March 21, 1853, *Hurja Papers*; Nichols, *Franklin Pierce*, pp. 255–57, 263–64.

3. Walker to Buchanan, Washington, D.C., April 28, 1856, *Buchanan Papers*; see also "Memoir of Robert John Walker," *Walker Papers*.

4. Walker to Buchanan, Washington, D.C., April 28, 1856, *Buchanan Papers*.

5. *An Appeal for the Union, Letter from the Hon. Robert J. Walker*, New York, September 30, 1856, p. 1.

6. *An Appeal for the Union*, p. 6.

7. *An Appeal for the Union*, p. 5 and *passim*; "Memoir of Robert John Walker," *Walker Papers*.

8. "Memoir of Robert John Walker," *Walker Papers*; Walker to Buchanan, New York, October 3, 1856, *Buchanan Papers*; Buchanan to

Walker, Wheatland, Pa. October 6, 1856, *Miscellaneous Papers; De Bow's Review*, Vol. XXI, pp. 591–92, contained the gist of the Walker arguments. New York *News,* October 4, 1856; Nevins, *Emergence of Lincoln,* Vol. I, p. 65.

9. Walker to Buchanan, New York, October 3, 1856, *Buchanan Papers;* Forney to Sanders, Philadelphia, October 13, 1856, *Sanders Papers.*

10. Wilkins to Buchanan, February 11, 1857, *Sanders Papers;* May to Walker, Baltimore, February 10, 1857, *Walker Papers;* Washington *Sun,* February 15, 1857; New York *Tribune,* February 15, 1857.

11. New York *Tribune,* February 3, 4, 6, 13, 17, 1857, contain many references to opposition. The last number assured the nation that Buchanan "will invite no man into his cabinet with unclean hands"; *An Appeal for the Union,* p. 4.

12. New York *Tribune,* February 12, 13 and 17, 1857, the southern senators who expressed support for Walker, other than Rusk and Clay, were Fitzpatrick of Alabama, Reid and Biggs of North Carolina, and his old friend, Albert Gallatin Brown of Mississippi; Claiborne, *Mississippi,* p. 422.

13. *Toombs, Cobb, Stephens Correspondence,* pp. 395–97.

14. New York *Tribune,* February 16, 17, 18, 19, 21, 1857; see also *National Intelligencer* and New York *Herald* for the same days.

15. Lillie to Eugene Bache, Washington, D.C., March, 1857, *Walker Papers;* a delightful portrait of the turmoil endemic to the Walker household is found in the *Ross Wilkins Papers.*

16. New York *Herald,* March 23, 1857.

17. Walker to Cooke, Washington, D.C., April 6, 1857, *Walker Papers;* New York *Tribune,* March 21, 25, 26, 27, 1857; March 24, 1857; New York *Herald,* March 27, April 1, 1857; the latter reports that Walker "repeats his opinion that Kansas will be a free state."

18. Walker to Buchanan, April 28, 1856, *Buchanan Papers;* New York *Tribune,* April 2, 1857; *Harper's Weekly,* Vol. I, April 11, 1857, noted "what a future Mr. Walker has before him! . . . Let us suppose that he succeeds in pacifying Kansas, and piloting it into the Union on terms which will coincide with public anticipation. . . . Let us assume that he will put an end to the . . . squabbles of the Freestate men and the Pro-slavery men . . . what reward would be too high for such a man?"

19. Colfax to Robinson, April 8, 1857, *Walker Papers;* New York *Herald,* April 1, 7, 1857, had James Gordon Bennett expressing fear "that before this Kansas imbroglio is six months older, he will be sorry

that he [went] to . . . Lecompton"; New York *Tribune*, April 2, 1857, doubted whether Walker had "a proper appreciation of the difficulties he will be compelled to confront."

20. New York *Herald*, April 7, 1857; New York *Tribune*, February 21, 1857; Paul Gates, *Fifty Million Acres, passim,* for a comprehensive treatment of land companies; *Harper's Weekly*, Vol. I, April 11, 1857, p. 229, described the Pacific R.R. Co. as a "stock-jobbing operation, and parties concerned were tainted with the peculiar fragrance which stock-jobbing exhales. It hurt Walker."

21. New York *Evening Mirror*, April 1, 1857; the New York *Tribune*, March 28, 1857, in an editorial entitled "Acceptance of Walker" stated the radical northern view of the appointment. It questioned the reason Walker had received "unlimited discretion as to the means to be employed in maintaining order and peace in Kansas." It assumed that power had been given to advance the cause of slavery. But it concluded, "we shall not prejudge Mr. Walker. His antecedents are unfavorable; but we shall not assume that he will aid in trampling three-fourths of the people of Kansas under the feet of the remaining fourth—it will be time enough to believe this when we cannot help doing so." The *Irish News*, March 31, 1857, cheered, "It must be regarded as no common indication of devotion to a political creed when—for the sake of illustrating and exhibiting the strength, justice and equalizing power of that creed on a society whose under-currents, lashed and goaded by fanaticism in the name of freedom, and by bullyism in the guise of benevolence, break the surface into portentiously rugged and lawless features—such a man as Mr. Walker accepts such an office." The New York *Herald*, April 4, 1857, which felt little sympathy for Walker, insisted he ought to accept the China Mission rather than Kansas. The New York *Tribune*, March 31, 1857; Cremwell to Black, Harrisburg, February 1, 1858, *Black Papers,* indicates that other Democrats felt Kansas was crucial to Democratic survival. Cremwell observed once the Kansas fat was in the fire, "I have come finally to this conclusion—not alone on my own Judgment, but by conference with good men, who act deliberately and decide justly—that if Kansas be admitted on the Calhoun Lecompton Constitution, without modification . . . it will knock our Democratic Party, *far,* 'to the other side of Jordan' in Pennsylvania."

12. A PIGMY ON THE PRAIRIE

1. The New York *Tribune*, April 20, 21, 23, 27, 1857; Corcoran to Walker, April 11, 1857, *Corcoran Papers,* asked permission to sell 155

shares of Chicago, St. Paul and Fond du Lac; Corcoran to Walker, April 16, 1857, *ibid.*; Corcoran to Riggs & Co., April 18, 1857, *ibid.*, deposits 600 shares of Texas, Western R.R. stock, to Walker's account, quoted value $30,000; Corcoran to Walker, April 18, 1857, *ibid.*, seeks sale of Chicago, St. Paul and Fond du Lac stock and 30 shares of Texas, Western R.R.; Corcoran to Walker, April 22, 1857, *ibid.*; Cass to Stanton, March 31, 1857, *Walker Papers*, explains that the appointment of Stanton was "due to the new Governor, Mr. Walker, that he should have for his Secretary a man known to him and in whom he has confidence, and your selection is desired by him."

2. The London *Daily News*, April 14, 1857.

3. The Lecompton, Kansas *Union*, April 11, 1857; *Herald of Freedom*, April 18, 1857; New York *Tribune*, April 24, 1857; New York *Times*, May 1, 1857, commends Walker for "high patriotism"; Walker to Buchanan, March 26, 1857, *Kansas Historical Publications*, 1889–1896, p. 290, neatly expresses the administration view of the Kansas problem. Walker states: "I understand that you and all your Cabinet cordially concur in the opinion expressed by me, that the actual bona fide residents of . . . Kansas, by a fair and regular vote, unaffected by fraud or violence, must be permitted, in adopting their state constitution, to decide for themselves what shall be their social institutions."

4. The New York *Times*, May 13, 1857; *Kansas Weekly Herald*, May 23, 1857; New York *Tribune*, May 13, 1857; St. Louis *Intelligence*, May 23, 1857, concluded "The Kansas troubles are over—They were, from the beginning, nothing but a stock jobbers war between Pro-Slavery and Free State Speculators—some making 'big strikes' for town sites, corner lots and eligible quarter sections, and others 'going it strong' for the offices of the future State. . . . Governor Walker will have a pleasant time. Grim-visaged war hath soothed its wrinkled front, and speculation is the order of the day."

5. The New York *Tribune*, May 13 and June 4, 1857; St. Louis *Morning Herald*, May 15, 1857, editorialized "He seems to look at the present difficulty not as a partisan, but as if desirous, only that right shall prevail, and the true voice of the people be heard"; the poem entitled "Affectionately Addressed to Robt. J. Walker, Governor of Kansas" is to be found in the Library of Congress and in the New York *Tribune*, April 28, 1857; Martha had wished to have a book of her poetry published at the time of Walker's appointment. Her brother, though expressing doubt about the necessity of rushing publication agreed to give the publishers "the necessary guarantees against loss." Walker to Cooke, April 6, 1857, *Walker Papers*.

6. Walker to Douglas, New York, January 9, 1857, *Douglas Papers,* expressed the belief that Douglas's territorial policy must "ultimately prevail." Walker had also aligned himself with the Dred Scott decision prior to its delivery by declaring his hope that the Supreme Court would deny Congress the right to control slavery in the territories. Walker asserted before the Covode hearings that Douglas had urged, "You must go Bob. I feel intensely on this. The whole success of the Kansas-Nebraska Act in that territory is to a great extent dependent upon your consenting to go. I beg it of you." Quoted in House Report 648, Thirty-sixth Congress, first session, pp. 105–06; see also Russel, *Improvement of Communications,* pp. 150–67 and 187–201; Nevins, *Emergence of Lincoln,* Vol. I, pp. 144–46; Milton, *The Eve of Conflict,* p. 262; Rainwater, *Mississippi: Storm Center of Secession 1856–1861,* pp. 46–47.

7. Chicago *Tribune,* May 25, 1857; New York *Tribune,* June 1, 1857; *Kansas Weekly Herald,* May 30, 1857; Gates, *Fifty Million Acres,* pp. 109–10.

8. The New York *Tribune,* June 4, 1857.

9. The New York *Tribune,* June 4, 1857; New York *Times,* June 1, 1857. Subsequently, the city of Leavenworth received a bill for the liquor consumed. It was paid only after severe protest. *Quindaro Chindowan,* May 27, 1857.

10. *Kansas Historical Publications,* 1889–1896, p. 238; "Broadside to the People of Leavenworth County, June 3, 1857," the copy in *Hurja Papers,* pledges fair election. *Kansas Weekly Herald,* June 6, 1857; Lecompton, Kansas *Union,* June 12, 1857.

11. *Kansas Historical Publications,* 1889–1896, pp. 335–36.

12. *Kansas Historical Publications,* 1889–1896, p. 336; New York *Tribune,* June 8, 1857.

13. Nevins, *Emergence of Lincoln,* Vol. I, p. 155; Morris, "R. J. Walker in the Kansas Struggle," *Master's Essay, University of Chicago,* p. 16; *Overland Monthly,* Vol. 5, December, 1870, pp. 544–56.

14. Walker to Buchanan, Lecompton, June 28, 1857, *Buchanan Papers,* also contains the revealing anecdote, "When first passing through Lawrence some . . . Black Republicans told me the violent pro-slavery men, if I went for submitting the constitution to the people, would assassinate me or drive me from Lecompton. I told them I had fixed the exact date for running, namely when General Harney (Commander of the Federal Troops) ran first." Nevins, *Emergence of Lincoln,* Vol. I, p. 155; *Overland Monthly,* Vol. 5, December, 1870, p. 550; Morris, *Walker in the Kansas Struggle,* p. 39.

15. The New York *Tribune,* June 22, 1857; *Kansas Weekly Herald,*

July 11, 1857; *Herald of Freedom,* November 14, 1857, records the emphasis with which Walker had disassociated himself from the pro-slavery wing of the party.

16. House Report 648, Thirty-sixth Congress, first session, Walker admitted his intentions quite candidly before the Covode Committee. *Kansas Historical Publications,* p. 345; Rainwater, *Mississippi, 1856–61,* p. 47, is mistaken when he asserts "Walker desired that Kansas should become a slave state." He is correct when he adds, "He . . . directed his energies towards making Kansas a Democratic state"; *Richmond South,* June 6, 1857; *The Herald of Freedom,* June 27, 1857.

17. Leavenworth *Times,* June 21, 1857; Brown, *Reminiscences of Gov. R. J. Walker in Kansas,* pp. 27, 42–44, and *passim.*

18. Walker to Buchanan, Lecompton, June 28, 1857, *Buchanan Papers;* New York *Tribune,* June 15, 1857.

19. *Kansas Historical Publications,* p. 339, Walker consistently refused to oppose existing territorial laws. He took the position that the franchise alone was a legitimate relief. His determined impartiality was amply illustrated in his actions pertaining to the establishment of "Banks of issue" in the Territory. Commenting on his appointment of L. A. Boling to inspect the Atchison, Kansas branch bank, he noted, "Upon his report to me that all requirements of the law have been complied with I shall issue the proclamation required permitting the bank to do business . . . I cannot . . . omit this opportunity to say, that if I had any discretion in the matter, I would not sanction the establishment of any bank of issue in the territory." See Walker to J. P. Walker, August 3, 1857, *Walker Papers;* Walker to Boling, August 3, 1857, *ibid.*

20. *Kansas Historical Publications,* pp. 35–64; Morris, *Walker in the Kansas Struggle,* pp. 41–47; *Detroit Free Press,* July 22, 1857, commented, "The Lawrence abolitionists have no fear that they will not be permitted to vote for or against the constitution. They know . . . that Kansas will at an early day enter the Union as a free democratic state. It is this that the Lawrence abolitionists fear." Walker defended his action by claiming that if the Lawrence action had been permitted, it would have provoked a rash of similar outbreaks. Harney to Walker, July 16, 1857, *Miscellaneous Papers;* Douglas to Walker, Chicago, July 21, 1857, *ibid.,* approved the action taken by the Governor as "maintaining the supremacy of the law."

21. The New York *Tribune,* July 4, 1857; *Kansas Weekly Herald,* July 4, 1857; Gates, *Fifty Million Acres,* p. 109 and pp. 129–30.

22. *Kansas Historical Collections,* p. 345; *The Herald of Freedom,* July 18, 1857.

23. *Kansas Historical Collections,* p. 359; Walker's speech, November 10, 1857, *Walker Papers,* protested that the North accused him of seeking to make Kansas slave, while the South accused him of wishing it free. He chose only to permit Kansas to find its own fate.

13. HE WILL NOT PRESUME

1. Roy Franklin Nichols, *The Disruption of American Democracy,* pp. 75–78; Philip G. Auchampaugh, *James Buchanan and His Cabinet on the Eve of Secession,* Chapter I; Allan Nevins, *The Emergence of Lincoln,* Vol. I, pp. 61–64.

2. Black to Van Dyke, Pittsburgh, November 15, 1856, *Black Papers; Toombs, Cobb, Stephens Correspondence,* pp. 382–83.

3. Douglas to Walker, Chicago, July 21, 1857, *Miscellaneous Papers;* Wise to Robert Tyler, Richmond, January 9, 1857, *Tyler Papers;* Nichols, *The Disruption of American Democracy,* p. 62; "Diary and Memoranda of William L. Marcy, 1857," *American Historical Review,* Vol. XXIV (1918–19), p. 647.

4. *Kansas Historical Collection,* pp. 322–23, in which Cass asserted it was the "duty of the government . . . to secure every resident . . . the free and independent vote . . . to decide their own destiny . . ."; Manuscript in John Appleton's handwriting, June, 1857, notation by Jeremiah Black, *Black Papers,* supports Walker's Topeka speech. Some evidence of the first disagreement in cabinet is evident in Aaron V. Brown to Walker, Washington, D.C., July 8, 1857, *Miscellaneous Papers,* which states, "Your inaugural was well received here and read with general approbation. Not so however some of your *speeches* particularly the Topeka one"; *Toombs, Cobb, Stephens Correspondence,* pp. 392, 400–01, 404–06; Cobb argued as late as July 21, 1857, "Walker I am satisfied has acted in concert and cooperation with our friends throughout," *ibid.,* p. 407.

5. Brown to Walker, Washington, D.C., July 8, 1857, *Miscellaneous Papers,* expressed concern lest Walker's Kansas pronouncements "might make the spirit of much discontent in the South." Brown urged Walker to make it clear that though Kansas "would come in as a *free state . . .* he should fix the record so, that it may not appear to have so come in by the administration having recommended any matter of submitting the constitution to the decision of a *horde of imported* votes . . ."; Cobb to Walker, Washington, D.C., July 27, 1857, *ibid.,* observed "No one desires that Kansas should come into the Union with a constitution that does not meet the approval of her people. . . . When she applies

for admission, it is the right and duty of Congress to know that the Constitution reflects the will of a majority of her bona fide citizens. I do not say that a vote of ratification at her polls is the only mode of furnishing that information—but I will say that it would seem the most satisfactory." John A. Dix to Walker, New York, June 16, 1857, *ibid.*, Dix, who accepted the Treasury department in the twilight days of the administration, described the Walker inaugural as "able, liberal & fair." He concluded, "I am satisfied that, with the exception of a few fanatics, north and south, there is an earnest desire in the community at large, that these dissentions shall be healed in the mode you have indicated— by a fair & unbiased vote of 'the *bona fide* resident settlers of Kansas.' "

6. Buchanan to Walker, Washington, D.C., July 12, 1857 (copy made by Eugene Cooke), *Hurja Papers;* also cited in Covode Committee, *op. cit.;* the foregoing letter indicated that Buchanan, along with the members of cabinet, had no clear idea what constituted "bona fide residents." Henry S. Foote, *Casket of Reminiscences,* pp. 114–15, discussing the period states, "I soon learned, from the lips of Mr. Jacob Thompson and others, that though Mr. Buchanan had been much galled and mortified by the course pursued toward him in the Southern States, he was resolved to stand firmly by Governor Walker and non-intervention in Kansas, whatever might be the consequences . . . to himself personally, or to the future prosperity of his administration." Thompson to Claiborne, June 3, 1878, *Claiborne Papers,* states "I never could tolerate Walker. He was a man devoid of opinions of his own, controlled by any man who had will & decision."

7. Thompson to Black, July 4, 1857, *Black Papers.*

8. The Charleston *Mercury,* June, 1857; the *Mercury* was not alone in its attacks. The Richmond *South,* June 6, 1857, insisted, "Under any circumstances the loss of Kansas would be a grievous calamity for the South; but to have it snatched from our grasp by the stealthy manipulation of a politician who affects a frank and honest purpose, is an insult and a wrong which we cannot bear with patience"; *ibid.,* June 20, 1857, continued, "don't every man outside of a lunatic asylum know, that Kansas is now under the control of pro-slavery men and that the convention will be composed of that material? Do you not know that the abolitionists north are now pouring into that territory thousands of mercenaries to vote down the pro-slavery convention? The thing is beyond the possibility of a doubt—the President and his cabinet are against the south. Not that they dislike the South or love abolitionism, but the necessities of the situation requires that the South shall be sacrificed, and the sacrifice will be made"; Natchez *Free Trader,* August

14, 1857, stated its preference to "see the party rent into ten thousand atoms and sent hurling into eternal oblivion before it would consent to 'Let Kansas Go,' if it is to be accomplished through the treachery of a Democratic Administration or officials. We love the South more than party"; New Orleans *Delta*, June, 1857, observed "Slavery in Kansas is becoming an obsolete idea under the Buchanan cum Walker cum Stanton influence"; the South Carolina *Times*, June, 1857, agreed with the New Orleans *Crescent* that Walker's acts proved "he is probably the most unscrupulous, heartless, and unprincipled man in the United States—"; see the Richmond *South* for months of June and July to trace the rising crescendo of denunciation. This secessionist organ went so far as to warn, "If Mr. Buchanan attempts to shield Walker, he will only expose his body to a mortal stroke. There is no divinity about the person of a President which the Democracy are afraid to violate"; *Star of Empire*, June 20, 1857; Louisville *Weekly*, July 1, 1857; Baton Rouge *Advocate*, July 23, 1857, Walker could not have been unaware of these attacks. Kansas newspapers published ample quotes from eastern and southern journals. The *Herald of Freedom*, June 27, 1857.

9. The New York *Tribune*, June 27, 1857; Haywood J. Pearce, Jr., *Benjamin H. Hill, Secession and Restoration*, pp. 24–27.

10. The Mississippi *Free Trader*, July 3, 1857; Rainwater, *Mississippi, 1856–61*, pp. 47–48; *Quindaro Chindowan*, November 21, 1857.

11. Buchanan to Walker, July 12, 1857, *Hurja Papers*, assured Walker, "The strictures of the Georgia and Mississippi conventions will . . . pass away, and be speedily forgotten"; Cobb to Walker, July 27, 1857, concluded that Walker "had been too harshly judged both in Georgia and Mississippi," *Miscellaneous Papers*; Foote, *Casket of Reminiscences*, pp. 116–17.

12. Douglas to Walker, Chicago, July 21, 1857, *Miscellaneous Papers*; Pearce, *Benjamin H. Hill*, pp. 28–30, indicates that Joseph E. Brown, the Democratic nominee for Governor in Georgia, refused to be trapped by his American party rival, Hill, into a flat denunciation of Walker; Nichols, *The Disruption of American Democracy*, pp. 114–15; *Toombs, Cobb, Stephens Correspondence*, p. 408.

13. Cobb to Lamar, Washington, D.C., July 27, 1857, *Miscellaneous Papers*.

14. The Charleston *Mercury*, June, 1857, *passim*; Richmond *Enquirer*, June 20, 1857, July 8, 1857; also St. Louis *Morning Herald*, June 14, 1857, observed, "so far as Governor Walker is concerned his course is a plain one. Kansas must be governed according to the laws which the Constitution of the United States has extended over it.

We think that it can be governed accordingly. We think these usurpations upon, and rebellions against those laws can be suppressed"; Louisville *Courier*, July 29, 1857.

15. The Richmond *Examiner*, July 14, 1857; Virginia *Sentinel*, July 16, 1857; Walker to Buchanan, Lecompton, June 28, 1857, *Buchanan Papers*, urged "we must have a Slave state out of the Southwestern Indian Territory & then calm will follow. Cuba will be acquired with the acquiescence of the North. . . . Cuba (& Puerto Rico if possible) should be countersigns of your administration & it will close in a blaze of glory."

16. The New Orleans *Courier*, July 18, 1857; Baton Rouge *Advocate*, July 23, 1857, contains a stinging attack upon Claiborne. It placed the blame for Southern difficulties upon know-nothing opposition to repeal of the Missouri Compromise; *True Delta*, July 24, 1857, echoed Claiborne's sentiments when it observed, "the South does much talking, is profuse of vituperation of individuals, and, finally, is satisfied to do nothing when her bravest talkers are installed in snug offices"; the *Southern Rights* of Athens, Ga., July 19, 1857, defended the reasonableness of Walker's position and warned the South against allowing herself to be "drawn in the wake of interested or tricky politicians"; Cassville, Georgia *Standard*, July 18, 1857, attacked the Milledgeville resolutions describing Walker's course "as steering between the two extremes." They concluded it was not "the Governor but the Kansan that would make Kansas free."

17. L. M. Keitt to Quitman, Monmouth, July 23, 1857, *Quitman Papers*; see also letter of Senator James M. Mason of Virginia, Winchester, July 22, 1857 to the editor of the *South*, in which he concludes that "if it will be effected by the numerical forces or organized majorities, operating against the usual laws which govern emigration; and it will present a new and most instructive lessen (sic) to the Southern States." A perusal of the radical fire-eating organs, the St. Louis *Republican*, Jackson *Mississippian*, Richmond *South*, Charleston *Mercury*, Vicksburg *Sentinel*, and New Orleans *Delta*, for the months of June to September, 1857, makes it evident that the issue for them was that of majority rule *vs.* minority rights. They thought the aggrieved minority had a right to invoke "the right of revolution as a defense."

18. Bigler to Buchanan, St. Louis, July 9, 1857, *Black Papers*; Jonah Hoover to Pierce, July 7, 1857, *Pierce Papers*, informed his former chief that most respectable opinion supported the action followed by the administration.

19. The New York *Tribune* and New York *Evening Post*, *passim*, for June, July, August, and September, 1857, are excellent examples

of the shifting editorial policies of two radical northern journals. See also Chicago *Tribune*, July 14, 1857.

20. The Boston *Journal*, August 6, 1857; it is worth noting that the ultra journal, St. Louis *Republican*, June 10, 1857, took the same stance; New Hampshire *Sentinel*, July 20, 1857; New York *Herald*, June 10, 15, July 20, 1857; Philadelphia *Press*; Springfield, Illinois *Sentinel*; Detroit *Free Press*; Chicago *Times*; Pittsburgh *Post*; Buffalo *Courier*; Louisville *Democrat*; Dubuque *Express, passim,* for June, July, August, September, and October, 1857; all treated the controversy as one involving party survival and majority rule. All vigorously supported Walker.

21. Butterfield to Pierce, Concord, July 30, 1857, *Pierce Papers*; also New York *Times*, June 10, 1857.

22. Vaux to Black, Philadelphia, September 2, 1857, *Black Papers*; also Nichols, *The Disruption of American Democracy*, p. 204.

23. Bigler to Black, Clearfield, August 26, 1857, *Black Papers*; Black draft of letter to Philadelphia Democratic meeting, September 25, 1857, *ibid.*

24. Black to Walker, Washington, D.C., August 1, 1857, *Black Papers*.

25. Nichols, *The Disruption of American Democracy*, pp. 119–21; Morris, *Robert J. Walker in the Kansas Struggle*, pp. 52–54; Walker to the People of Kansas, Lecompton, October 19, 1857, *Hurja Papers*.

26. Nevins, *Emergence of Lincoln*, Vol. I, pp. 234–39 and 255.

27. Brindle to Black, Lecompton, January 27, 1858, *Black Papers*.

28. Buchanan to Black, November 18, 1857, *Black Papers*; Washington *Union*, November 18, 1857; there exists in the *Black Papers* an undated version of the original article. It approves the Lecompton constitution and the behavior of Walker. Perhaps Black found the conjunction too incongruous or thought that a pat on the back after a stab in the back was too much.

29. Gwin to Buchanan, undated, *Gwin Papers*; Black to Governor Packer of Pa., Washington, D.C., December 26, 1857, opposed selection of Judge John C. Knox for post of Attorney General of Pa., as "he refuses to go along & support the Buchanan Administration on the all-important slavery issue"; New York *Tribune*, November 27, 28, 1857; New York *Times*, November 27, 28, 1857 and December 2, 1857.

14. PRINCIPLE ABANDONED

1. Nichols, *The Disruption of American Democracy*, pp. 129–30; New York *Herald*, December 1, 2, 3, 1857; *Overland Monthly*, Vol. V, 6, pp. 554–56; Stanton to Walker, Lecompton, January 8, 1858, *Miscel-*

laneous Papers; Kansas Historical Publications 1889–1890, pp. 421–32.

2. Woodward to Black, Philadelphia, December 4, 1857, *Black Papers;* Black to Governor Packer, Washington, D.C., December 26, 1857, *ibid.;* New York *Tribune*, December 9, 1857.

3. Hughs to Black, Somerset, December 21, 1857, *Black Papers;* Heffley to Black, Berlin, December 18, 1857, *ibid.;* Banks to Black, Lewiston, December 12, 1857, *ibid.;* Knox to Black, Germantown, December 21, 1857, *ibid.*

4. Stanton to Walker, Lecompton, January 5, 1858, *Miscellaneous Papers; Overland Monthly*, Vol. V, 6, p. 555.

5. Edwin Stanton to Black, Washington, D.C., October 26, 1857, *Black Papers;* Stanton to Black, San Francisco, April 16, 1858, *ibid.*

6. Walker to Black, Washington, D.C., February 12, 1858, *Black Papers;* J. A. Bayard to Black, Wilmington, November 23, 1857, *ibid.*, found the Senator from Delaware strongly supporting the Eldridge claim. *Corcoran Papers, passim* for 1857 and 1858.

7. Buchanan to Black, January 20, 1858, *Black Papers;* Walker to Black, Washington, D.C., February 12, 1858, *ibid.;* Gwin to Buchanan, undated, *Gwin Papers;* Claiborne, *Mississippi*, pp. 422–23; Ascher, *The New Almaden Mine*, pp. 119–20; *The National Cyclopaedia of American Biography*, Vol. XVIII, pp. 11–12; *Bulletin of the American Institute of Mining Engineers*, 53, May, 1911.

8. Walker to Forney, Hoboken, February 6, 1858, *Dreer Papers.*

9. "Democratic Protests Against the Lecompton Fraud," *Kansas Collected Speeches and Pamphlets*, Vol. 6 (1858); Walker to Forney, Hoboken, February 6, 1858, *Dreer Papers;* Philadelphia *Bulletin*, February 24, 1858; New York *Daily News*, February 17, 1858.

10. "Mr. Walker's Mission in Kansas," 1858 speech in *Walker Papers;* Speech, November 10, 1857, *ibid.; Report of the Committee on Federal Relations Relative to the Admission of Kansas into the Federal Union* (Austin, 1858).

11. Black's Manuscript Editorial on Forney's Tarrytown Speech on Kansas, September, 1858, *Black Papers;* see also Forney to Black, Washington, D.C., May 6, 1857, *ibid.*, which gives ample evidence that Forney had fallen out with the administration over patronage. Webster to Black, Philadelphia, December 24, 1857, *ibid.*, implies that efforts were made to conciliate Forney when the conflict over Kansas erupted. Webster observed, "Forney's reply to your proposition is 'that if twenty years active service in the Democratic Party, and in the interests of Mr. Buchanan, is no guarantee of his continued devotion to the great principles of an organization, then he has lived in vain. That he would con-

sider himself humiliated if we had to make such a declaration in his paper *at the present time,* and *on mere expectation.'* This is, as you know, what I feared. . . . If the pursuit of an object is a greater pleasure than its possession, I think the maxim must have one exception, at least, and that is the public printing."

12. Gwin Memorandum, undated, *Buchanan Papers; William English Papers, passim,* makes it evident that he saw his amendment as a way of assuaging southern sensibilities; Nevins, *Emergence of Lincoln,* Vol. I, pp. 296–301; *National Intelligencer,* May 2, 1858.

13. Copy of Contract between Walker and Janin, May 22, 1859, *Walker Papers;* Tucker and Townsend to Walker, June 4, 1860, *ibid.;* "Memorandum of Agreement, July, 1860," *ibid.;* Leftwich, "Robert J. Walker," *Publications of Mississippi Historical Society,* Vol. VI, p. 369; Claiborne, *Mississippi,* pp. 422–23; Nevins, *Emergence of Lincoln,* Vol. II, p. 174.

14. *John Covode Papers,* though sketchy in its coverage, contain ample evidence of his interest in railroad promoting and his urgent desire to have an amenable government in Washington. They also indicate that Douglas Democrats as well as Republicans thought well of the investigation. One is almost led to wonder if Walker had been intent upon provoking such an investigation.

15. Buchanan to Walker, Washington, D.C., July 12, 1857, *Hurja Papers,* is a copy in the handwriting of Eugene Cooke. The copy of which Walker spoke was in the possession of his sister Martha.

16. Typewritten transcript of the Covode Testimony, *passim, Walker Papers;* Buchanan to Walker, Washington, D.C., July 12, 1857, *Hurja Papers;* New York *Tribune,* April 18, 19, 1857; New York *Herald,* April 18, 19, 21, 23, 1857; New York *Times,* April 19, 1857.

17. Receipt retaining Caleb Cushing in New Almaden Mine case, September 20, 1857, *Hurja Papers;* Charles S. Sydnor, *A Gentleman of the Old Natchez Region Benj. L. C. Wailes,* p. 278; Gwin to Claiborne, May 6, 1879, *Claiborne Papers; The Diary of Orville Hicks Browning,* p. 369.

15. A SIXTY-YEAR-OLD PUBLIC MAN

1. James R. Gilmore, *Personal Recollections of Abraham Lincoln and the Civil War,* pp. 1, 29. Although Gilmore is factually unreliable, his description of Walker's sentiments is borne out by other sources. See *Continental Monthly,* Vol. II, October, 1862; Vol. I, June, 1862, in which Walker states that victory depended upon the "Northing of the South."

Vol. II, September, 1862, demanded that the leaders of secession be punished; Vol. IV, November, 1863, advocated total reeducation to make the southerner fit to rejoin the Union; Vol. II, October, 1862, supported Lincoln's program of reconstruction.

2. Gilmore, *Personal Recollections,* p. 30; *Continental Monthly,* Vol. V, April, 1864; Vol. II, November, 1862, in which Walker observed, "Slavery must die, that the Union and liberty may live forever." Vol. II, October, 1862; Vol. I, March, 1862, emphasized the degrading effects of slavery upon both northern and southern white labor.

3. Gilmore, *Personal Recollections,* p. 32; Cushing to Walker, September 11, 1861, *Hurja Papers; Continental Monthly,* Vol. I, June, 1862, notes, "There is something intensely American in such phrases as manifest destiny, mission and call." Vol. II, November, 1862, contains an article in which Walker described his vision of a transcendent Union under the leadership of the "sublime Anglo-Saxon," Vol. IV, July, 1863.

4. The New York *Tribune,* April 20, 22, 1861; New York *Herald,* April 20, 22, 1861; New York *Times,* April 20, 22, 1861; Gilmore, *Personal Recollections,* p. 35; Walker to Bradford, Duganne, & Talmadge, Hoboken, September 19, 1861, *Hurja Papers,* repeats similar sentiments and adds a demand for "severe punishment for treason."

5. Jordan, *Robert J. Walker,* p. 379; *Continental Monthly,* Vol. II, September, 1862, happily announced, "we have been obliged to print three times the number for which we anticipated sale." Some confusion exists as to whether Gilmore and Walker persuaded Greeley to contribute articles to the magazine and established themselves as the source of advance information on administration policy for the *Tribune* editor. No article written by Greeley appeared in the *Monthly,* nor does there exist any supporting data for Gilmore's recollection. See Gilmore, *Personal Recollections,* pp. 40, 49; William Hale, *Horace Greeley, Voice of the People,* pp. 255–57 and 260; Carl Sandburg, *Abraham Lincoln, the War Years,* Vol. I, pp. 402–03; Roy P. Basler, *The Collected Works of Abraham Lincoln,* Vol. VIII, pp. 578 and 591.

6. "Memoir of Robert John Walker," *Walker Papers; Continental Monthly,* Vol. I, 4, p. 470.

7. *Continental Monthly,* Vol. II, 5, p. 644; Walker to Daggett, Hoboken, September 28, 1861, *Hurja Papers.*

8. *Continental Monthly,* Vol. II, 2, pp. 226–27; *The* (London) *Times,* April 25, 1863, carried an article which indicates that Walker's attacks had not gone unnoticed by the British. It reported: "The press overflows with denunciations of the English Government and people. . . . One of the most violent of these declaimers is the Hon. Robert J. Walker

. . . who . . . expresses himself . . . in the *Continental Monthly:* 'England is now building, in the cause of slavery . . . , a great fleet of iron-clad pirate vessels, which are intended to prey on our commerce. . . . Are the English mad, demented, or besotted, that they suppose we intend to endure such deliberate aid of our enemies. . . . We are not a people to stop and reason nicely on legal points, when they are enforced in the form of fire and death!'"

9. *Continental Monthly,* Vol. II, 2, p. 230; Vol. II, 1, p. 107, entitled, "Warning to Britain," concluded, "There is even a stronger king than cotton here; we may call him King Market. Let King Market once lay hands on you, and whereas you were before only broken, then you will be ground to powder."

10. *Continental Monthly,* Vol. II, 4, p. 426; Vol. III, 2, p. 104.

11. *Continental Monthly,* Vol. II, 5, p. 573; Walker to Brooks, Washington, D.C., July 3, 1862, *Hurja Papers,* revived the "funnel theory"; Walker to Lincoln, July 29, 1862, *Robert Todd Lincoln Papers,* indicates that Walker forwarded various of his emancipation articles to Lincoln. Walker wrote: "My friend, Mr. Arnold, the member from Chicago has informed me, that you had expressed satisfaction with my first letter advocating your gradual emancipation measure; I now enclose . . . my second letter, and I am confident, that, with proper efforts, Maryland will initiate this policy. As I shall continue the discussion of this question . . . it would give me much pleasure to see you at anytime and place you may be pleased to indicate." The foregoing hardly supports the idea that there was frequent communication between Lincoln and Walker. It makes Gilmore's descriptions of an intimate relationship doubly suspect.

12. Walker to Brooks, Washington, D.C., July 3, 1862, *Hurja Papers.*

13. The New York *Tribune,* January 15, 1863; *Continental Monthly,* Vol. 2, p. 743; New York *Times,* February 6, 1863.

14. "Memoir of Robert John Walker," *Walker Papers.* Under the guidance of Martha the *Continental* became, among other things a repository for her odd theories of poetry and of her poems. One can only conclude after reading them that filial affection is no judge of poetic talent. Walker to Cooke, January 25, 1863, *Hurja Papers.*

15. Chase to Walker, March 30, 1863, *Chase Papers;* Chase to Walker, March 30, 1863, *Miscellaneous Papers;* Seward to Mary Walker, April 16, 1863, *Hurja Papers.*

16. The New York *Tribune,* January 15, 1863.

17. The New York *Tribune,* January 15, 1863; see also *National Intelligencer,* January 14, 1863; the letter also contains the following

paragraph, "I have contended, during the last fourth of a century, that all State bank currency is unconstitutional. This Rebellion will demonstrate the truth of that proposition, and the question ultimately be so decided by the Supreme Court of the United States. . . . State banks will fall before judicial action, as well as nullification . . . secession, and the whole brood of kindred heresies. . . . To permit the States to provide the circulating medium, the money of the country, is to enable them to furnish the sinews of war, and clothe them with a power to overthrow the Government."

18. The New York *Tribune*, January 15, 1863; March 6, 1863, gives ample evidence that Walker had entrance into the highest governmental circles. It contained the social item, "Col. Forney held his annual reception after the adjournment of Congress at his house on New Jersey Avenue last evening. About a hundred members of Congress, Cabinet officers, and Generals, were present, among them Secretary Seward, the Secretary of the Interior, Mr. Ushur, Postmaster-General Blair, Gen. Heintzelman, Gen. Cochrane, Prof. Bache, and nearly all the Senators. During the evening, Robert J. Walker, in response to a war sentiment eloquently uttered by the host, spoke at great length upon the great measures of the XXXVIIth Congress. . . . The sentiments voiced were not calculated to upset Congressional dignity." See also David Donald (ed.), *Inside Lincoln's Cabinet: The Civil War Diaries of Salmon P. Chase*, p. 72 and Roy P. Basler (ed.), *The Collected Works of Abraham Lincoln*, Vol. V, p. 451, which indicates administration use of Walker's legal talent.

19. *War of the Rebellion, Official Records of the Union and Confederate Armies*, Series II, Vol. II, p. 1127, Walker to Seward, December 16, 1861, warned during the Trent controversy, "I would assume it is a fact that all who during the present crisis would precipitate us unnecessarily into a war with England are at heart allies of the Southern rebellion and traitors. With such a war . . . the Union . . . may be dissolved and the separate Confederate Government established."

20. Amos E. Taylor, "Walker's Financial Mission to London on Behalf of the North 1863–64," *Journal of Economic and Business History*, Vol. III, February, 1931, p. 296, emphasizes that one of his qualifications was the notorious fact that he was "not entirely guided by the highest ethical considerations, his methods were picturesque and his weapons of aggression in most cases effective." "Walker Expense Account," *General Accounting Bureau*, lists a total of $29,402.35. The amount does not seem unreasonable given the scope of his activities during the period abroad. New York *Tribune*, March 11, 1863, reported

that the Supreme Court had voided the Castillers claim on the grounds of fraud. The paper noted, "Among the interests affiliated with the Fossatt interest, . . . is that of the Hon. Robert J. Walker, the value of which is of course greatly augmented by this decision. The net annual income . . . is estimated to be not far from half a million." Cushing to Walker, Newburyport, April 30, 1865, *Hurja Papers*, indicates that Walker still looked for ways of further exploiting the New Almaden Mine. Exactly how much Walker finally obtained for his share of the mining interest is difficult to ascertain. Claiborne, *Mississippi*, p. 423, cites the accepted figure of $500,000. It seems likely that the figure was obtained from William Gwin. See Gwin to Claiborne, May 6, 1879, *Claiborne Papers*. Given the extensive financial difficulties Walker experienced after 1865, it is likely that he received far less.

21. Walker to Chase, Hoboken, April 1, 1863, *Chase Papers*.

22. Wallace and Gillespie (ed.), *The Journal of Benjamin Moran* Vol. II, p. 1148; Walker to Chase, March 24, 1863, *Chase Papers*, stated, "I think our relations with England can be made *cordial*, but Louis Napoleon is our enemy, so far as he dare be."

23. Worthington Ford (ed.), *A Cycle of Adams Letters 1861–1865*, Vol. I, p. 277; *Charles Francis Adams Diary*, April 20, 1863, April 21, 1863, May 19, 1863, in *Adams Papers*; Walker to Chase, March 24, 1863, *Chase Papers*, asked for a letter from Seward to Adams "so that I might communicate freely with him, not only about *financial* but *diplomatic* affairs, and to act, as regards the latter, in correspondence with his views." Journal of *Benjamin Moran*, Vol. II, p. 1148, cites the circumstances which provoked Adams' amusement. "After breakfast Walker told an interesting anecdote certain to please . . . Adams. 'He said that nearly 20 years ago he met Mr. [John Q.] Adams on Pennsylvania Avenue in front of a book store, both of them being on their way to the capitol at the time. Mr. A. asked him to go into the shop for a minute or so, for said he, I am going to buy a Diary, the one I have been using having been filled this morning. Mr. Walker said he had often thought of buying one. 'Do so now,' said Mr. Adams, 'and write in it here, that John Quincy Adams predicted here in Washington this day that 40 years hence there will not be a slave in the U.S.' Mr. Walker said he had remarked that was impossible, but that he would remember it without a written record. At the period of the utterance of the prophecy he looked upon it as a wild assertion no man then living would see fulfilled; but now he believes he will live to see it.' "

24. *Journal of Benjamin Moran*, Vol. II, p. 1152; Walker to Chase, April 28, 1863, *Chase Papers*, reported, "I have seen many English

Gentlemen, including some old acquaintances, and breakfasted with Cobden and Foster, M.P. Both are devoted to England but believe its true interest will be promoted by our success, and by maintaining peace . . . the tone of Palmerston & Russell is improved. Horsman, who made the last violent speech, is a *Tory* & has no influence. . . . The terrible rebuke of Milne was well received. He is a Liberal & relative of Earl Russell. He is very friendly to our country & will do us good in Parliament & with the Cabinet."

25. Walker to Chase, April 28, 1863; Aspinwall to Chase, April 25, 1863, emphasized "We think he [Walker] will render great service in helping stem the current of ignorance & misapprehension so generally prevalent in Europe." Walker to Chase, London, May 15, 1863, asked: "In the event of a war with England, would we sequester, confiscate, or suspend payment of the principal or interest on our public debt held here as menaced by some of the newspapers?. . . We must, in my opinion continue to pay without interruption. . . . A contrary principle, while it would impair our credit, tarnish our honor, would save us nothing." Chase to Walker, Washington, D.C., May 14, 1863, *Chase Papers;* Cobden to Walker, May 1, 1863, *Miscellaneous Papers; Hughes* (ed.), *John Murray Forbes,* Vol. II, pp. 42–43.

26. Walker to Chase, April 28, 1863, *Chase Papers,* sets forth several reasons for avoiding war with Britain. "1st . . . we shall derive no revenue from *duties* & you will have *no gold* with which to pay the interest on our public debt . . . 2nd . . . our finances will be overthrown, legal tenders become unavailable to meet our . . . expenses & pay our troops . . . 3rd . . . The blockade will be broken & Southern Cotton . . . exported at the present value of nearly a billion dollars . . . 4th . . . The independence of the South will be acknowledged . . . 5th . . . England joins the South, so will France, taking Mexico as her share . . . Look on *that* picture, . . . & who can hesitate, unless national honor force us to the contest."

27. Walker to Chase, May 1, 1863; see also Walker to Chase, Liverpool, May 4, 1863, which urged, "Let us have at least 200,000 black troops in the field, they should be rewarded for gallant deeds, & encouraged in every way. Appeals should be made (oral & printed) to their love of liberty, & of their race, they should be reminded how they are charged by the South with loving their chains, & how they are accused by them of cowardice—Let them wipe out the lie, on the battlefield, in the blood of their calumniators & enslavers, & prove that they are not chattels." Walker to Chase, May 8, 1863, expresses pleasure at Adjutant General Thomas' speech encouraging the organization of black regiments, *Chase Papers.*

28. Walker to Chase, London, May 15, 1863, *ibid.*

29. Harrington to Walker, April 21, 1863, *Harrington Papers;* Harrington to Walker, April 21, 1863; Chase to Aspinwall and Forbes, May 30, 1863; Chase to Walker, May 29, 1863, *Chase Papers;* New York *Times,* May 2, 1863; *The* (London) *Times,* July 13, 1863.

30. Walker to Chase, May 8, 1863, *Chase Papers;* Walker to Chase, May 1, 1863, *ibid.*

31. Walker to Chase, September 24, 1863, *Chase Papers;* Walker to Chase, May 1, 1863, *ibid.;* in Walker to Chase, July 3, 1863, *ibid.,* he offers military advice on how to attack Vicksburg. "Here let me make a suggestion founded on local knowledge. If Vicksburg is not taken & you cannot pass it, then if the canal (not the old one) across the point & out of the range of the Confederate guns, cannot from the character of the soil be constructed, why not build (confidentially) in the North, a marine railway, to be laid down at the place, with or without partial digging across, so as to pass boats over, with or without guns, & do the same thing if necessary, from below or above Port Hudson, beyond the Confederate guns." *Charles Francis Adams Diary,* May 18, 1863 and June 16, 1863.

32. Walker to Chase, London, June 12, 1863, *Chase Papers,* gives a detailed analysis of the French attitude toward the Union war effort. Walker believed that Napoleon had approached Palmerston with a proposal for joint recognition of the Confederacy, but had been refused for "the alleged reason that it would only more thoroughly unite all parties at the North in the war for Union. There was a deeper reason. France has no Canada bordering on our Union & can live without our markets or supplies." Confidentally, he wrote Chase that Napoleon no longer "regarded the dissolution of the Union as certain." Chase to Walker, Washington, D.C., July 10, 1863, *Miscellaneous Papers,* reports, "Your last letter [that of June 12, 1863] reached me nearly two weeks ago. . . . I read it to the President who was much pleased."

33. Walker to Chase, June 27, 1863, *Chase Papers;* see also Walker to Chase, July 25, 1863, *Chase Papers;* Walker to Chase, London, June 12, 1863, *Chase Papers,* describes his delight with the Grierson raid through Mississippi, especially as it permitted him to plot the five hundred mile dash through country that he knew intimately; *Charles Francis Adams Diary,* July 9, 1863.

34. Chase to Walker, Washington, D.C., July 14, 1863, *Autograph Collection.*

35. Chase to Aspinwall and Forbes, May 14, 1863, noted "I do not regret that you find European capitalists indisposed to make offers for large loans." Chase to Walker, May 29, 1863, *Chase Papers,* concluded

"A loan is no longer desirable in Europe . . ."; Walker to Chase, London, May 22, 1863, *ibid.*, agreed with the Secretary's policy and anticipated that once the war had ended American obligations would exceed in value those of Britain. "They would rest on the basis of a continent . . . I am willing to record the prediction, that at the close of this century . . . our wealth would exceed that of the whole world at this time." Chase to Cisco, September 24, 1863, *ibid.*

36. Robert J. Walker, *Jefferson Davis and Repudiation, passim; Continental Monthly,* Vol. IV, 2, August, 1863, p. 223; Walker to Chase, April 28, 1863, *Chase Papers,* urged that Lincoln reissue the proclamation of freedom to the slaves for its propaganda effect in England, *"but warning them against any injury* by them to *women & children,* or *even to their masters except in defence of liberty and life."* For a bitter southern attack upon Walker which did not hesitate to recollect Walker's stand on repudiation, see Anonymous, *A Familiar Epistle to Robert J. Walker, passim;* for the effect of the essay on the continent see Consul General, Frankfurt A.M., September 10, 1863, *Dispatch 92, ibid.;* Consul General, Frankfurt A.M., September 16, 1863, *Dispatch 94, ibid.,* expresses particular pleasure at Walker's publication of a Davis letter in which he referred to the "blood of the Judas Iscariots and Shylocks flowing in the veins of the Rothschilds." Such sentiments, if known to the Rothschilds, were not, he wrote, "calculated to help the currency of Southern Securities."

37. Robert J. Walker, *American Slavery and Finances, passim.*

38. Walker to Chase, London, July 18, 1863, *Chase Papers;* Bright to Walker, Rochdale, July 27, 1863, *Miscellaneous Papers.*

39. Walker to Chase, July 25, 1863, *Chase Papers;* Walker to Chase, July 30, 1863, *Chase Papers,* in which the New York riots were discussed. Walker asserted, "The N. York riots, called here a *revolution,* constitute the sole remaining hope of slavedom, but the outrages of the mob . . . excites universal disgust. These wretches will persecute the blacks into popularity. . . . That was a strange speech of Archbishop Hughes, to a crowd of traitors and brutal assassins. If I am not greatly mistaken, the riots will destroy the Copperhead party, by whom no doubt they were instigated." Bright to Walker, Rochdale, July 27, 1863, *Miscellaneous Papers,* in which the British liberal writes, "The New York riot is serious *as a riot*—but it must tend to bring all native Americans more into harmony with the Govt. & with the policy of abolition— for it would seem as the Irish hatred of the negro had as much to do with the outbreak as hostility to the conscription."

40. *The Journal of Benjamin Moran,* Vol. II, p. 1201; *Charles Francis Adams Diary,* April 6, 1863, expresses disdain for Miles.

41. "A Memoir of Robert John Walker," *Walker Papers*.

42. Walker to Chase, London, November 6, 1863, *Chase Papers*.

43. Walker to Chase, London, November 6, 1863, *ibid.; The Journal of Benjamin Moran*, Vol. II, p. 1222; *Continental Monthly*, December, 1863, p. 713, gives a full description of both the trip and of Walker's series of novel experiments. It concluded: "Some years ago, this gentleman had the scientific curiosity to descend to the bottom of the sea, in a new diving apparatus . . . and recently he has been driven through a tunnel on a railway, by the pneumatic process. . . . He seems to be not only ready to welcome all valuable improvements in science and mechanics, but is ready . . . to take the risks of dangerous exploration . . . for the promotion of progress."

44. *Journal of Benjamin Moran*, Vol. II, p. 1231, described "Ever since R. J. Walker went up in the balloon he has been spitting blood. This arises from the sudden change from warm to cold and the failure to take the necessary preparations to keep up the temperature."

45. *Continental Monthly*, December, 1863, p. 716, has Walker stating, "To thrust a State back into the Union, & clothe it with all its former constitutional privileges, while the masses of the people are still hostile to the Federal authority, would envince a degree of recklessness, and even insanity. . . . But when a State is fit to return, and may properly and safely be received, let her be welcomed cordially and heartily, without . . . reminiscence of her sad and disastrous error. . . .We cannot create a State in the midst of a hostile population, . . . but we can favor, encourage and build up the loyal minority . . . so as to make it the majority." Also, *Charles Francis Adams Diary*, October 24, 1863.

46. *Continental Monthly*, December, 1863, p. 717.

16. THE SEARCH

1. Undated Associated Press dispatch, *Walker Papers*; "Memoir of Robert John Walker," *ibid*.

2. Walker to Chase, London, July 25, 1863, *Chase Papers*; Ephraim D. Adams, *Great Britain and the American Civil War*, Vol. II, pp. 117–51.

3. Walker to Chase, July 25, 1863, *Chase Papers*; Walker, *Jefferson Davis and Repudiation*, pp. 46–47.

4. Clay to Walker, St. Petersburg, August 15, 1863, *Walker Papers*.

5. *Journal of Benjamin Moran*, Vol. II, p. 1239, 1243, and 1249, in which Walker is described as "an obstinate old man." Foote, *Casket of Reminiscences*, pp. 126–29; Adams to Walker, December 10, 1863, *Miscellaneous Papers*; Walker, *Slavery and Finances*.

6. Walker to Chase, August 7, 1863, Walker to Chase, September 5, 1863, Walker to Chase, September 24, 1863, in which Walker describes his pamphlets as an effort to "stimulate European investments." Walker to Chase, December 9, 1863; Walker to Chase, December 19, 1863; Walker to Chase, December 23, 1863; Walker to Chase, February 26, 1864; Walker to Chase, February 20, 1864, *Chase Papers;* Murphy to Walker, Frankfurt am Main, January 18, 1864, *Walker Letters,* in which Murphy, Consul General at Frankfurt informed Walker that despite bad news from home, American stocks advanced one-half percent and "about the only business done yesterday was in American securities." Consul General, Frankfurt A.M., *Dispatch 92, State Department,* June 12, 1863, describes Walker visits to European bankers; Baltimore *Sun,* November 30, 1867.

7. Walker to McCulloch, June 28, 1865, *Hugh McCulloch Papers;* a copy of this letter is also located in the Mississippi Department of Archives.

8. Baltimore *Sun,* November 30, 1867; New York *Tribune,* December 3, 1867; Robert J. Walker, *Our National Finances, passim.*

9. The Baltimore *Sun,* November 30, 1867; New York *Tribune,* December 3, 1867.

10. Seward to Stanton, February 13, 1865, Stanton to Walker, February 14, 1865, Pallen to Walker, March 25, 1865, *Miscellaneous Papers;* New York *Times,* March 29, 1865, April 19, 1865; E. C. Kirkland, *Peacemakers of 1864,* pp. 71–72.

11. Walker to McCulloch, Washington, D.C., June 28, 1865, *McCulloch Papers.*

12. *Journal of Benjamin Moran,* Vol. II, p. 1340; Walker to Dudley, February 17, 1864, *Walker Papers,* says health prevents journey to Edinburgh; Walker to Dudley, March 1, 1864, *ibid.;* Walker to Dudley, Nice, March 12, 1864, *ibid.,* states health has improved but that eyesight was failing. Moran to Eggleston, Cadiz, April 22, 1864, *State Department Records.*

13. Walker to Corcoran, Washington, D.C., April 9, 1867; Corcoran to Walker, August 23, 1866; Memo of May 24, 1867; Memo of June 6, 1868, *Corcoran Papers;* W. W. Corcoran, *A Grandfather's Legacy,* p. 286.

14. Walker to Corcoran, Washington, D.C., April 9, 1867, *Corcoran Papers;* Walker to Clay, New York, October 4, 1866, *Miscellaneous Papers;* Rowland, *Jefferson Davis,* Vol. VII, p. 95; New York *Times,* February 23, 1866; Thompson to Walker, May 20, 1866, *Hurja Papers; 71 United States (4 Wall),* Mississippi *vs.* Johnson, p. 475; Alexander A. Lawrence, *James Moore Wayne Southern Unionist,* p. 211.

15. *73 United States (6 Wall)*, State of Georgia *vs.* Stanton.

16. Greeley to Lawrence, Beloit, Wis., December 16, 1866, *Greeley Papers*.

17. Corcoran, *A Grandfather's Legacy*, pp. 268 and 286; "Memoir of Robert John Walker," *Walker Papers*.

18. Fortieth Congress, Third session, *H.R. 35*, p. 12; Mickles to Fish, January 3, 1876, *Hamilton Fish Letterfile*, sets forth the substance of these accusations. "The exposure of the Ring frauds being the order of the day, I would call your attention to the purchase of Alaska. A person may know things which he may not be in a situation to prove, but I do not hesitate to say that by that operation, we the people, were swindled out of millions of dollars. Govr. Seward, Cassius M. Clay, and Thurlow Weed, all poor before, became rich directly after the purchase." Clay, he charged, had passed the Russian desire to sell the territory to Seward and Weed who, "always like the Jew Fagin watching for something hanging out, suggested . . . a price far in excess of" Russian hopes. Walker, hired as a lobbyist, receiving $25,000, the balance, "amounting to millions went into the pockets of the trio."

19. W. A. Dunning, "Paying for Alaska," *Political Science Quarterly*, Vol. XXVII, pp. 385–86; Benjamin P. Thomas, *Russo-American Relations 1815–1867*, pp. 158–62; John Bigelow, *Retrospections of an Active Life*, Vol. IV, pp. 216–17; Stevens to Seward, April 11, 1867, reports "I congratulate you & I rejoice at your safe deliverance. I hope the after birth is easy," *Seward Papers*; Richard N. Current, *Old Thad Stevens*, p. 313.

20. Clay to Seward, Vol. 21, Despatches, Russia, Despatch 241, April 1, 1867, *Seward Papers*.

21. Walker to Seward, Washington, D.C., February 9, 1868, Vol. 73, *Seward Papers*; Charles C. Tansill, *The Purchase of the Danish West Indies*, pp. 126–27; Bille to Danish Foreign Office, Washington, D.C., February 4, 1868, *Danish Foreign Office Records, 1867–1868* (Rigsarkivet, Kobenhaven), forwarded to the Danish foreign office the Washington *Chronicle* articles which Bille, the Danish envoy to Washington characterized "as the best and most detailed statements for the acquisition of St. Thomas." He thought them "worth reading and perhaps will be a beginning of a change in the public opinion, on which the ratification of the treaty depends." As for Walker, Bille concluded, though he was not at his "greatest and without a political post, he is not yet politically insignificant."

22. Walker to Seward, July 2, 1868; Seward to Johnson, July 2, 1868, *Johnson Papers*, urges the use of Presidential influence to insure the support of the Democratic congressmen.

23. Walker to Johnson, New York, March 30, 1866, *Johnson Papers*, also expressed acute concern over the final disposition of the New York collectorship. He stated, "When I left Washington the contest for the collectorship *seemed* to be narrowed down between my friend Mr. Smythe & Mr. Davis (the anti-Seward) Republican candidate. Mr. McCulloch has *no objection to* Mr. Smythe altho he may not be his first choice. Rest assured, in the present aspect of our political affairs, you should appoint to the collectorship, a Johnson *Republican.* . . . The appointment of a Democrat will keep back wavering Republicans."

24. Walker to Reverdy Johnson, February 22, 1867, *Johnson Papers.* Reverdy Johnson forwarded this letter to the President.

25. "Memoir of Robert John Walker," *Walker Papers;* Reverdy Johnson, Walker, Senator Thomas C. McCreery of Ky., Samuel J. Randall, May 26, 1868, "confidential" appeal, *Hurja Papers.*

26. Walker to Newton, New York, July 6, 1868, *Johnson Papers;* A. C. Flick, *Samuel Jones Tilden*, p. 172; Stewart Mitchell, *Horatio Seymour*, pp. 425–26, and 449.

27. Walker to Grant, Philadelphia, September 25, 1869, *Miscellaneous Papers;* Robert J. Walker, *Annexation of Nova Scotia and British America;* New York *Times*, April 25, 1869; Porter to Walker, Washington, D.C., September 16, 1869, *Hurja Papers.*

28. Hyde to Walker, Washington, D.C., November 29, 1867, indicates Walker's growing difficulty in meeting his debts; Judgments *vs.* Walker, indicates that the sale of *Woodley* and its household effects were made to secure $43,000 with which to retire the bulk of indebtedness. Walker to Hyde, October 3, 1868, authorizes sale of *Woodley;* Hyde to Walker, October 14, 1868; Hyde to Walker, December 19, 1868; Hyde to Walker, December 22, 1868; Corcoran to Duncan S. Walker, September 30, 1868; Duncan S. to Corcoran, January 18, 1869; Corcoran to Duncan S., January 21, 1869, acknowledges liquidation of indebtedness, *Corcoran Papers;* "Memoir of Robert John Walker," *Walker Papers;* Washington *Evening Star*, October 25, 1869; Frank Carpenter, *Carp's Washington*, pp. 174–75.

Bibliography

MANUSCRIPT MATERIAL

Chicago Historical Society, Mason Brayman Papers.

Columbia University Microfilm, Adams Family Papers; Jeremiah Black
Papers; J. F. H. Claiborne Papers; General Records of the Treasury;
Andrew Jackson Papers; Robert Todd Lincoln Papers; John Quitman
Papers; Martin Van Buren Papers.

County and Church Records, Pennsylvania, Cumberland County Assessments, East Pennsboro; Cumberland County, Record of Deeds; Northumberland County, Deed Book "F" Sunbury; Northumberland
County, Deed Book "I" Sunbury; Records of Christ Church, Philadelphia.

Daughters of American Revolution Records, Washington D.C., D.A.R.
Lineage Book LVI.

Detroit Public Library, Ross Wilkins Papers.

Harvard University, George M. Bancroft Papers.

Huntington Library, California Historical Document VII.

Indiana University, Autograph Collection; William English Papers;
Hugh McCulloch Papers.

Library of Congress, Blenheim Roll; J. F. H. Claiborne Papers; William
W. Corcoran Papers; John J. Crittenden Papers; Caleb Cushing
Papers; Andrew Jackson Donelson Papers; Hamilton Fish Letterfile;
Andrew Jackson Papers; Andrew Johnson Papers; William Marcy
Papers; Franklin Pierce Papers; James K. Polk Papers; George N.
Sanders Papers; Nicholas Trist Papers; John Tyler Papers; Martin
Van Buren Papers; Robert J. Walker Papers; Reuben Walworth
Papers; Gideon Welles Papers.

Mississippi State Department of Archives and History, Albert Gallatin
Brown Papers; J. F. H. Claiborne Papers; Governor Papers, Series
'E'; Robert J. Walker Papers.

Missouri Historical Society, George Harrington Papers.

National Archives, General Accounting Bureau Records; General Records of the Department of the Treasury; Letters Received: 1843–1849 Secretary of the Treasury; State Department Records.

New York Historical Society, Robert J. Walker Papers.

Newberry Library, Illinois Central R.R. Papers.

New York Public Library, George M. Bancroft Papers; Horace Greeley Papers.

Pennsylvania Historical Society, Autograph Collection; James Buchanan Papers; Salmon P. Chase Papers; Lewis Coryell Papers; George M. Dallas Diary; George M. Dallas Papers; F. J. Dreer Papers; Genealogy of the Bache Family; Genealogy of the Dallas Family; Henry Gilpin Papers.

Pennsylvania State Archives, Patent Book "A"; Pennsylvania Archives, 5th Series, Vol. VI.

Private Collections, Emil Hurja Papers; Robert J. Walker Letterbook.

Rigsarkivet, Kobenhaven, Denmark, Danish Foreign Office Records, 1867–1868.

Rochester University, William Seward Papers.

Southern Historical Collection, University of North Carolina, J. F. H. Claiborne Papers.

University of California, William M. Gwin Papers; E. G. Squier Papers.

University of Chicago, R. D. Douglas Papers.

University of Pennsylvania, Alumni Records.

Western Pennsylvania Historical Society, John Covode Papers.

ESSAYS AND UNPUBLISHED MATERIAL

Ascher, Leonard W. *The Economic History of the New Almaden Mine, 1845–1863* (Dissertation, University of Southern California).

Dodd, William E. "Robert J. Walker, Imperialist," *Randolph-Macon Bulletin* (1914).

Dunning, William A. "Paying for Alaska," *Political Science Quarterly*, Vol. XXVII.

Eichert, Magdalen. "Some Implications Arising from Robert J. Walker's Participation in Land Ventures," *Journal of Mississippi History*, Vol. XIII.

Hamilton, Holman. "Texas Bonds and Northern Profits: A Study in Compromise, Investment, and Lobby Influence, *Mississippi Valley Historical Review*, Vol. XLIII.

Hamilton, William B. and Nuremberger, Ruth K. "An Appraisal of J. F. H. Claiborne with his Annotated 'Memoranda' (1829–1840)," *Journal of Mississippi History*, Vol. VII.

Harris, Neil. *Not by Deportment: A Re-examination of the Locus and Extent of Jacksonian Patronage* (Senior Essay, Columbia College, 1957).

Jordan, H. Donaldson. "A Politician of Expansion: Robert J. Walker," *Mississippi Valley Historical Review*, Vol. XIX.

Learned, H. B. "The Establishment of the Secretaryship of the Interior," *American Historical Review*, Vol. X.

Leftwich, George J. "Robert J. Walker," *Mississippi Historical Society Publications*, Vol. VI.

McPherson, Hallie Mae. *William McKendree Gwin, Expansionist* (Dissertation, University of California).

Miles, Edwin A. "Franklin E. Plummer, Piney Woods Spokesman of the Jackson Era," *Journal of Mississippi History*, Vol. XIV.

———— *Robert J. Walker—His Mississippi Years* (Masters Essay, North Carolina University, 1949).

Morris, A. B. *R. J. Walker in the Kansas Struggle* (Masters Essay, University of Chicago, 1916).

Persinger, Clark E. "The Bargain of 1844 as the Origin of the Wilmot Proviso," *Annual Report of the American Historical Association*, Vol. I.

Sioussat, St. George L. "Andrew Johnson and the Early Phases of the Homestead Bill," *Mississippi Valley Historical Review*, Vol. V.

Taylor, Amos E. "Walker Financial Mission to London on Behalf of the North 1863–64," *Journal of Economic and Business History*, Vol. 3.

Thompson, E. Bruce. "Reforms in the Penal System of Mississippi, 1820–1850," *Journal of Mississippi History*, Vol. VII.

Tick, Frank H. *Political and Economic Policies of R. J. Walker* (Dissertation, University of California Los Angeles).

Winston, James E. "The Lost Commission: A Study in Mississippi History," *Mississippi Vally Historical Review*, Vol. V.

———— "Robert J. Walker, Annexationist," *The Texas Review*, Vol. II.

PUBLISHED MATERIALS

Adams, Ephrain D. *Great Britain and the American Civil War*. New York, 1925.

Adams, John Q. *Memoirs*. Philadelphia, 1874.

Anonymous, *History of the Susquehanna and Juniata Valleys*. 1886.

Anonymous, *Nine Years of Democratic Rule in Mississippi 1838–1847*. Jackson, 1847.

Aptheker, Herbert. *American Negro Revolts*. New York, 1943.

Auchampaugh, Philip G. *James Buchanan and His Cabinet on the Eve of Secession*. Duluth, 1926.

Baldwin, Joseph G. *The Flush Times of Alabama and Mississippi*. New York, 1957.

Basler, Roy P. (ed.) *Abraham Lincoln: His Speeches and Writings*. New York, 1946.

―――― *The Collected Works of Abraham Lincoln*. New Brunswick, 1955.

Bassett, J. S. *Correspondence of Andrew Jackson*. Washington, 1926–1935.

Beccaria, Caesare Bonesama. *Essays on Crimes and Punishments*. London, 1767.

Bell, Herbert C. (ed.). *History of Northumberland County, Pennsylvania* (1891).

Blaine, James G. *Twenty Years of Congress*. Norwich, 1884.

Blatzell, E. Digby. *Philadelphia Gentlemen*. Glencoe, 1958.

Bronson, Howard G. *History of the Illinois Central Railroad to 1870*. Urbana, 1915.

Brown, George. *Reminiscences of Governor R. J. Walker* (1902).

Burnham, W. Dean. *Presidential Ballots 1836–1892*. Baltimore, 1955.

Butler, W. A. *A Retrospect of Forty Years, 1825–1865*. New York, 1911.

Carpenter, Frank. *Carp's Washington*. New York, 1960.

Catterall, Helen T. *Judicial Cases Concerning American Slavery and the Negro*. Washington, 1926–37.

Chase, Lucien B. *A History of the Polk Administration*. New York, 1850.

Claiborne, J. F. H. *Life and Correspondence of John A. Quitman*. New York, 1860.

―――― *Mississippi as a Province, Territory and State*. Jackson, 1880.

Coleman, Chapman Mrs. *Life of John J. Crittenden*. Philadelphia, 1873.

Colton, Calvin (ed.). *The Private Correspondence of Henry Clay*. New York, 1856.

Commager, Henry S. (ed.). *Democracy in America*. New York, 1947.

Connelley, William E. *Kansas Territorial Governors*. Topeka, 1900.

Corcoran, William W. *A Grandfather's Legacy*. Washington, 1879.

Craven, Avery. *The Growth of Southern Nationalism*. Baton Rouge, 1953.

Crippen, Lee F. *Simon Cameron*. Mississippi Valley Press, 1942.

Davies, Arthur. *An Outline of Empire of the West as Foreshadowed in the Correspondence of Robert J. Walker and Arthur Davies, M.P.* London, 1852.

De Voto, Bernard. *Year of Decision: 1846.* Boston, 1943.

Dickey, Dallas C. *Seargent S. Prentiss, Whig Orator of the Old South.* Baton Rouge, 1946.

Dickinson, John R. (ed.). *Speeches, Correspondence of the late Daniel Dickinson.* New York, 1867.

Donald, David (ed.). *Inside Lincoln's Cabinet: the Civil War Diaries of Salmon P. Chase.* New York, 1954.

Egle, William H. *History of Pennsylvania.* 1876.

Eiselin, Malcolm Rogers. *The Rise of Pennsylvania Protectionism.* Philadelphia, 1932.

Flick, A. C. *Samuel Jones Tilden.* New York, 1939.

Foote, Henry Stuart. *Casket of Reminiscences.* Washington, 1874.

Ford, Worthington (ed.). *A Cycle of Adams Letters 1861–1865.* Boston, 1920.

Garraty, John. *Silas Wright.* New York, 1949.

Garrison, George P. (ed.). *Diplomatic Correspondence of the Republic of Texas.* Washington, 1908.

Gates, Paul. *Fifty Million Acres.* Ithaca, 1954.

Gilmore, James R. *Personal Recollections of Abraham Lincoln.* 1882.

Godcharles, Frederic A. *Freemasonry in Northumberland and Snyder Counties, Pennsylvania.* 1911.

Going, C. B. *David Wilmot, Free Soiler.* New York, 1924.

Graebner, Norman A. *Empire on the Pacific.* New York, 1955.

Hale, William. *Horace Greeley, Voice of the People.* New York, 1951.

Hayes, John L. *A Reminiscence of the Free Soil Movement in New Hampshire 1845.* Cambridge, 1885.

Heilman, Grace E. and Levin, Bernard S. *Calendar of Joel R. Poinsett Papers.* Philadelphia, 1941.

Henry, Robert S. *The Story of the Mexican War.* New York, 1950.

Hughes, Sarah Forbes. *John Murray Forbes.* Boston, 1899.

Isely, Jeter. *Horace Greeley and the Republican Party.* Princeton, 1947.

James, Marquis. *Andrew Jackson the Border Captain.* New York, 1933.

——— *Andrew Jackson, Portrait of a President.* New York, 1940.

——— *The Raven: A Biography of Sam Houston.* Indianapolis, 1929.

Jameson, J. F. (ed.) *Correspondence of John C. Calhoun.* Washington, 1899.

Kehl, James A. *Ill Feelings in the Era of Good Feelings.* Pittsburgh, 1956.

Kirkland, Edward C. *Peacemakers of 1864.* New York, 1927.

Lawrence, Alexander A. *James Moore Wayne Southern Unionist.* Chapel Hill, 1943.

McCormac, Eugene I. *James K. Polk.* Berkeley, 1922.

McGrane, Reginald C. *William Allen: A Study in Western Democracy.* Columbus, 1925.

Meginess, John F. *Biographical Annals of the West Branch Valley.* 1889.

Meigs, William M. *The Life of Charles Jared Ingersoll.* Philadelphia, 1897.

Milton, George Fort. *The Eve of Conflict.* New York, 1931.

Mitchell, Stewart. *Horatio Seymour of New York.* Cambridge, 1938.

Moore, John B. *Works of James Buchanan.* Philadelphia, 1909.

Myers, Margaret G. *The New York Money Market.* New York, 1931.

Nevin, Alfred. *Men of Mark of Cumberland Valley, Pennsylvania.* 1876.

Nevins, Allan. *Emergence of Lincoln.* New York, 1952.

––––––– *Ordeal of the Union.* New York, 1947.

––––––– *Polk Diary.* New York, 1929.

––––––– *The Diary of Philip Hone, 1825–1851.* New York, 1927.

Nichols, Roy Franklin. *Franklin Pierce.* Philadelphia, 1958.

––––––– *The Disruption of American Democracy.* New York, 1948.

Paul, James C. N. *Rift in the Democracy.* Philadelphia, 1951.

Pearce, Haywood J. *Benjamin N. Hill, Secession and Restoration.* Chicago, 1928.

Pease, T. C. and Randall, J. G. (ed.). *The Diary of Orville Hicks Browning.* Springfield, 1925.

Phillips, Ulrich B. (ed.). *Toombs, Cobb, Stephens Correspondence.* New York, 1911.

Phillipson, C. *Three Criminal Law Reformers: Beccaria, Bentham, Romilly.* London, 1923.

Quaife, Milo (ed.). *Polk Diary.* Chicago, 1910.

Rainwater, Percy L. (ed.). "Letters to and from Jacob Thompson," *Journal of Southern History,* Vol. VI.

––––––– *Mississippi: Storm Center of Secession 1856–1861.* Baton Rouge, 1938.

Robbins, Roy M. *Our Landed Heritage, The Public Domain, 1776–1936.* Princeton, 1942.

Roseboom, Eugene H. *A History of Presidential Elections.* New York, 1957.

Rowland, Dunbar. *Jefferson Davis, Constitutionalist, His Letters, Papers and Speeches.* Jackson, 1923.

––––––– *Mississippi the Heart of the South.* Chicago, 1925.

Rupps, I. D. *History of Cumberland County.* undated.

Russel, Robert E. *Improvement of Communications with the Pacific*

Coast as an Issue in American Politics, 1783–1864. Cedar Rapids, 1948.

Sandburg, Carl. *Abraham Lincoln, The War Years.* New York, 1940.

Schlesinger, Arthur, Jr. *The Age of Jackson.* Boston, 1953.

Schurz, Carl. *Speeches, Correspondence, Political Papers.* New York, 1913.

Sears, L. M. John Slidell. Durham, 1925.

Sellers, Charles G., Jr. *James K. Polk: Jacksonian, 1795–1843.* Princeton, 1957.

Sherwood, Foster H. *The Role of the Supreme Court in American Government and Politics 1835–1864.* Berkeley, 1957.

Simpson, Henry. *The Lives of Eminent Philadelphians.* Philadelphia, 1859.

Sioussat, St. George L. "Heiss Papers," *Tennessee History Magazine,* Vol. II.

———— "Letters of James K. Polk to Andrew J. Donelson, 1843–48," *Tennessee History Magazine,* Vol. III.

———— "Letters of James K. Polk to Cave Johnson," *Tennessee History Magazine,* Vol. I.

Smith, Justin. *The War with Mexico.* New York, 1931.

Smith, William E. *The Francis Preston Blair Family in Politics.* New York, 1933.

Sprague, William Buell. *Annals of the American Pulpit.* New York, 1857.

Sydnor, Charles H. *Benjamin L. C. Wailes.* Durham, 1938.

Tansill, Charles C. *The Canadian Reciprocity Treaty of 1854.* Baltimore, 1922.

———— *The Purchase of the Danish West Indies.* Baltimore, 1932.

Thomas, Benjamin P. *Russo-American Relations 1815–1867.* Baltimore, 1932.

Tyler, Lyon G. *The Letters and the Times of the Tylers.* Richmond, 1885.

Van Deusen, Glyndon G. *The Jacksonian Era.* New York, 1959.

Varle, Charles. *Complete View of Baltimore.* Baltimore, 1843.

Walker, Robert J. *American Slavery and Finances.* London, 1864.

———— *An Appeal for the Union.* Washington, 1856.

———— *Annexation of Nova Scotia and British America.* Washington, 1869.

———— *Jefferson Davis and Repudiation.* London, 1863.

———— *Letter on the Annexation of Texas.* 1844.

———— *Our National Finances.* Washington, 1867.

Walker, Robert J. *Speech of Hon. R. J. Walker at the Banquet to Louis Kossuth at Southampton.* London, 1851.

—— *Speech of Mr. Walker of Mississippi on the Bill Presented by Himself Limiting the Sale of the Public Lands to Actual Settlers.* Washington, 1837.

—— *1845 Treasury Report.* Washington, 1846.

—— *1846 Treasury Report.* Washington, 1847.

—— *1847 Treasury Report.* Washington, 1848.

—— *1848 Treasury Report.* Washington, 1849.

Waters, Raymond, jr. *Alexander James Dallas.* Philadelphia, 1943.

Wender, Herbert. *Southern Commercial Conventions.* Baltimore, 1930.

Wharton, Anne H. *In Old Pennsylvania Towns.* Philadelphia, 1920.

White, Leonard. *The Jacksonians.* New York, 1956.

Williams, Amelia W. and Baker, Eugene C. (ed.). *The Writings of Sam Houston 1813–1863.* Austin, 1938.

Woodford, Frank B. *Lewis Cass.* New Brunswick, 1950.

Zeamer, J. *One Hundred and Seventy-fifth Anniversary of the Silver Spring Presbyterian Church.* Cumberland, 1909.

Index